Homecoming

In Honor of
Joanne Currie
in
memory of her mother
Maud House

HOMECOMING

THE ART AND LIFE OF WILLIAM H. JOHNSON

RICHARD J. POWELL

Introduction by
MARTIN PURYEAR

The National Museum of American Art
Smithsonian Institution, Washington, D.C.
in association with
W. W. Norton & Company
New York   London

To my mother, Eliza Hughes Powell

Published on the occasion of the exhibition *Homecoming: William H. Johnson and Afro-America, 1938–1946,* National Museum of American Art, Smithsonian Institution, Washington, D.C., 13 September 1991–1 March 1992

Trade paperback edition published in the
United States of America by W. W. Norton & Company
500 Fifth Avenue, New York, NY 10110

Project Director: Steve Dietz
Editor: Terence Winch
Editorial Assistant: Deborah Thomas
Designer: Margaret Sartor

Typeset by Graphic Composition, Inc., Athens, Georgia
Printed and bound by South China Printing Company,
Hong Kong

Cover: *Li'l Sis* (see fig. 178).
Back Cover: William H. Johnson (detail; see fig. 50)
Half-title page: *Man in Vest,* ca. 1939–40. Oil on canvas, 30 x 24 in.
Contents page: William H. Johnson (see fig. 33).
Frontispiece: *I Baptize Thee* (see fig. 164).

Library of Congress Catalog number 91-052670

Powell, Richard J., 1953–
Homecoming: the art and life of William H. Johnson / Richard J. Powell: introduction by Martin Puryear. p. cm.
Includes bibliographical references and index.
ISBN 0-8478-1421-1—ISBN 0-937311-00-6 (pbk.)
1. Johnson, William H., 1901–1970. 2. Afro-American painters—Biography. I. Title.
ND237.J73P69 1991   91-52670
759.13—dc20   CIP

ISBN 0-937311-00-6 (NMAA pbk)
ISBN 0-395-31127-9 (pbk)

The National Museum of American Art, Smithsonian Institution, is dedicated to the preservation, exhibition, and study of the visual arts in America. The museum, whose publications program also includes the scholarly journal American Art, has extensive research resources: the databases of the Inventories of American Painting and Sculpture, several image archives, and a variety of scholarly fellowships. For more information or a catalogue of publications, write: Office of Publications, National Museum of American Art, Smithsonian Institution, Washington, DC 20560.

Contents

Foreword

t is hard to believe that so accomplished a modernist as William Henry Johnson remains to be "discovered" by general audiences after a generation of avid new interest in American art of this century. Several of the reasons for his relative obscurity are explained in this meticulously researched new study by Dr. Richard J. Powell— racial prejudice, years of expatriation, lack of gallery sponsorship, and stylistic change or "fickleness" that made it difficult for audiences to follow his career.

To these reasons, however, must be added the fact that the vast majority of Johnson's lifework has been concentrated in one place, the National Museum of American Art, during the period in which histories of American modernism took shape. In 1966– 67, as Johnson was languishing in a Long Island asylum after two decades of confinement, Adelyn Breeskin and David Scott, respectively curator and director of the museum, arranged with the Harmon Foundation for the transfer of more than one thousand paintings, drawings, and prints by Johnson—the largest number of objects by any single artist in our collection. Soon after, the museum distributed scores of works to historically black colleges and museums and presented an exhibition surveying Johnson's career. These efforts to make him known, however, were too isolated to compensate for the near total absence of art-market activity that would have kept Johnson's work constantly in the public eye, had the works been more widely available. Since Johnson's work did not enter major museum and private collections, he was, through general ignorance of his art, edited from the history of modernism as it evolved. This excellent new book on Johnson, and the exhibition of his late work that accompanies it, are offered as a corrective to this edited history.

We like to imagine that the sheer quality of fine works of art is sufficient to persuade audiences of their worth, but in truth we are all conditioned by the assumptions we inherit, and an "obscure" artist is assumed to be less worthy of attention until his case is forcefully made. This is the only way to account for the radical reversals in artists' reputations that sometimes occur, as with Van Gogh's transformation from outcast to art star. It is greatly to the credit of Adelyn Breeskin and David Scott that they saw through Johnson's obscurity to recognize the heightened spiritual and political energy of his art. With similar insight, they also acquired for the museum the remainder of the estates of two other great American artists, Henry Lyman Sayen and Romaine Brooks, who, like Johnson, still await their place in the story of American art of this century.

One other aspect of Johnson's work hampered the museum's efforts to make him more widely known. He painted on unstable supports—plywood, burlap, paperboard—that deteriorated through years of neglect while Johnson was confined in the asylum. Even after the museum acquired his lifework, convinced of its significance for American art, only a few dozen works were restored and accessible to public audiences. The museum's conservation staff experimented with a number of new techniques for stabilizing them, at first with mixed results, but more recently with considerable success. The conservation of Johnson's art is an ongoing project requiring unusually laborious procedures, and many years will be required to reclaim all the wonderful paintings that still await attention. The exhibition, "Homecoming: William H. Johnson and Afro-America," presents many newly conserved paintings never before shown publicly. They greatly expand our knowledge of Johnson's work and demonstrate that he produced not just an occasional dazzling image, but a large body of consistently strong paintings.

The question that remains as this volume goes to press is whether Johnson will be assessed as a major American modernist or a major *black* modernist. During the 1940s and 1950s, when the Harmon Foundation championed his work, he was invariably described as a "Negro artist." Today's social climate, in which aspects of racial identity are being reinterpreted as ethnicity, makes it easier for general audiences to respond to Johnson's neoprimitive formal style and African-American subjects. But there is no denying that his self-consciousness as a black artist intensified over his career and that the last works he made—the Fighters for Freedom series—constitute a powerful statement about race and politics in America, not to be understood without recourse to the darker history of prejudice and oppression.

These insistent late works, which deliberately avoid the charm of an accommodating style, must be considered an integral part of his oeuvre, a final declarative comment on his lifelong concerns. Had he stopped painting before doing the Fighters for Freedom, we could more easily integrate his art into the nonpolitical story of modernist style. Coming at the end of his career, however, they provide a retrospective lens through which his entire production is refocused, leading us to see even the earliest self-portraits as essays in identity and the agitated Scandinavian landscapes as evidence of a troubled inner world.

Will Johnson remain within the ghetto of the "Negro artist" or emerge as a painter of range and power who recast his personal experience as a profoundly moving national history? It is surely unfair to assess Johnson's art solely through the lens of race, however strongly it affected the direction of his career, including his expatriation and his choice of subjects. His racial identity, however, was more a determinant than Degas's physical infirmity or Goya's deafness if only because it linked him to a profoundly significant aspect of cultural and national experience. To place Johnson accurately within the history of American art, we must first accept his experience as an essential part of American history. This would be a true "homecoming" for all of us.

To Dr. Richard J. Powell, whose penetrating narrative reveals Johnson's art and life with new clarity, we owe a profound thanks; Johnson could ask no more sympathetic and insightful a biographer and critic. Steve Dietz, chief of publications at the National Museum of American Art, and his staff brought the highest level of commitment to the production of this book. Dr. Virginia Mecklenburg, the museum's chief curator, worked closely with guest curator Powell on the exhibition that accompanies the publication. Many more members of the museum staff worked to assure the highest standards for both the publication and exhibition, which we all hope will win new friends and appreciation for a great American painter.

Elizabeth Broun
Director
National Museum of American Art
Smithsonian Institution

Preface

By almost every standard, William Henry Johnson (1901–1970) can be considered a major American artist. Yet, for too many years, his art has been invisible to Americanists and modernists, both in art historical studies of American and modern painting and in survey exhibitions of this work. With a few exceptions, this invisibility has persisted in spite of the regular and widely acclaimed showings of Johnson's work throughout the United States and abroad, beginning with the many accolades that Johnson reaped from his first major shows in the early 1930s, and continuing in recent times with the high praise that his work has received in numerous theme exhibitions and related publications.

William H. Johnson was an African-American artist at a time in United States cultural history—1926 through 1946—when the two descriptives, *Negro* and *artist*, were rarely (if ever) paired with seriousness by most white critics; yet this only explicates part of the problem. While racism certainly interfered with substantive support for most black artists during those years, it is nonetheless true that in the same time period the art world *did* enthusiastically support three of this century's most celebrated black American artists: realist sculptor Richmond Barthé, folk artist Horace Pippin, and narrative modernist Jacob Lawrence. Although the mainstream art world's unwillingness to focus on, celebrate, and support more than a few exemplary African-American artists at any given moment is one explanation for the lack of broader recognition of Johnson in America, it does not fully explain the absence of a sustained, critical inquiry into his work.

While American racism certainly played a key part in Johnson's invisibility, there are other factors which, when combined, all worked toward erasing his mark on modern American art. The first, and perhaps most obvious, was his expatriate status. Just at that moment in history—the 1930s—when American painters and sculptors were beginning to banish from their minds the defeatist notions of cultural inferiority and flex their artistic muscles on an equal par with their European contemporaries, Johnson was immersed in a life and art (first in France and later in Scandinavia) that were light years away from the American scene. While debates over what constituted an authentic American art raged in various parts of this country, Johnson focused his artistic concerns not on issues of nationalism, but rather on issues of cultural integrity.

Another factor that has unquestionably contributed to William H. Johnson's absence from the larger picture of modern American art is his artistic eclecticism. In a career of just twenty years, Johnson, at every significant juncture, subscribed to a myriad of aesthetic positions, ranging from the conservative ideals of the "Academy," the painterly approach of the post-Impressionists, the emotionally charged technique of northern European Expressionism, the rhythmic, African-American mode of painting, and, finally, to a school of colorful, signlike, narrative art. Although these transitions in Johnson's relatively short career were logical (and perhaps even necessary) steps in his passage from art student to professional painter and then to visual chronicler of Afro-America, many critics unfortunately interpreted them as signs of his stylistic fickleness. While Johnson was admittedly eclectic at the beginning of his career, by 1935 his aesthetic vision was quite consistent. Johnson's stylistic turns after the middle 1930s were the direct consequence of his ever-shifting surroundings, his career-long allegiance to experimentation, and his adherence to a basic, twentieth-century impulse in art for growth through continuous, significant change. Though art historians rarely acknowledge it, eclecticism forms the core of a great deal of artistic production in the twentieth century.

A third factor in Johnson's invisibility to American collectors and critics during his lifetime was simply a matter of fate. Although Johnson was active in the New York art scene from the early to middle 1940s, his departure for Denmark in 1946, his subsequent mental breakdown, his hospitalization back in the United States, and, tragically, his incapacitation for the rest of his life removed him and his work from the world of modern American art for at least a quarter of the century.

The 1971 retrospective at the Smithsonian Institution's National Collection of Fine Arts—now the National Museum of American Art (NMAA)—brought Johnson's work back into the public eye. Now, twenty years later, the time seems right for a reexamination of his life's work, one that frames Johnson's art in the larger context of international art and culture during the years between the Great Depression and the end of World War II.

William H. Johnson, 1901–1970, the exhibition catalogue that accompanied the 1971 retrospective, was for many years the only available publication on the artist. The late Adelyn D. Breeskin, the catalogue's principal author and former NMAA twentieth-century art curator, had a formidable task in reconstructing the life and career of an artist whose history—aside from his more than one thousand art works—was more or less confined to a thick, yellowing scrapbook of fragmented letters, foreign-language clippings, and unidentified photographs. Breeskin (and assistant curator Jan K. Muhlert) accepted the challenge by preparing an extensive bibliography of published reviews (mostly from American newspapers), assigning dates to and cataloguing many of the previously undocumented works, and developing a chronology for the itinerant, ever-traveling Johnson. Subsequent research undertakings—especially in the reassigning of dates for many of Johnson's works, the interviews with contemporaries of the artist, and the contextualization of the work in a specifically European and/or African-American cultural sphere—have corrected many of the inaccuracies, and expanded upon the findings, of the 1971 catalogue.

Homecoming: The Art and Life of William H. Johnson builds on the pioneering work of Breeskin, Muhlert, and succeeding authors, and attempts to add to this diverse literature a synthesis, in which the products of Johnson's artistic imagination, his intentions, his biography, and contiguous zones of cultural data are all marshalled together as a way of understanding his contribution to modern American art. This examination of Johnson's art and life—inseparable in my mind—promises to revise the most commonly held view of William H. Johnson—that of the artist as tragic isolate—and replace it with an image of the artist that, while cognizant of his personal trials and singular path in art, shows his constant explorations and perennial discoveries of self and place. From the earliest to the very last paintings, Johnson infused his work with a searching, introspective quality that held as its ultimate ideal his subjects' sense of oneness with the outer and inner environment. This philosophical niche, whether realized in tumbling and contorted scenes of the French Riviera, in bold areas of color and brushstroke in the depictions of Danish fishermen, or in interlocking wedges of quiltlike patterns and shapes from an imaginary South Carolina and Harlem, always came back to Johnson, through subject matter, in his notion of home. It is this uncanny, self-actualizing aspect of William H. Johnson's art, and its dogged survival in spite of all of the attendant misfortunes and neglect, that make his art and life a triumph rather than a tragedy.

It should come as no surprise that primitivism and spirituality—two of this century's most elusive concepts in artistic thought—were the philosophical vehicles for Johnson's eternal quest for home in his work. Johnson, as a self-conscious "artist of color," understood the importance of his cultural roots—and those of other, kindred, marginalized peoples—in the formulation of an authentic, self-locating, artistic expression. As Joshua C. Taylor eloquently wrote in his Foreword to Breeskin's 1971 catalogue, in Johnson's mature work the artist essentially "found a union with the imagination of others, as earlier [i.e., referring to his European works] he had found a union with the world he saw." That both of these phases of primitivism necessitated a spiritual grasp of the others and the worlds under his scrutiny is again borne out in the way Johnson always connected with the various people he encountered on his trips, making himself completely at home during his travels, whether in France, Scandinavia, North Africa, New York City, or South Carolina.

It is with this sense of the artist coming to terms with the environment and its inhabitants, its folkways and, especially, its *spirit*, that the idea of "homecoming" becomes a kind of coda for William H. Johnson's art and life. Although Johnson was not alone among twentieth-century artists in his quest for spiritual and physical contacts with particular locales and cultures, his methods for making those linkages—first, through the international language of expressionism and, later, through the attitudes, styles, and aesthetic sensibilities of urban and rural African-American folk culture—individuated his direction, eternally casting it and him in the role of pilgrim. Johnson's pilgrimage, however, was not the Sisyphean labor of someone who is never fulfilled or at peace. In his journeys, every stop and every way station—from Cagnes-sur-Mer to Kairouan, from Hamburg to

William H. Johnson in his studio, Kerteminde, Denmark, ca. 1931

Harlem—became an oasis of sorts, a place to celebrate common bonds and spiritual ties, and, in the parlance of Johnson's own African-American community, a *homecoming*.

William H. Johnson's career-long ambition to express "the rhythmic" and "the spiritual" aspects of his inner and outer worlds stands as a testament to the far-ranging influence of African-American cultural values on many American moderns. Johnson's search for a conducive place to paint and live—shaped by his culture, his temperament, and his times—provides us with yet another view of art in America: one that increasingly offers up a complex, multi-valenced picture of enterprise, change, desire, and elucidation in the American artistic imagination. But William H. Johnson's art and life do more than merely illustrate an American way of painting: they record the artistic contributions of a world-class citizen and the genius of a man for whom self-awareness and creativity were equivalent to being.

Richard J. Powell
Durham, North Carolina
September 1990

Acknowledgments

Fortunately, in my ten years of researching William H. Johnson's work and life, I have encountered many people (on both sides of the Atlantic) who, with perhaps some of his same sense of "the rhythmic and spiritual" in life, have rallied me on and encouraged me at every step. From the very beginnings of my research, as a graduate student at Yale University, professors and fellow students prodded me to look at these works in different ways, to ask previously unfathomed questions about Johnson, and to finish my dissertation so that I could then go about the task of bringing Johnson's brilliant art and extraordinary life to a wider audience. My two principal advisors at Yale, Professors Robert Farris Thompson and Jules David Prown, provided sound suggestions at various stages of my research and, more importantly, served as scholarly role models. Dwight D. Andrews, Ramona Austin, Rebecca Bedell, John Blassingame, Sylvia A. Boone, Joseph Brown, S. J., Rae Linda Brown, Robert Bunselmeyer, Susan Fillin-Yeh, Henry Louis Gates, Jr., Vera Kutzinski, Sholomo Levy, Charles Martin, Etta Onat, Vincent Scully, Robert Stepto, Rebecca Stone-Miller, John Szwed, Deborah G. Thomas, Judith Wilson, Beryl Wright, and Rebecca Zurier all played invaluable parts in those first, exploratory investigations into Johnson's world. Among the readers and advisors outside Yale University to whom I am also indebted are: Lois Marie Fink, Curator of Research, National Museum of American Art, Smithsonian Institution; Øystein Hjort, Professor of Art History, University of Copenhagen, Denmark; Richard A. Long, Professor of Interdisciplinary Studies, Emory University; Kristine Stiles, Assistant Professor of Art History, Duke University; and Peter Wood, Professor of History, Duke University.

My colleagues in the Department of Art and Art History at Duke University have all helped to create an environment that encourages scholarship and intellectual growth. For each of them, our wonderful support staff, and my students, I am eternally grateful.

A number of fellowships enabled me to focus my energies for extended periods of time on research and writing: Visiting Graduate Fellowship, Smithsonian Institution, 1982; Yale University Fellowship, 1984–85; Fulbright Grant for Graduate Study Abroad, 1984–85; Predoctoral Fellowship, Smithsonian Institution, 1985–86; Ford Foundation Dissertation Fellowship, 1986–87; and Duke University Department of Art and Art History Grant, 1989–90. The past and present administrative staffs of the Fulbright Commission in Copenhagen, Denmark—John Berg, Barbara Lehman, Anne Meulengracht, and Mette Skakkebæk—were especially helpful during my stays in Denmark.

During my two sojourns to Scandinavia (from September 1984 to June 1985 and in June 1990), members of the museum and arts community helped facilitate my research endeavors. I would like to thank, in particular, Torben Lundbæk, Poul Mørk, and Kirsten Ramløv of the National Museum of Denmark's Department of Ethnography; Inger Sjørslev of the University of Copenhagen's Department of Ethnography; Hanne Finsen, Chief Curator, Ordrupgaard Collection, Charlottenlund, Denmark; Kristof Glamann, Director, Carlsberg Foundation, Copenhagen, Denmark; Per Svein Hovdenakk, Curator, Sonia Henie and Niels Onstad Art Center, Høvikodden, Norway; and Erland Porsmose, Director, Kerteminde Museum/Johannes Larsen Museet, Kerteminde, Denmark.

While a Predoctoral and Dissertation Fellow at the Smithsonian Institution's National Museum of American Art, former and current members of the curatorial and research support staffs were instrumental in my museum-based research. In addition to Lois Fink, I thank Tom Bower, the late Adelyn D. Breeskin, Cecilia Chin, Charles Eldredge, Gwendolyn Everett, Roberta Geier, Margaret Harman, Lynda Roscoe Hartigan, Robert Johnston, Melissa Kroning, Patricia Lynagh, Martina R. Norelli, Harry Rand, and Charles Robertson. Arthur Breton, Liza Kirwin, and Garnett McCoy of the Archives of American Art, Smithsonian Institution, were also very helpful during this research phase. This book (and the accompanying exhibition) would not have been possible without strong support and belief in this project from the National Museum of American Art's Director, Elizabeth Broun, and its Chief Curator, Virginia Mecklenburg. The entire staff of the NMAA's Office of Publications, especially Steve Dietz, Terence Winch, Carole Broadus, Deborah Thomas, and interns Mary Coffey and Elizabeth Peck, shepherded this book from beginning to end, for which I am extremely indebted. Special thanks also go out to Margaret Sartor, for her beautiful and sensitive book design.

The family and close friends of William and Holcha Krake Johnson, both in the United States and in Scandinavia, supplied me with an abundance of information. Relatives and acquaintances of the couple to whom I owe much thanks include Lillian Cooper, Johanna Voll, James H. Johnson, Gregers Krake, William Cooper, Lewis Harriton, Carol Cartwright, Helga and Niels Ejsing, Ernestine Brown, Isla Meyers, Sigrid Bondo, Torbjørg Bondo, Bothild Hagstrøm, Johanne-Marie Esbjerg, Onni Fahrenholtz, Eivind Tjensvoll, Helge Nilausen, Niels Hansen, Turid Riste, and Liv Drabløs.

I express my gratitude to the following persons—and to those whom I have inadvertently left out—who, in various ways, helped me to realize this book: Tage and Gulle Aamodt, Barbara Adams, Maya Angelou, Bob and Inger Bæhr, the late Romare Bearden, Tritobia Benjamin, Camille Billops, Sylletta and Søren Birk, Robert Blackburn, Bill Broom, Selma Burke, Ronald and Ditte Burns, Charlotte Carter, Floyd Coleman, Francis Costa, Narcissa Dargan, David C. Driskell, Tina Dunkley, James Early, Sverre Engeset, Michel and Geneviève Fabre, Sharon Farmer, Ric and Ulla Fisher, Bernard Gardi, Abigail Booth Gerdts, Delores Gore, Leslie King Hammond, Else Steen Hansen, Mogens Helmer Hansen, Ves and Nece Harper, Joseph Hawthorne, Judith Hayward, Janet Headley, Henry Hensche, Earl Hooks, the late Hans Hviid, Gunvor Jeppsen, G. Wayne King, Lone Kühlmann, Else Larsen, Jacob and Gwendolyn Knight Lawrence, James Lewis, Nadja Lonnert, Mario and Hanne Di Lucci, Pearl McCleese, Karin and Bendt Meisel-Joensen, Per Mossin,

Kåre Mathiasson, Jostein Nerbøvik, Frank Nichols, David Nye, Svanhild Øvrelid, David Page, Michael Panhorst, James T. Parker, Martin and Rachelle Puryear, Helen J. Rennie, the late Gary A. Reynolds, Jock Reynolds, Maria Eugenia Garrido Saavedra, Herbert Sanborn, Renee Boser Sarivaxevanis, David W. Scott, Frantzen Sennett, Teresa Singleton, Elka Spoerri, Inngunn Steinnes, Jeffrey and Marta Reid Stewart, Tara Tappert, Prentiss Taylor, Barbara Thompson, Ambassador and Mrs. Terence Todman, Laura Trusedell, Lars Tvedskov, Leo Twiggs, Nils Valnes, Barry Vann, Gudmund Vigtell, Jerry Waters, John Wetenhall, Jeanne Zeidler, and Nancy Zuschlag. My agent, Marie Dutton Brown, and my close friends, Michael and Teresa Grana, were indispensable "anchors" and my foremost advocates during the final days of labor on this book.

My family has endured my many periods of creative isolation over the past few years with understanding, support, and patience. And my wife, C.T., has also tolerated me at my highest—and lowest—points in the writing process. For loved ones, I am especially grateful, and glad to be back home.

R. J. P.

Introduction
By Martin Puryear

first encountered the work of William H. Johnson in the collection of Fisk University, where I had gone to teach twenty years ago. While looking through the collection I was drawn to a group of perhaps a half dozen works on paper—gouaches and serigraphs, as I recall—by an artist whose work I'd never seen before. The works depicted black life, usually in scenes typically southern and rural. They were bold, direct, and full of absolutely fearless color, laid down flat, with little or no modeling. The work had an intuitive sense of design, such as I'd always admired in children's art or in the art of "outsiders"—people who are compelled to make images without benefit of formal training (and usually with little direct experience of art at all). Despite their candor and directness, however, the works seemed anything but naive. Something savvy and sophisticated about these pictures gave them an oddly modern quality.

Very shortly afterwards I saw an exhibition of William H. Johnson's work at the National Collection of Fine Arts (now the National Museum of American Art) in Washington, D.C. Here was a revelation: the exhibition's large body of work confirmed my suspicion that Johnson was a far more complicated artist than the works I'd seen at Fisk, with their simple directness, would suggest. These were sophisticated modern paintings, done when Johnson lived in France, Denmark, and Norway, and they were painted earlier than the Fisk works. They were done in a variety of styles, all loosely expressionistic—landscapes, portraits of ordinary people, an occasional still life. As I walked through the exhibition I discovered that behind this many-faceted output, and the evolving vision it revealed, was a human story nearly as fascinating as the paintings.

William H. Johnson began life as a young man with an uneasy racial identity in Florence, South Carolina, and nothing he saw in the black community there gave him any hope that his own life wouldn't also be one of unrelieved anonymity. Yet years later, as a worldly expatriate in Europe, Johnson would embrace his racial difference and see it as the source of his uniqueness and strength as an artist. "I myself feel like a primitive man," he would say, "like one who is at the same time both a primitive and a cultured painter."

This remark, made in a 1935 interview, seems a succinct enough expression of Johnson's feelings about himself, but it also introduces a number of contradictions. For the European avant-garde "the primitive" embraced a creative principle that would form the basis for a succession of stylistic advances in western art. Primitivism valued the radical, the unrefined, the raw. It described a direction away from sophistication, taste, and conventional notions of beauty, while at the same time it assumed an awareness of these notions as its point of departure. Against the background of this rarefied and very European sense of the primitive, William H. Johnson, despite his academic background and obvious skill, was able to construe the African and American Indian elements of his ancestry as something of special value. Through European eyes he was able to see himself anew.

Of course he was not a true primitive in either the tribal sense or with respect to his level of sophistication, and his remark reveals more than a trace of calculated awareness of just how exotic he felt as an artist of color living in Nordic Europe. What I feel his declaration reflects most accurately, however, is his racial dilemma as a black artist moving between several worlds, on terms that are never stable. The way Johnson negotiated this dilemma—black American artist in a Eurocentric culture—is at the heart of his achievement.

Johnson's intense vitality was his greatest gift as an artist, and I feel that when his work is considered as a whole, this vitality becomes the real focus of his painting, regardless of what is actually depicted on the canvas. Style for him seems to have been a conduit, a carrier for this enormous creative energy. The various forms his work took during his years in Europe seem to have been the means by which he tried to understand himself in the face of constantly changing circumstances.

When Johnson first arrived in Europe, his excitement at being abroad unlocked something in his painting. At first he would put the subject of the painting itself into violent motion, like the crazily tumbling landscapes he painted early on in Cagnes-sur-Mer in southern France. Later in Scandinavia, where he married and settled into a more stable existence, he painted serene landscapes and harbor scenes, but with energetic strokes of bold thick color. In France, he expressed an admiration for Chaim Soutine; in Scandinavia, he admired Edvard Munch. While it is possible to see the influence of these and other European painters on his work, the peculiar spirit of his paintings is his own.

In 1939, when Johnson returned to New York after thirteen years abroad, his work again reflected the change almost immediately. Whereas in Europe he painted mostly landscapes, back in America he devoted himself almost exclusively to human figures. He painted the people he observed around him in New York, and he painted scenes from memory of rural southern life. He made a remarkable series of pictures depicting black army life, and some of his finest works from this time were scenes from the Bible.

Perhaps this latest transformation was rooted in the shock of having finally come full circle; or perhaps, once he found himself back in the United States, the expressionist bravura from Europe seemed overblown to Johnson. Whatever the impulse, he painted these last pictures with a calmer hand and with flat colors, put down with more deliberation. Now the energy and vitality would reside in the subjects themselves, rather than in the gusto with which the paint was applied.

Johnson's people were boldly, but carefully painted against stark backgrounds, and color was let loose in a way he'd never done before. Color and pattern—in women's dresses, prisoners' stripes, checkerboard floor tiles, plowed fields, the clothing of saints, anything that caught his fancy—throbbed and hit the eye hard. He captured motion, gesture, posture—rendered all as staccato pattern. And, if they happened to be caught in a still moment, his people stared back, as though returning Johnson's own searching gaze. These paintings are Johnson's triumph: Although they were painted at a time when he began to suffer tragic misfortunes, they still have a lyrical, if somewhat fatalistic, poetry, and behind their honest directness beats a deeply felt warmth for his people.

The simplicity and directness had been hard won. He journeyed a long way and learned to speak as an artist in many tongues. In the end he came home to find his own voice and his own way of telling about that which was his own. At any point in William H. Johnson's journey there are rewards and pleasures and truths. Johnson's homecoming is as honest and clear as a mirror.

I know my God and rejoice in
him every day. Trusting him
for my journey, I am not
ashamed of his name or afraid
of hellfire, for I have been
killed dead and made alive
again and am fireproof, rejoicing
every day and waiting for him
to carry me home.

Anonymous African-American,
ca. 1929, from *God Struck
Me Dead* (1969)

The Gate City
1901–1918

ike so many small towns in turn-of-the-century America, Florence, South Carolina, was a solidly capitalistic hamlet, whose visions of grandeur were limited only by the realities of its location and political influence.[1] Florence's transition from a gathering of farmers and small businesses to a small but burgeoning town was sparked in 1851 by its selection as the future site for rail connections between Wilmington to the northeast and Charleston to the south. The arrival of the railroad in 1853, symbolized by the creation of a major railway station, spurred immediate growth and contributed to the Pee Dee region's swift recovery from the economic dislocations of the Civil War (fig. 1). By the early 1900s, Florence was a bustling center of commerce and commuters, moving hundreds of people and tons of freight daily through its endless network of wooden crossties and steel railroad tracks.

The Atlantic Coast Line Railroad Company (ACL) held dominion at the turn of the century over most of the region's transportation needs. With Florence's position as one of the principal headquarters for the ACL, the town gained much in the way of economic incentives from railroad officials, railroad-related jobs for Florence citizens, and the steady patronage of local businesses by railroad-affiliated people. The ACL also meant increased employment options for the common folk of Florence County, giving them viable alternatives to the hard and unpredictable world of farming and sharecropping. But those who left the fields to enter day labor and domestic service reaped relatively little of the economic prosperity that the railroad brought to Florence.

Florence's Board of Trade plunged head-on into those first, optimistic years of the twentieth century, proudly prefacing its 1911 city directory with such promotional headlines as "FLORENCE, S.C., The Gate City of the Pee Dee Section," "FLORENCE—The Bale-to-the-Acre County," and "FLORENCE, S.C., A Future Manufacturing Center." Florence's almost self-willed sense of ambition transformed it into a place where, at least for some of its citizens, there was the possibility of political advancement and economic growth.

For Henry and Alice Johnson, however, the Board of Trade's celebratory tone had very little relevance to their reality in Florence. The Johnsons, like countless other African-Americans at the turn of the century, lived in a humble, inconspicuous manner. They worked hard, earned very little money, and maintained respectful and subservient relations with Florence's whites. Henry, who shoveled coal as a "fireman" for the Florence division of the ACL railroad, and Alice, who worked as a domestic in various Florence homes, found themselves in the distant background of the Florence Board of Trade's rosy picture of affluence and progress.

Although blacks made up well over half the population of Florence County around the turn of the century, they were virtually ignored by state and local government in matters of public education, health, and community development. Around 1900, for example, annual state allocations for public education in Florence County averaged out to $5.55 for each white student, while for a black student the amount was $1.30. As these statistics suggest, illiteracy was commonplace in Florence. In 1910, nine of every hundred whites in the county and four times as high a percentage of blacks—thirty-six of each hundred—could not read or write. Sickness and mortality rates mirrored these racial inequities in education, for South Carolina and the entire South were part of a segregated system that provided separate and inferior public services and accommodations for blacks.[2] Indeed, black citizens of the "Gate City of Eastern South Carolina" were well aware that this so-called entranceway to opportunity seemed to have a sign above it that read "for whites only."

Henry and Alice Johnson were certainly no strangers to these social peculiarities. Born and raised in South Carolina during the 1870s, when the state experienced its most tumultuous years of racial strife and political change, the Johnsons would have had at least some knowledge of just how much political and social progress had been gained, then lost, for blacks on the heels of the Reconstruction. Although Florence was relatively free of the political strife and almost daily occurrences of racial repression that characterized the post-reconstructed South in the 1880s and 1890s, the region was not without incidents of lynchings and racial violence.

In 1898, just four years after Henry and Alice were married, Florence and its neighboring counties witnessed one of the most notorious instances of white violence toward blacks. In Lake City, a town about twenty miles south of Florence, in the neighboring county of Williamsburg, a collection of white citizens voiced their disapproval of the federal appointment of a black man, Fraser B. Baker, as postmaster of the city. Vocal protests soon gave way to a bloody confrontation between an anonymous mob of angry whites and Baker, culminating in the burning down of Baker's home (which also served as the post office), the murder of Baker and his youngest child, and multiple gunshot injuries sustained by Baker's wife and three of their six children. The community, black and white, rallied together to provide Mrs. Baker and her five surviving children with food, medical attention, and shelter, yet the racial overtones of this horrific incident remained in people's minds for a long time. Although newspaper editorials and community spokespersons publicly condemned the racism that precipitated the tragedy at Lake City, no one stepped forward to provide any names of the members of the mob.

Oddly enough, there were many blacks in Florence and in the surrounding area who felt that the Lake City lynching was not just outrageous, but an aberration—a strange turn of events that escalated into a full-blown tragedy because of Baker's unwillingness to be subservient. Although most people felt sorry for the Baker family, the overriding opinion among many was that Baker's determination to hold on to his federal appointment constituted a death wish. The call for blacks to abdicate all political aspirations, as well as any claims for basic civil rights, had already been sounded: first, by post-Reconstruction white militia bands and gun clubs, who intimidated blacks with violence; and second, by conservative black leaders like Booker T. Washington, whose response to this racially motivated violence was to advise their fellow blacks to accept their lowly status in the segregated South and to confine their ambitions to the agricultural and vocational education sectors. For instance, only one month prior to the Baker lynching, the prominent black South Carolina minister Richard Carroll told a black congregation in Sumter, South Carolina, to forego politics and stay on the farm. Ironically, this speech was made in conjunction with the local Emancipation Day festivities.[3]

1. A.C.L. Passenger Station, Florence, South Carolina, ca. 1915

As Negroes who earned their board and keep from the railroads and kitchens of Florence, Henry and Alice Johnson must have thought often about the precarious position that any blacks would put themselves in if they, like Fraser B. Baker, were to make known their aspirations and desires for social equality. Henry and Alice possibly wondered in the aftermath of the Baker family tragedy if they, as blacks working for whites, could avoid the fatal mistake of revealing too prideful a side of their character, much less a sense of self-worth and individuality. Perhaps Henry and Alice also felt a particular sadness for the Baker's murdered infant and three critically wounded children, since Alice, like so many women during this period, had herself already lost several children to stillbirths and early childhood diseases.[4]

But life in turn-of-the-century Florence offered blacks more than just hard labor, second-class status, and an undercurrent of fear and unease. In Florence and throughout the South, the black church provided its membership with spiritual and secular release from the racial insults and class-based affronts that blacks experienced almost daily. The Johnsons' home church, Mount Zion African Methodist Episcopalian, sponsored cookouts, bazaars, revivals, and other events for the black community in Florence. Although these church-sponsored events and services were only temporary respites from the day-to-day realities of living under a separate and unequal system, their exclusive, all-black social structure, impenetrable by white institutions, gave blacks the chance to express themselves freely and passionately, without fear of white criticism or retaliation. Mount Zion A.M.E.'s pastor, the Reverend W. T. Williams, and Trinity Baptist Church's pastor, the Reverend E. R. Roberts, remained in the spiritual and political forefront of Florence's

black community for many years. For a brief period, Reverend Roberts also published Florence's first and only black newspaper, *The Baptist Herald*.

Besides the black churches and the black press, other black institutions in Florence, such as some of the medical practices, provided a few black men and women with an opportunity to advance, economically and socially, as well as to serve as leaders of Florence's black community. In the eyes of their fellow blacks, and even among some whites, local black physicians such as Dr. William Francis Holmes were also educators, politicians, businessmen, and arbitrators. They served as living, flesh-and-blood role models for the poorer and less educated members of their race, with whom, however, they still shared a segregated, second-class existence.

One profession in Florence that was entirely dominated by blacks, yet served both a black and white clientele, was midwifery. This time-honored profession was comprised exclusively of elderly black women who, because of the medical profession's indifference to obstetrics, developed an expertise in caring for women in childbirth. Even when Florence's medical community changed its thinking and began to provide regular care to expectant mothers, local midwives still enjoyed wide popularity. Although lacking medical training and an understanding of the latest medical advancements, midwives made up for these deficiencies with years of "hands-on" training, an acquired knowledge of traditional folk medicine, and a personable, woman-to-woman rapport with their patients. Sadly enough, Florence's infant mortality rate was not significantly reduced either by its midwives or by the rest of the medical community until well into the first quarter of the twentieth century.

Mary Wilson, one of Florence's best-known midwives at the turn of the century, attended to Alice Johnson during the delivery of her first baby to survive childbirth. Alice, who had previously experienced difficulties in carrying her children to full term, successfully gave birth to a baby boy, William Henry Johnson, on 18 March 1901.[5]

Not long after Alice Johnson gave birth to "little Willie," rumor-mongering neighbors in Florence questioned whether the wavy-haired, fair-skinned child was, in fact, fathered by brownskin Henry Johnson.[6] The fact that Alice's subsequent offspring—Lacy, Lucy, James, and Lillian (born in 1910, 1913, 1914, and 1916, respectively)—all looked more like their father, in coloring and features, lent further credence to these speculations. Furthermore, Alice's job as a domestic, which placed her in close and constant contact with whites, also put her at risk of being subjected to the sexual advances of her white male employers. Women in Alice's position often fell prey to rape by their employers—such assaults were among the unspoken realities of a racially, economically, and sexually stratified society. These women had no hope of any legal recourse and, if a child was conceived from the rape, the women and their families coped with the situation to the best of their abilities. Though, in private, idle tongues would click in disapproval and dismay, the black community's public position was generally one of acceptance and understanding of these mixed-race children as part of the social and racial reality of the South.

On the other hand, Alice Johnson, with her dark mahogany complexion and abundance of thick black hair, probably was of American Indian and African-American ancestry, and it is quite possible that she and Henry shared some element of caucasian ancestry as well (fig. 2).[7] Moreover, interracial connections—covert or overt, forced or free—had a far longer and broader history in South Carolina than residents cared to acknowledge, and it was not uncommon for racial traits from previous generations to show up visibly in later offspring.

Whatever its origins, growing up with the mark of the white race across his face profoundly affected Willie. Because of the overheard whispers from gossiping neighbors and the cruel taunts of other children, Willie would often assume a distant and disinterested attitude toward those around him. This sense of individuality and, at times, a brooding self-introspection, were no doubt reinforced by Willie's lengthy status, until age nine, as the Johnson household's only child. As the eldest, pre-adolescent boy of a growing brood of younger Johnson children, Willie increasingly thought of himself as beyond his siblings' playful, childish world, and alone in his perceptions of self. Thirteen-year-old Willie, in the roles of babysitter, household helper, and all-around assistant to "Mom Alice,"

2. Alice Smoot Johnson, ca. 1940

3. William H. Johnson, 1918

as she was called, and her husband Henry, had already acquired an air of independence and self-sufficiency that would stay with him as he matured.

As his siblings grew older and more independent, Willie supplemented his household chores with odd jobs in and around Florence's railroad station and at the recently opened Young Men's Christian Association, where Mom Alice also took employment as a cook. With money made from running errands for the engineers at the Transfer Shed Station to retrieving and stacking bowling pins at the YMCA's bowling alley, Willie contributed what he could to the family's meager income. Henry Johnson, who in his early years had worked as a railroad fireman and day laborer, started working for the Florence Steam Laundry during this period.

When not helping out at home, working at the Transfer Shed Station, or at the YMCA, Willie attended Florence's all-black elementary school, the Wilson School. Leona M. Webster, daughter of one of the school's teachers and a teaching assistant at Wilson, recalled many years later that Willie was one of her students and that, even then, he had demonstrated some artistic talent. Miss Webster, upon noticing a loose piece of paper on Willie's desk one day, picked it up and was pleasantly surprised to find drawn on it a remarkable likeness of herself. When she questioned Willie about it, he admitted to being the artist.[8] Although sketching was not officially part of the Wilson School's curriculum, an artistically inclined teacher at the Wilson School, Louise Fordham Holmes (wife of the Florence physician and the Wilson School's interim principal, Dr. William Francis Holmes), often incorporated music, art, and poetry into her daily instructions. Willie, who was one of Louise Fordham Holmes's students, could have easily been introduced to sketching in her classes.[9]

It was because of these early encounters with the arts, the timely exposure to a few black professionals, as well as a keen awareness of the trains, travelers, and the comings-and-goings of different people in Florence, that Willie soon realized there was life and culture beyond the Gate City. In an ordinary day at the Transfer Shed Station or at the YMCA, Willie could see all kinds of people—commuters, train officials, conductors, common laborers, vacationers, salesmen, politicians, and businessmen—going about life with a purpose and single-mindedness that he found fascinating. Family members recall that

Willie was forever picking up discarded newspapers from the railroad station and pondering over *Mutt and Jeff* and the other comic strips. They also remember that Willie loved to sketch cars and trains with pencil and paper, and that he looked forward to those intermittent visits from his namesake, Uncle Willie Smoot, who was a Pullman porter on the New York City/Miami train route.

Smoot was particularly fond of Willie, his oldest nephew. During stops in Florence, Smoot would drop off delicacies, such as Florida oranges, to his sister Alice and the children, and would keep his nephew Willie captivated for hours with funny stories about strange encounters on the train and unusual sights along the way. Smoot also told Willie and the others about his life in New York City and the many opportunities that were available there for blacks.

No doubt it was Smoot's influence on an already impressionable Willie that prompted the teenager to first consider leaving his family and home in Florence to seek out job opportunities in New York City. In Florence as well as in other black communities, the advantages of knowing a Pullman porter were innumerable; the most practical advantage was having someone to rely on for ready access to interstate transportation and a vast network of economic resources and community information throughout black America. Through Smoot, the younger Willie soon realized that certain lifestyles and career choices were simply impossible if he decided to remain in a small, segregated, southern town like Florence.

During and following World War I, there was a virtual exodus by blacks from the nation's farms and small towns, all of them drawn by the opportunities promised in America's urban centers. Although young, optimistic, and still uncertain about what he wanted to do with his life, Willie sensed that he too would have to join this exodus if he wanted to attain any of his dreams. He also knew that there was a place for him in his uncle's Harlem home. Sometime around 1918, with his family's blessings and farewells fresh in his mind, a seventeen-year-old William H. Johnson boarded a train at Florence's celebrated railroad station, bound north (fig. 3).

Artistic Beginnings
1918–1926

The Harlem of 1918, when William H. Johnson first arrived there, was a community in transition. Mingling about in upper Manhattan with the vague sense of bearing witness to a community on the threshold of a bigger, brighter tomorrow were all kinds of people—recently arrived black migrants from the rural South and the West Indies; race-conscious supporters of the Jamaican-born black nationalist Marcus Garvey; small-scale and big-time entrepreneurs in pursuit of World War I-era dollars; and Negroes—thousands and thousands of Negroes. Whether this historic moment was plainly articulated by the public relations people in the pages of the African-American newspaper *The New York Age*, or subconsciously conveyed in the swagger and style of a dapper U. S. Army soldier in Harlem's all-Negro regiment, the notion that Harlem was just then embarking on a cultural and economic climb permeated the air.[1]

Even working-class blacks, like Johnson's uncle, Willie Smoot, and his wife, Rebecca, were cognizant of an expanding job market and understood the short-range opportunities that this economic spurt provided for their nephew William and the rest of Harlem's ever-increasing population. Because jobs in manual labor and in the service sector were relatively plentiful at this time, it was not long before recent-arrival William H. Johnson took on a succession of them: hotel porter, short-order cook, and stevedore. The money that Johnson earned on these assorted jobs paid for his lodgings and board in the Smoot household (at 146 West 128th Street) and helped with his family's expenses back home in Florence, South Carolina.[2]

Oddly enough, it was during this early New York period, while Johnson struggled to achieve a level of economic self-sufficiency, that he began to contemplate a previously unimaginable career as a newspaper cartoonist. Johnson was inspired in this ambition by his own childhood memories of copying the comic strips and was further encouraged by the wide popularity and mass appeal of this all-American, popular art form.

Johnson may even have had the idea of pursuing a career as a cartoonist in the fall of 1921, when he applied for admission to the School of the National Academy of Design. Along with completing a registration form and paying an admission fee, Johnson and the other applicants were required to make on-the-spot drawings from an antique sculpture, under the supervision of a school proxy. Apparently Johnson's self-taught practice of copying various comic-strip characters (Maggie and Jiggs of *Bringing Up Father* and Mutt and

4. Charles Louis Hinton's Preparatory Class at the School of the National Academy of Design, ca. 1921–22. Charles Louis Hinton (second from right, front); Francis Costa (second from right, rear); William H. Johnson (center, rear)

Jeff of *Mutt and Jeff*) prepared him well for this drawing exam, for he was admitted on 4 October 1921 to the preparatory class of the school.[3]

An aspiring cartoonist like Johnson, or a young artist with loftier aims, had several choices in 1921 for art study in New York. Notable among these choices were the Art Students League and the School of the National Academy of Design. At the relatively progressive Art Students League, students controlled faculty hiring, had a major voice in the formulation of the curriculum, and, in general, directed the tenor of the school toward contemporary trends in art. In contrast, art instruction at the School of the National Academy of Design was essentially a by-product of the Academy's older, more established membership of professional artists. Although students at the school had always played an important part in the Academy's programing, the school's curriculum was very much tied to the conservative tenets of an academic tradition in American art, an artistic point of view long espoused by the Academy's members.

The two art schools also differed in amounts of tuition charged, and this certainly accounted for the kinds of students who enrolled in each school. Because the Art Students League was a student-managed, privately endowed school, the burden of institutional costs fell on the students. In 1921, tuition fees at the Art Students League ranged from nine dollars to thirteen dollars per month, so it was more likely that wealthier, more affluent students would enroll there. In order to maintain a nonprofit, tax-free status, the School of the National Academy of Design charged its students no tuition and very low equipment fees. Consequently, the student population at the School of the National Academy of Design (known as the N.A.D.) was predominately of a working-class background.

In the school's preparatory class, which was mandatory for all beginners, students received a general orientation, an explanation of the proper procedures for advancement, and an introduction to methods and materials. Unlike the advanced classes, the preparatory class was regularly supervised by an appointed instructor who served as an advisor to the students, guiding them through the first few months of their Academy experience.

Johnson's appointed instructor for the preparatory class, Charles Louis Hinton (1869–1950), was himself a former N.A.D. student, as well as the recipient of the prestigious title of "Academician" by N.A.D. members. A fairly successful sculptor of allegorical themes, Hinton had been teaching at the school for over twenty years by the time Johnson came under his supervision. According to Johnson's school records, he quickly advanced under Hinton's aegis from the introductory "Antiques-on-Probation" level to the more advanced "Antiques-in-Full." Johnson's receipt, at the end of the 1922 spring term, of an Honorable Mention for his work on the antiques attested to his quick and relatively facile drawing ability at this early stage in his development.

A photograph of the 1921–22 preparatory class shows a young and relaxed Johnson standing along with instructor Charles Louis Hinton and other first-year N.A.D. students (fig. 4). One of Johnson's first-year classmates, Francis Costa, recalled that, in spite of Hinton's insistence that the first-year students in the preparatory class draw the antique sculptures over and over again until they drew them correctly, there was the general attitude among students that these exercises did have some value that would ultimately unite them as a group.[4]

The characteristic camaraderie of the art academy is reported in the reminiscences of countless American artists. From Thomas Cole to Robert Henri, the image of portfolio-carrying students, collectively engaged in sketching sessions, traveling throughout America and abroad, conversing in bars and sidewalk cafes, and rolling around on studio floors in impromptu wrestling matches, was a standard one.

At the School of the N.A.D., this exuberant community feeling, with its atmosphere of unbridled collective energy, was often more than the average person could bear.

5. *Life Study of H.T. Wong,* ca. 1923. Pencil on paper, 9½ x 7½ in.

Artist Ilya Bolotowsky, former N.A.D. student and friend to William H. Johnson, recalled that friendly rough-housing among students frequently turned into violent fist fights. During one unsupervised class, for example, Bolotowsky got into a fight with a fellow student who ended up breaking his nose. Former N.A.D. student Helen Rennie, one of the few women from that period in attendance at the school, remembered how the mostly male and high-spirited student body would often wreak havoc in her classes. Johnson's classmate Francis Costa also remembered that it was not unusual to find art students at the school who were adept at both painting *and* boxing.[5]

In a Danish newspaper interview some thirteen years after that first year at the N.A.D., Johnson talked briefly about his student days, fondly remembering how students immersed themselves in the day-to-day experiences of art study, and how the N.A.D.'s structure was similar to that of the European academies. Johnson also described the N.A.D. as a place where, for the first time in his life, he closely interacted with people of different

races, nationalities, and religions. "In the artistic realm," said Johnson, "race ultimately isn't very important."[6]

Indeed, in Johnson's first year at the N.A.D., he encountered a culturally diverse student population, with many students hailing from the Lower East Side, the Bronx, Chinatown, Little Italy, Harlem, and other New York ethnic enclaves. Besides Johnson, Costa, Bolotowsky, and Rennie, other students who were enrolled that year included future painters Raphael Soyer and Paul Cadmus, soon-to-be-known Harlem Renaissance genre painter Malvin Gray Johnson, and future art historian and critic Meyer Shapiro. In the years that followed, Johnson was joined at the N.A.D. by such future New York art world notables as Luigi Lucioni, Gregorio Prestopino, Arshile Gorky, Theodore Roszak, and Ernie Bushmiller (creator of the classic newspaper comic strip *Nancy*).

Although it is not known exactly when Johnson decided to abandon his goal to become a cartoonist, by the spring of 1923 he was exhibiting works in the N.A.D. Student Association Exhibition, as well as swiftly advancing through the N.A.D.'s Life-in-Full classes. His teachers during the 1922–23 winter and spring terms, Charles Courtney Curran (1861–1942) and George Willoughby Maynard (1843–1923), were longstanding members of the Academy and proponents (in their teaching and art) of the "Academy Ideals." These ideals, which stressed proficiency in the rendering of an idealized human form, were the school's philosophical bedrock.[7] That Johnson was more than competent in these ideals is evident from his being awarded the school's second prize that year for a still-life painting. Johnson's small pencil drawing (ca. 1923) of fellow student Hong Ting Wong not only shows Johnson's firm grasp of portraiture, but also demonstrates his acceptance of classical principles and proportions in art (fig. 5).[8]

George W. Maynard died on 5 April 1923. His replacement at the school, painter Charles Webster Hawthorne (1872–1930), brought a radically different notion of art instruction, figure painting, and aesthetic priorities to the

6. Charles Webster Hawthorne, n.d.

N.A.D. Although born in the Midwest, Charles Haw-thorne was raised in the small New England village of Richmond, Maine, where his father was the captain of a merchant ship (fig. 6).[9] Hopes of becoming an artist led Hawthorne, in 1890, to New York, where he studied at the Art Students League with painters George DeForest Brush, H. Siddons Mowbray, and Frank Vincent DuMond. In 1896, Hawthorne began studies with painter William Merritt Chase and shortly thereafter became a valued teaching assistant at Chase's art schools in New York City and Shinnecock, Long Island. For the next twenty years, Hawthorne supplemented his formal art education with painting excursions to the Netherlands and Italy. After Chase closed his two schools in 1898, Hawthorne opened

7. Charles W. Hawthorne's Life-in-Full Class at the School of the National Academy of Design, ca. 1923–24

his own summer school in Provincetown, Massachusetts, in the following year, calling it The Cape Cod School of Art. In conjunction with the opening of his school came a wider recognition of Hawthorne as a brilliant colorist and perceptive figure painter. His sub-jects—rugged Portuguese fishermen and their catch of the day, wide-eyed children, cor-pulent businessmen, and women wearing flowing, pastel-colored day gowns—were her-alded for their "sympathetic insight into character."[10] But it was especially the popularity of Hawthorne's ideally located Cape Cod School, and his reputation as an inspiring teacher of art, that made him a legend in his own time.

Although Johnson could have very easily chosen to work with one of the other three life-class instructors at the school, he began the 1923–24 term with Hawthorne. Former students recalled that, unlike other instructors, Hawthorne would willingly demonstrate various life painting techniques in front of his classes: a simple, yet generous gesture that endeared him to many students (fig. 7).[11]

Johnson's first efforts under Hawthorne are a series of "life compositions" (now lost), with titles such as *Serenity, Struggle, Tyranny,* and *Liberty.* The titles of these life com-positions are indicative of a typical collection of academic, figural allegories, so that we may assume that Johnson, at least at the beginning of the 1923–24 term, was still very much a product of the Academy.

The Academy's reliance on literary and narrative devices, drawing-as-a-building-block in art, and the careful pre-planning of compositions were all being gradually undermined, however, by the teaching methods and art techniques of Charles Hawthorne. In his classes both at the N.A.D. and his school on Cape Cod, Hawthorne challenged many of the aesthetic assumptions that his fellow Academicians took for granted and supplanted these "ideals" with concepts that, in retrospect, seemed to point his students toward modernist tenets in art.

Hawthorne differed from his N.A.D. colleagues with his particular approaches to painting and color and in his de-emphasis of drawing. "I don't say much about drawing," Hawthorne was fond of stating, "because I think drawing the form and painting are better separated."[12] Hawthorne made his sense of the distinction between the two clearer with his opinion that "no amount of good drawing will pull you out if your colors are not true." At the N.A.D., where the continuity of the academic tradition was contingent upon developing proficiency in drawing the human figure, Hawthorne's attitude was blasphemy. Former Hawthorne acolytes at the school, like Ilya Bolotowsky and Helen Rennie, recalled that tensions often arose between them and the more conservative instructors, especially when these students began to echo Hawthornelike sentiments in the presence of the Academicians.[13] Hawthorne himself was well aware of how his points of view put him at odds with his colleagues. "Each time I feel like saying 'forget drawing,'" Hawthorne quipped, "[it] only adds . . . to my already bad reputation."

Instead of drawing, Hawthorne emphasized the primacy of color in painting, frequently advising his students to "overdo in color rather than be weak." He urged them to "see brilliant color, then paint it a little more brilliant than you see it." Hawthorne constantly intoned to his students the visual concept of "spots of color." Hawthorne's "spots," somewhat like Pointillism for the Impressionists, were the foundation of form, rather than something applied to the form. By emphasizing the expressive materiality of color, Hawthorne subverted the Academy's adherence to an art of painted illusions and surface decorations.

Along with color, Hawthorne stressed that students should avoid an overly rational approach to art and instead strive for spontaneity and expressive emotion. "Good painting," Hawthorne preached, "is an excitement, an aesthetic emotion." "We must train ourselves to keep and preserve our fresh and youthful vision. If we do we'll be great artists— if we don't we'll be academicians."

In another jab at the Academicians, Hawthorne told students to go beyond the elegant subjects and lofty themes of their teachers and to "see the beauty of the ugly" and the "beauty of the commonplace." In response to the allegorical figures and Arcadian settings in paintings by artists like George Maynard, Charles Curran, and others, Hawthorne insisted that "anything is painter's fodder" and that it is the artist's responsibility to raise the mundane to the level of the profound.

These statements, in spite of their wit, seemed somewhat incongruous, since Hawthorne was himself an Academician and one of the most respected painters among the art establishment in the 1920s. The ultimate irony was that these anarchistic words were rarely, if ever, followed by the artist himself. In *Summer Millinery*, an oil-on-board painting of 1915, the moody, introspective quality of Hawthorne's scene and his palette of muted pastels and somber earth tones stand in direct opposition to his oft-repeated description of "good painting" as "an excitement" or "aesthetic emotion" (fig. 9). Similarly,

8. *Self-Portrait*, ca. 1923–26. Oil on canvas, 29¾ x 23¾ in.

9. Charles W. Hawthorne, *Summer Millinery*, 1915. Oil on board, 61¼ x 48 in.

10. Charles W. Hawthorne, *The Fish and the Man*, 1925. Oil on canvas, 40¼ x 39¾ in.

one might argue that one of his major canvases, *The Fish and the Man*, rather than paying tribute to the "ugly" and the "commonplace," actually transforms the plain old man into a heroic, handsome figure, and his fish into a luminous, glittering trophy—an artistic metamorphosis not very different from those executed by Hawthorne's fellow Academicians (fig.10). Still, one perhaps can see how both paintings could be interpreted as ennobling, expressive works, conceived and executed in a manner that celebrates the mundane in life and revels in the act of painting and in the allure of color. Elizabeth McCausland, writing about Hawthorne in 1947, also noted these "conflicting pulls" within the artist. "His choices of subject and style," she writes, ". . . showed an oscillation which reflects the response which he (like most artists of the time) made to the pressures from conservatism, on the one side, and from the proponents of artistic change, on the other. . . ."[14]

Although Hawthorne did not follow his own edicts in his artistic creations, the effects of his teachings, lectures on painting, and words of advice reverberated from generation to generation of former Hawthorne students, giving them the philosophical artillery to combat the conservative art mainstream. One can only imagine that William H. Johnson, being an art world outsider to the debates and battles between the traditionalists and the moderns, would have been oblivious to this discourse, motivated instead to simply perfect his talent, get his certificate from the school, and then find an art-related job. But like many other art students, Johnson soon fell under Hawthorne's spell, moving gradually away from making precise, tight little drawings and, instead, toward painting those proverbial "spots of color."

One of Johnson's earliest known paintings from his student years, a *Self-Portrait* from around 1923–26, clearly documents Hawthorne's influence on Johnson (fig. 8). Almost unabashedly, Johnson's *Self-Portrait* embodies Hawthorne's "spots of color" concept, articulated here as the chromatic building blocks for Johnson's face, plaid shirt, and the murky background. Johnson's use of the palette knife in *Self-Portrait*, which contributes to the spotty, patchlike quality of his painting, links this work directly to Hawthorne, who was legendary for encouraging its use over the paintbrush.

In spite of the linkage that Johnson's *Self-Portrait* has with Charles Hawthorne's teachings, the painting's overall effect and formal characteristics still made the basic accommodations to conventional portraiture. The painting's jewel-like, luminous core of impressionist colors (yellows, pinks, and greens) is perhaps the only area of departure from standard academic painting. Otherwise, Johnson's use of dark brown, maroon, and black shadings for the figure, along with his subtle, compositional overtures to portraiture "in the grand manner," situate his *Self-Portrait* squarely within art establishment norms.

In another early figure painting by Johnson, known today only from a photograph in an old N.A.D. School catalogue, Johnson's explorations into Hawthorne's concepts of painting are even more obvious (fig. 11). This *Nude Study*, reminiscent of the faceted, shattered qualities of compositions painted by Cézanne and other European moderns, illustrates Johnson's youthful awareness and adept handling of a cubist idiom; at the same time, it shows Johnson's academic anchoring and his unwillingness to venture too far afield from reality.

Johnson's earliest known still life not only reflects Hawthorne's guidance but, indirectly, the teachings of Hawthorne's mentor, painter William Merritt Chase (fig. 12). Chase's fascination with the perceived materiality of brass, tin, and ceramics also appears in Johnson's *Still Life*, though, in Johnson's painting, this fascination is tempered by Hawthorne's counsel to avoid meticulous details and "pretty painting." Broad brushwork in *Still Life* obscures both the exact patterns on the depicted delft ware and the exact types of fruit scattered throughout. Nevertheless, Johnson's grasp of what Hawthorne referred to as "the right note of color" helps one to distinguish ceramic from tin, as well as citrus fruit from pome fruit.

Following his initial classes with Hawthorne in the 1923–24 winter-spring terms, all of Johnson's remaining classes at the School of the N.A.D. were under Hawthorne's supervision. In addition, Johnson followed his teacher for the next three summers (1924–26) to the Cape Cod School of Art in Provincetown.

Although the tuition at the Cape Cod School of Art was fifty dollars for an eight-week summer session—almost twice as high as the tuition at the already expensive Art Students League—Johnson earned his tuition, as well as money for his food and lodgings, by working as the school's all-around handyman. From carrying Hawthorne's painting equipment to and from classes, to regularly helping to maintain Hawthorne's cinder tennis courts behind the artist's Provincetown home, Johnson became one of the essential human cogs in the summer school machinery. This work/study arrangement also fostered the development of a close relationship between Hawthorne and Johnson. Hawthorne had served as an inspiring art teacher and mentor to literally hundreds of young aspiring art students in his lifetime, yet he was especially moved by Johnson's abilities and felt that he would do whatever he could to assist the young black artist, particularly in light of Johnson's meager circumstances.

Prentiss Taylor, who was a student at the Cape Cod School of Art during the summers

11. *Nude Study*, ca. 1925. Oil on canvas, dimensions and whereabouts unknown

12. *Still Life*, ca. 1923–26. Oil on canvas, 25⅜ x 31⅞ in.

of 1924 and 1925, remembered that Johnson was not alone in his adulation of Hawthorne and that among many of the students there was a kind of unspoken competition for the teacher's attention and approval. One Friday morning, for example, Hawthorne gathered his students for the weekly painting demonstration. Taylor recalled that Johnson was one of three students that day who eagerly set up the easel, laid out the painting materials, and attended to Hawthorne's every anticipated wish. Taylor remembered fellow student Alice Harold Murphy wryly commenting that the three students fawning over Hawthorne reminded her of a contemporary version of "the Adoration of the Magi," with Johnson obviously playing the part of the black king.[15]

13. Group photo from the Cape Cod School of Art, 1925. William H. Johnson (second from left, front); Hong Ting Wong (right, front); Helen J. Rennie (left of center, rear)

A photograph from Helen Rennie's scrapbook shows Johnson as part of a group of casually dressed art students at the Cape Cod School of Art (fig. 13). Also included in the large group photograph is Johnson's N.A.D. classmate and former life model, Hong Ting Wong. According to Rennie, students who wanted to work closely with Hawthorne, or who needed a reprieve from their working-class, rough-and-tough classmates at the N.A.D., often went to Provincetown in the summers, if they could afford the relatively stiff tuition.[16]

Helen Rennie, Prentiss Taylor, and other former Cape Cod students recalled that while Johnson was very much a part of Hawthorne's classes and outdoor painting excursions, he did not really participate in the extracurricular activities at the school. Although ostensibly a "member of the group," as seen in this photograph, Johnson did not join the other students in their social gatherings after class, nor did he participate in their weekend dances, picnics, and dates. Certainly the racial and sexual attitudes of most Americans at that time provide one explanation for his nonparticipation in these student activities. But other factors, which have to do with Johnson's personality and mechanisms for coping, may also explain his absence.

Both Helen Rennie and Prentiss Taylor remembered that, in spite of the friendly, relaxed atmosphere at the Cape Cod school, Johnson would rarely interact with his fellow students, nor would he engage them in conversation. "As far as this photograph is concerned," Rennie recalled, "Johnson just happened to be around at the time, and somebody encouraged him to take part. Otherwise, he probably wouldn't have been included." If someone spoke to Johnson, he would often answer them in a decorous manner, all the while maintaining an unduly reserved, almost solemn bearing. At first, the other students attributed his cool, emotional distance to a natural aloofness; later, however, they thought that Johnson may have wanted to convey a more mature self-image by appearing

14. *New York Times* rotogravure of Charles W. Hawthorne's class at the Cape Cod School of Art, William H. Johnson (far left), 10 August 1924, sec. 5, p. 6.

stand-offish because he was self-conscious about being slightly older than the others.[17]

They also sensed that he was uncomfortable whenever questions arose concerning his racial background. And given the free license that, historically, many whites felt they had in relationship to blacks, one can assume that Johnson was frequently asked about his race, and probably without a lot of tact or sensitivity. And no doubt, his fellow students were not quite sure what to make of him: talented, handsome, with a tawny complexion and wavy black hair, this quiet African-American man could have easily "passed" for Latino, Indian, Middle Eastern, or any combination of these.

And conversely, Johnson must have wondered how he—Southern-born, working-class, under-educated, and racially mixed—could best cope during the summers with these white, relatively affluent, yet unpredictable young men and women. And his answer was probably to retreat into the background of this seemingly casual but class-conscious milieu, where he could function with whites as blacks had always: as silent or, at least, low-key participants in society. Johnson could fully partake of the art and information from the painting sessions with Hawthorne but, in potentially problematic social situations, whether after school or in town, simply abstain from participating, and instead disappear into his rented room.

In spite of these minor but still important interpersonal challenges for Johnson, his summers at Cape Cod provided him with a welcomed escape from his regular routine of formal art classes, menial jobs, and inner-city living back in New York (fig. 14). Although no landscapes, watercolors, or other works of art are known to exist from Johnson's Provincetown experience, selected works painted several years later in the south of France hark back to the Provincetown teachings of Hawthorne (fig. 15). Johnson's watercolor, from around 1928–29, of the landscape on the Mediterranean island of Corsica recalls Hawthorne's following recipe for painting out of doors:

Make your canvas drip with sunlight. You cannot reproduce nature out of doors for it is impossible to do what you see; you have to approximate by a convention. . . . Exaggerate to give the impression inside that you feel outside. Key your work higher than nature really seems to be, and when you take it indoors and hang it upon the wall, it will come nearer to the truth or to the way you want it to appear.

Hawthorne's insistence on a subjective reality, especially in relation to a *plein-aire* world of visual material, was affirmed in his own watercolors.[18] Unlike other instances where

Hawthorne's statements and aesthetic deeds diverge from one another, watercolors such as *New Hampshire Lake-Raymond* perfectly illustrate Hawthorne's directives to his art students (fig. 16).

In Johnson's *Piana, Corsica,* the pigments drip and congeal with an artistic abandon that reminds one of Hawthorne's axiom: "a good watercolor is a happy accident." Hawthorne's instructions to neither make a watercolor "too precious" nor to "bother about the object but [to place] the spots of color against each other," also seem to be Johnson's motivation in this French landscape. Notwithstanding Johnson's familiarity by 1929 with a whole corpus of figurative, expressionist artists and art works in Europe, Hawthorne's teachings clearly set a precedent for much of Johnson's early work in watercolor and in the landscape genre.

Under Hawthorne's tutelage, Johnson distinguished himself as one of the N.A.D.'s most promising art students. In the three years that Johnson studied with Hawthorne, he received numerous honors as well as cash prizes that totaled in excess of three hundred dollars.

During the 1925–26 terms, Johnson's fifth and final year at the N.A.D., he applied for the school's most coveted award, the Pulitzer Traveling Scholarship. Founded by Joseph Pulitzer, the newspaper editor, publisher, and philanthropist, the fifteen-hundred-dollar traveling scholarship was awarded annually to "the most promising and deserving" student from an accredited art school in the United States. Although other students were theoretically eligible, it was an unspoken assumption that the jury for the scholarship (which was comprised entirely of N.A.D. members) would select a student from the School of the N.A.D.

Johnson's school record was outstanding and his work with a variety of N.A.D. teachers (Hinton, Maynard, Curran, and Hawthorne) confirmed his understanding of the "Academy Ideals." In spite of his achievements, however, Johnson lost the Pulitzer Traveling Scholarship to fellow N.A.D. student Umberto Romano. Although the twenty-year-old Romano was also a Life-in-Full student of Hawthorne's, he had an even more influential advocate in the long-time school instructor and Academician Ivan G. Olinsky.[19]

There were many who felt, however, that Johnson was the most deserving applicant for the scholarship. Years later, Ilya Bolotowsky reaffirmed that Johnson was "one of the most gifted art students" he had ever seen and that his losing the scholarship to Romano was probably because of racial prejudice and because everybody knew that Johnson was a "Hawthorne favorite." Francis Costa concurred with Bolotowsky but also felt that the jurors were more likely—as a result of class prejudice—to pick a student from an affluent background (Romano's father was a businessman) rather than a student, like Johnson, of working-class origins.[20]

Charles Hawthorne, who felt strongly about Johnson's potential as an artist, was obviously disappointed in the jury's choice. But rather than resign himself to the jury's decision, he personally raised about one thousand dollars among his friends and colleagues to finance Johnson for a year of independent art study in Paris.[21]

15. *Piana, Corsica*, ca. 1929. Watercolor on paper, 24 x 18¾ in.

16. Charles W. Hawthorne, *New Hampshire Lake-Raymond*, 1927. Watercolor on paper, 13¹⁵⁄₁₆ x 19 ¹⁵⁄₁₆ in.

17. William H. Johnson's 1926 passport photograph

Hawthorne's encouragement of Johnson to pursue an extended course of independent art study in Paris was more than simply that of a concerned teacher for a talented student—there were deeper implications at work. Hawthorne knew that no matter how talented Johnson was, he would have difficulties advancing in a racially biased environment. Hawthorne also realized that the New York art world was a microcosm of the larger society, and (as seen already in the jury's decision concerning the scholarship) it would not support a young black artist in the same way it would a similarly talented white youth.

Paris, in 1926, was both the mecca of the art world and a cultural magnet in Europe for people of many different nationalities and ethnic backgrounds. Because of the good exchange rates for U.S. dollars, Americans were also moving to Paris by the droves, especially drawn to its post-World War I atmosphere of artistic freedom, intellectual inquiry, and social abandon. Black Americans, especially in the performing arts, had been working in Parisian nightclubs, amusement halls, theaters, and cabarets for much of the decade, contributing significantly to the city's cultural reputation. Henry Ossawa Tanner, a world-renowned painter of religious subjects and, in the opinion of many, *the* leading black American artist, had been a resident of Paris since 1891. With all of these factors in mind, Hawthorne advised Johnson that, as a young, gifted, and black artist, he would be virtually at home in a city like Paris.[22]

After securing an affidavit from Florence's Master in Equity, which verified his place and date of birth, William H. Johnson was issued a passport on 27 September 1926 (fig. 17). Accompanying Johnson to the passport office that day was his Aunt Rebecca, who also served as a witness to his identity. According to his passport application, Johnson had already made plans to travel to France by obtaining a porter's job on one of the many ships leaving New York's Port Authority. But since he still needed to raise some additional funds, Johnson remained in New York until November of that year, working part-time as a custodian in the studio of painter George B. Luks (1867–1933).

Although it is not certain exactly how or when Johnson met Luks, this celebrated member of the turn-of-the-century artists' group known as "The Eight" had been teaching in New York for several years and was widely perceived as one of the art scene's more colorful characters. Luks, a former newspaper illustrator and journalist, and the other members of his circle painted New York's demimonde, indigents, and common folk with a flair and passion that earned them another name—the Ash Can School. Among these painters, Luks was the most extroverted, often identifying with his subjects to such an extent that he himself became a part of their world of back-alley fist fights and lengthy alcoholic binges.[23] During Johnson's part-time employment with the elder artist, Luks's art followed a visceral, high-key approach, as seen in paintings like *The Miner*, that owes much to the bravura technique of seventeenth-century Dutch painter Frans Hals (fig. 18). In exchange for his custodial services, Johnson received both a small salary and a few painting lessons from Luks which, no doubt, reinforced the monetary and instructional offerings of Charles Hawthorne.

On the eve of Johnson's departure for Europe, his work was still basically the product of America's foremost art academy. His *Self-Portrait*, *Still Life* and, to a lesser extent, *Nude Study* fit comfortably within the boundaries of what was acceptable to the art establishment. Yet lying just beneath the surface and sense of tradition in these paintings was something offbeat and novel. A small rainbow of colors, a figure's penetrating glance, and subtle permutations of the artist's brushstroke and use of the palette knife all seemed to challenge "Academy Ideals" as they indicated a move toward self-expression. Though his work was still far from modernistic or expressionistic, the visual language of post-impressionism—strong colors, fluid painting, an immediacy of vision, and emotional empathy with the subject—had been drilled into Johnson by his teacher and mentor, Charles Webster Hawthorne. As he sailed for Paris, Johnson carried the ideological compass that would chart his direction in art for the next twelve years.

18. George B. Luks, *The Miner*, 1925. Oil on canvas, 61¼ x 50½ in.

19. *Vieille Maison*, ca. 1927. Oil on burlap, 24 x 20 in.

First Successes
1926–1930

Paris: it was some experience. new life. The Dôme. sit down with a "café," with Eye[s] open you see the world in Cavalcade. before a few hours I had met fellow artists from New York, Provincetown. . . . first winter in Paris, sharing James M. Whistler's first studio in Montparnasse—painting . . . as an independent man. . . . continued still-life, portrait painting, with many visits to art museums and galleries, with a little French on the side

William H. Johnson, ca. 1938

This reminiscence, written by William H. Johnson after twelve years abroad, looks back to the autumn of 1926 when, as an impressionable twenty-five-year-old, he arrived in Paris. This brief but poignant quotation describes how Paris was the setting for Johnson's self-discovery, as well as for his view of the world as an expressive, dynamic place. While most accounts of Paris in the 1920s recall the cultural "invasion" by Lost Generation literary figures, including Ernest Hemingway and F. Scott Fitzgerald, or by flamboyant, artistic personalities such as Gertrude Stein, Man Ray, or Josephine Baker, Johnson's memoir proudly recounts his following in the footsteps of artistic ancestors like the American expatriate painter James McNeill Whistler, the archetypal "American in Paris."

Johnson's first home in Paris, Whistler's former studio at 86, rue Notre-Dame-des-Champs, was situated within easy walking distance to Montparnasse's famous cafés, the studios of countless painters and sculptors, and the famed art school, l'Academie de la Grande-Chaumière. Although this Left Bank base provided the young artist with limitless opportunities for encountering the latest art works, painting techniques, and artistic lifestyles, the first paintings from Johnson's stay in Paris owed more to the French artists of the previous generation than they did to any of his contemporaries.

Vieille Maison and two still lifes (ca. 1927) recall the turn-of-the-century French impressionist paintings of Pissaro, Monet, and especially Sisley: three artistic giants who were well represented by numerous art galleries throughout Paris and in the nearby Musée du Luxembourg (figs. 19–21). In addition to these artists, the impact of Charles Hawthorne's teachings was also evident, as seen especially in Johnson's *Vieille Maison*, and in a candid snapshot of Johnson painting *Vieille Maison* under the towers of the

20. *Still Life*, 1927. Oil on burlap, 23 x 19⅛ in.

21. *Still Life*, ca. 1927. Oil on canvas, 32 x 25⅛ in.

22. Painting *Vieille Maison*, probably near Chartres, France, ca. 1927

cathedral at Chartres (fig. 22). While Johnson's formal overtures to a latter-day Impressionism and his thematic reliance on nature separated him from some of the more radical elements of the French art world, these elements of style also represented a degree of progress and a growing independence for the former Academician. In choosing to paint in a representational, yet high-key, faceted, and impasto manner, Johnson was casting his lot with a generic form of French modernism that, in part, comprised Paris's eclectic art scene, circa 1927.

These paintings and others were featured in Johnson's first solo exhibition in November 1927 at the Students and Artists Club on the Boulevard Raspail. Johnson was not the only black American artist exhibiting his paintings in Paris that season. Palmer C. Hayden (1890–1973), a custodian-turned-landscape painter and a 1926 recipient of a Harmon Foundation Gold Medal and cash award, was exhibiting his paintings at the same time at the fashionable Galerie Bernheim-Jeune.

In an interview for the Paris Edition of the *New York Herald* on the occasion of his exhibition, Johnson spoke about France, observing that its air was "more subdued," the tones "quieter," and the sky "a deeper blue" than he had experienced in the United States. "I must admit," Johnson nevertheless announced, "Paris in the winter does not inspire me at all. It is entirely too gray. I need . . . to have vivid color and contrasts before me to make me paint, which I hope to find on the Riviera. . . . To express a feeling on canvas, one must first *feel* it, and I don't feel the grayness surrounding us now."[1] By this time, Johnson had obviously decided to leave his Paris home of only one year to seek out the warmer climate and more colorful atmosphere of southern France.

Although not immediately apparent from Johnson's interview, another reason for his desire to move to the south of France (specifically, the town of Cagnes-sur-Mer) may have been that region's association with one of France's most celebrated artists, the Lithuanian-born, French-trained painter Chaim Soutine (1893–1943). Soutine's expressionistic landscapes of Céret and Cagnes—which entered into modern art consciousness in a series of critically and financially successful Left Bank exhibitions in the 1920s—were all the rage in Paris, especially after the American art collector and millionaire, Dr. Al-

bert Barnes, became Soutine's most ardent patron (fig. 23).
For many artists, including Johnson, Soutine's works became painted advertisements for the beautiful, sweeping
vistas of the south of France, as well as subconscious symbols of quick, glittery success in Paris's contemporary art
market.

Johnson's *New York Herald* interview hints at his
awareness of Soutine and his doubts about some other
contemporary artists. When asked by the interviewer
about "the modern painters" and their license to freely
interpret reality, Johnson stated that this approach was far
more appealing to him than one that seeks a photographic
interpretation of the world. "But unfortunately," Johnson
continued, "there is often a lack of sincerity among the
painters of today. They are seekers after sensational effects
and neither seek nor are capable of a profound emotion,
nor are they technically well equipped to carry out any

23. Chaim Soutine, *Landscape
at Cagnes*, ca. 1923–24.
Oil on canvas, 21⅛ x 25½ in.

serious conception." With the cubist, dadaist, surrealist, and international constructivist
painters all representing the radical fringe of the Paris art world, Johnson's comments
could be interpreted as voicing sharp opposition to these "moderns" and their collective
deconstruction of time-honored artistic conventions.

But in contrast, Chaim Soutine's handling of an expressive, autographic painting technique seems to have provided Johnson with a real alternative to what he perceived as
modernism's often emotional and technical shortcomings. This view of Soutine, expressionism in art, and Johnson's related struggle to "work out a style of [his] own" were the
primary topics of his August 1928 letter from Cagnes-sur-Mer to his teacher and mentor
Charles Hawthorne.

Johnson never mentions Soutine by name in his letter, but his description of "the real
spirited modern painters," who utilize "distortion," "elongation," and an "elution [*sic*] of
the reality," surely referred to Soutine, himself a former resident of Cagnes. "I am painting," wrote Johnson, ". . . the old villages, buildings, and streets. . . . I have a big space to
select from that gives me all the freedom that I need. Here the sun is everything." "I am
not afraid," he further explained to Hawthorne, "to exaggerate a contour, a form, or anything that gives more character and movement to the canvas." But in the same breath,
Johnson stressed his "great admiration for *the nature*" and concern that his "freedom"
not take him too far away from a perceived reality.[2]

These thoughts about Expressionism, Johnson's own coming to terms with modern
trends in painting, and the south of France as an inspiring site for art-making are all evident in Johnson's paintings from Cagnes-sur-Mer. The earliest of these, *Houses on an*

24. *Houses on an Incline, Cagnes-sur-Mer*, ca. 1927. Oil on canvas, 19¼ x 23½ in.

Incline, Cagnes-sur-Mer, maintains the luminous, jewel-like quality of his Parisian subjects, while incorporating subtle geometries via stark shadows and raking sunlight (fig. 24).

In *Village Houses, Cagnes-sur-Mer*, Johnson abandons altogether the proto-formalist tendencies of the earlier townscape and, instead, freely imposes a knowing distortion on the small, narrow streets of this typical, French Mediterranean-styled town (figs. 25, 26). The bending and swaying buildings, which form a kind of tunnel for the viewer, suggest a nervous energy and individual sense of rhythm that, up to this point, are absent from Johnson's work. In his letter to Hawthorne, he conceded that, in the process of making changes in his artistic outlook, he "worked like a fool to exploit some of [his] new enthusi-asm[s]" and, as seen in works like *Village Houses, Cagnes-sur-Mer*, that "it was not long before [he] grasped the significance" of it all.

The artistic trail blazed by Soutine eased Johnson's entry, with *Village Houses, Cagnes-sur-Mer*, into expressionist art territories. Yet Johnson's affinity for Soutine's painterly trademarks—viscous oil paint, topsy-turvy interpretations of architecture, and amorphic, wavering portraiture—should not be viewed as imitation. Paintings that at first appear to be of one spirit, such as Soutine's *Landscape at Cagnes* (see fig. 23) and Johnson's *Cagnes-sur-Mer*, are actually the products of two, very distinct sensibilities (fig. 27). For Soutine, the rugged, natural terrain and cockeyed buildings in *Landscape at Cagnes* express their disintegration via his diagnostic brushwork, virulent combinations of colors, and, most important, his elemental composition, in which the sky, mountains, and architecture are all given the same two-dimensional, gestural treatment. Johnson, on the other hand, employs a rhythmic, but consciously orchestrated distortion in *Cagnes-sur-Mer*, so that the earthquakelike effects seem to emanate from an underground source. Johnson's academicism shines through in his tumultuous, but composed view, while Soutine's iconoclastic position in modern French art is fully revealed in his riotous landscape.

Village Houses, Cagnes-sur-Mer and *Cagnes-sur-Mer* both exhibit what Johnson described in his letter to Hawthorne as a "reverence [for] the minute detail of the color variation in the sun light," and an "abstraction of pure form." These two townscapes strike a curious balance, with a fidelity to a particular architectural type offset by the revelation of Johnson's own excitable nature—or what one art critic, upon viewing these paintings in Johnson's circa 1929 exhibition at the Galerie Alban in nearby Nice, called

25. *Village Houses, Cagnes-sur-Mer*, ca. 1928–29. Oil on canvas, 31 x 25⅛ in.

26. Postcard, Cassis, France, ca. 1925

"un rythme personnel des courbes inattendues" (a personal rhythm from the unexpected curves).[3]

By the time of this latest exhibition in Nice, Johnson had lived in France for almost three years. Cagnes, his home for the last year and a half, was a frequently visited tourist spot along the French Riviera and a legendary hideaway for the weary gamblers and party-goers of Monte Carlo, Nice, and Antibes. From the majestic Grimaldi castle, tucked away in the mountainous "Haut de Cagnes," to the picturesque coast, running alongside a turquoise-colored Mediterranean, Cagnes was the destination for tourists, sun-worshipers, artists, and socialites alike.

Johnson's Riviera, unlike the idyllic playground depicted by American expatriates such as Harry Crosby or Gerald Murphy, was a bohemian world inhabited by society's marginalia: working-class French nationals, a collection of vagabonds of almost every imaginable race and creed, and an accompanying body of poverty-stricken artists and intellectuals hoping for greatness. Although racism occasionally reared its ugly head even within this cultural *bouillabaisse* (especially in response to the few Africans and African-Americans on this scene), Johnson, like many of his fellow blacks in Europe, found France's racism to be a far less insidious evil than the U.S. variety.

Artists of many different aesthetic and cultural persuasions counted high among the temporary residents of Cagnes-sur-Mer. The town's informality, inexpensive lodgings, brilliant light, and, of course, its reputation as the former home of such art legends as Soutine and Renoir, all gave it high marks for painters and other artists. One such artist was the Indianapolis-born, African-American painter Hale Woodruff, who for a brief time also lived and painted in Cagnes. Oddly enough, Woodruff never encountered Johnson during the time they both resided in that tiny resort town, and it was not until some fifteen years later, in New York, that these two former residents of Cagnes would actually meet.

Among the many artists that Johnson did encounter in Cagnes-sur-Mer during 1928–29 were the German Expressionist sculptor and printmaker Christoph Voll (1897–1939), his Danish wife Erna, and her unmarried sister, textile artist Holcha Krake (figs. 28, 29). When they first met Johnson, the three were on a holiday jaunt across Europe and were only passing through Cagnes. Their brief encounter with Johnson quickly developed into such an empathetic and friendly meeting that they invited him to join them on the next leg of their tour: a Mediterranean boat ride to the French island of Corsica.

En route to Corsica, Johnson learned about Christoph Voll's humble beginnings in a Munich orphanage, his disillusionment with the military during World War I, his move to Dresden after the war, and his involvement (as a student at the Dresden Kunstakademie) with a left wing, politically oriented group of German Expressionist artists, known

27. *Cagnes-sur-Mer*, ca. 1928–29. Oil on canvas, 23½ x 28½ in.

28. Christoph and Erna (Musse) Voll, Saarbrücken, Germany, ca. 1925

29. Holcha Krake, ca. 1920.

as the *Sezession: Gruppe 1919*. Johnson learned that in spite of Voll's relative youth as a practicing artist, his sculpture was considered by many to be among the most representative examples of new German art (fig. 30). Prior to meeting Voll, Johnson's notions of modern art were largely confined to artists and/or movements whose locus was Paris. But after meeting Voll, Johnson began to hear about the cultural significance of places such as Dresden, Mannheim, Stuttgart, and Berlin, and the previously unfamiliar names of important artists such as Otto Dix, Oskar Kokoschka, Ernst Barlach, and George Grosz.

Erna Krake, Voll's wife, was an art student at the Dresden Kunstakademie when she met her future husband. Erna's older sister, Holcha Krake (1885–1944), had actually begun the study of art before either Christoph or Erna. After following a general course of study within Denmark's network of nationalist, adult-education schools (known as the folkhøjskole), Holcha began an extensive, independent study of folk-weaving techniques and design theories throughout Europe.[4] Odd as it may seem, Voll, Erna, Holcha Krake, and the young black American painter Johnson all found enough common ground and interest in one another to form an impromptu band of kindred souls in art.

Suggested in Johnson's vibrating, contorted paintings of Corsica are the telltale signs of a more agitated emotional state than that normally conveyed in his art, evidently precipitated by his growing affection for one of his kindred traveling companions, Holcha Krake (see fig. 15). Observed from the vantage point of their respective races, cultural backgrounds, and ages (Johnson's twenty-eight to Holcha's forty-four), one perhaps could not find a couple as dissimilar as these two. Yet in a very short time, they had indeed fallen in love and were almost inseparable.

That this relationship may have had some initial moments of doubt and, subsequently, its share of trial runs and emotional tests, is suggested in a humorous little caricature of Johnson, drawn in Corsica by an unknown artist. Beneath the pen-and-ink sketch of Johnson as a demonic, wild-haired spectre is an inscription in French, which translates: "To Mephisto, perhaps a Cuckold!" (fig. 32).

In any event, Johnson and Holcha survived this implied (or actual) lapse of fidelity, as seems clear from a wistful account of that spring, written by Johnson many years later. In Johnson's remembrance of his and Holcha's time in Corsica, he wrote that they "painted together, . . . enjoyed the sun, the beauty of the landscape, and the simple peasant life" (fig. 31).[5] This idyllic period in the south of France may have reminded Johnson of his summers at the Cape Cod School of Art, which was also located by the sea in an informal, artistic setting. But Johnson's new-found sense of personal confidence, emotional openness, and artistic freedom in France, especially among his new European friends, was such that, by 1929, the image that he held of art and life in the United States had faded considerably.

Still, in correspondence with Charles Hawthorne, Johnson spoke of eventually returning to the United States, if only to see his family again and to exhibit his new paintings. "My mother writes [that] . . . she wouldn't mind if I should come back to the states," Johnson told Hawthorne, "but you know what you told me hold[s] good with me . . . so the first chance I get to settle down in France I will sure take advantage of it."[6] That Hawthorne had counseled Johnson to remain in Europe is the subject of another letter, in which Hawthorne wrote:

I will be interested to see what you've been doing and will probably see your canvases next winter when I get back. Very glad you are getting on so well, and I would advise you, if you can possibly arrange it, to count on making your home abroad. I feel that life will be much easier for you there. If you can come over, I would do so with the thought of finding some place to exhibit my things, and then returning to where I would be more comfortable, as, in New York, there is bound to be prejudice against your race.[7]

Probably Hawthorne's only model for a successful black artist was Henry Ossawa Tanner, whose self-imposed exile to France made expatriation, in Hawthorne's mind, the only viable way to be both a successful artist *and* black. And since Johnson had met Tanner shortly after arriving in 1926 and had seen for himself how well off Tanner was and how seemingly free of the effects of American prejudice, the thought of living abroad was definitely to be considered.[8]

After Corsica, Johnson left Cagnes to travel with the Volls and Holcha throughout Europe. The foursome made intermittent stops at selected art museums and other cultural institutions in France, Germany, Luxembourg, Belgium, and other European countries—with their travels documented in Johnson's old scrapbook of picture postcards. By mid autumn, however, the Volls had returned to Karlsruhe to begin a new session at the Kunstakademie, Holcha was back at home in Odense, Denmark, to assist her middle sister in caring for their widowed elderly mother, and Johnson was on a transatlantic freighter, heading for New York. But even as he worked his way across the Atlantic, an older, more mature and confident Johnson seemed fairly certain that the last three years were only the beginning of a new phase for him, and that the European experience, his new friends, a love interest, and his revised outlook on art, life, and the world would no doubt lead to ever more exciting terrain (fig. 33).

After docking in New York and reconnecting with friends and relatives, Johnson rented

30. Christoph Voll, *Nude, Ecce Homo*, 1926. Wood, 64¾ in. high.

31. Postcard, Évisa, Corsica, France, ca. 1925

32. Anonymous, *Caricature of William H. Johnson*, ca. 1929. Pen and ink on paper, 10 x 7⅞ in.

the top-floor loft of a garage in Harlem, at 311 West 120th Street. With his paintings of Chartres, Fountainbleu, Cagnes-sur-Mer, Corsica, and innumerable still lifes and portraits scattered about the room, he proceeded to do more paintings, in hopes of having enough for a solo exhibition somewhere in the city (fig. 34). One of his friends, former N.A.D. classmate Ilya Bolotowsky, sat for a portrait done in this "new," modern mode of Johnson's. The result shows how Johnson was still stylistically enamored of the quivering and quaking techniques of painter Chaim Soutine (fig. 35). Bolotowsky's rumpled outfit, lean build, and eastern European looks were physical features that easily fused with Soutine's methods of portraiture (fig. 36).

Similarly, two self-portraits by Johnson, with their painterly eruptions and seismographiclike brushwork, are also akin to Soutine's portraits (figs. 37, 38). The 1929 painting, however, with the large, foppish bow tie, lavalike rendering of the profiled face, and the swollen, searing eyes, extends beyond Soutine's distant, disintegrating portrayals and, instead, moves in the direction of a self-conscious, highly perceptive use of figural distortion. In this and many portraits from the 1929–30 period, Johnson demonstrates a genuine talent for realizing—without mollifying the self-expression and experimentation of his art—the very countenance and soul of each sitter.

George B. Luks, who had briefly employed the young artist just prior to his departure for France, met with Johnson several weeks after his return to New York. Seeing how much Johnson had advanced over the last three years, Luks suggested that he nominate Johnson for the Harmon Foundation's 1929 Award for Distinguished Achievements Among Negroes in the Fine Arts Field. Although Luks was a juror for the awards that year, and the nominations had already been closed for several months, he assured Johnson that he had as good a chance as any of the other nominees.

Luks contacted the Harmon Foundation and asked them to accept his belated nomination of Johnson, saying that he felt there was something "special" about Johnson and his work. Upon receiving the Harmon Foundation's official word that they would accept his application, Johnson submitted the 102nd and last application for the 1929 awards.[9]

The Harmon Foundation had been established in New York in 1922 as a "family organization through which constructive service might be rendered . . . through pride in achievement." American real-estate tycoon William Elmer Harmon (1862–1928) founded this philanthropic organization initially to assist small U.S. cities in building community playgrounds and recreation fields. The foundation later expanded its philanthropy to include student loans, pensions for health workers, and support for a variety of

33. William H. Johnson, ca. 1927

34. *Young Pastry Cook*, ca. 1928–30. Oil on canvas, 31¼ x 22⅝ in.

causes, including improvements for rural health clinics and the development of a Religious Motion Pictures Organization.[10]

The Harmon Foundation's presentation of medals and monetary awards for outstanding achievements among Negroes, co-administered by the Commission on Race Relations of the Federal Council of Churches of Christ in America, recognized excellence in literature, music, business, science, education, religious service, race relations, and fine arts. In the fine arts field, former award recipients included Johnson's fellow visitors to France, Palmer C. Hayden and Hale Woodruff; the Philadelphia portrait painter Laura Wheeler Waring; sculptor May Howard Jackson of Washington, D.C.; and the Chicago painter of colorful, black genre scenes, Archibald J. Motley, Jr. In the year he applied, Johnson competed against such up-and-coming talents as Allan Rohan Crite, Lois Mailou Jones, and sculptors Sargent Johnson and Augusta Savage.

In addition to Luks, the jury for the 1929 awards was comprised of sculptor Meta Warwick Fuller, art critic George Hellman, sculptor Karl Illava, and artist/illustrator Victor Perard. After deliberating in early December, the jury unanimously decided that Johnson should receive the Harmon Gold Medal and a four-hundred-dollar cash award. Two bronze medals were also awarded, one to Sargent Johnson and the other to painter/printmaker Albert Alexander Smith. In a published statement regarding Johnson and his work, the jury (which was probably quoting Luks) said: "We think he is one of our coming great painters. He is a real modernist. He has been spontaneous, vigorous, firm, direct; he has shown a great thing in art—it is the expression of the man himself."[11]

Following the announcement of the 1929 awards, several Harmon Foundation staff members paid a visit to Johnson's Harlem loft. In preparing a general news release about the gold medal winner, one staff member made detailed notes on what they saw:

A visit to him on a rainy day recently found him working in a very large room covering the entire top floor of [a] garage building and its walls lined with his Modern paintings. Rain was leaking through the roof in several places and water stood on the floor nearly everywhere except for a small space around his couch. In order to enter the room, one had to cross an improvised bridge over a pool of water. The bridge was from the top of an orange crate on which Mr. Johnson had, at some previous time, painted a portrait. He had just completed a self-portrait which stood on the easel. The room was entirely without electric lights, although empty sockets hung from the ceiling here and there. As the darkness approached, Mr. Johnson lighted a candle which stood in the neck of a bottle. The place was clean and orderly and while the furnishings

35. *Ilya Bolotowsky*, 1930. Oil on canvas, 24 x 19⅞ in.

36. Chaim Soutine, *Portrait of a Gypsy Boy*, ca. 1926. Oil on canvas, 18⅛ x 15 in.

37. *Self-Portrait*, ca. 1929.
Oil on canvas, dimensions and
whereabouts unknown

were most modest and the water on the floor at first very evident, Mr. John-
son's self-possession and joy at finding someone interested in what he was
doing made one forget these things and feel that he was a real genius and in
the finest surroundings.[12]

Although the above observations on Johnson's Spartan existence never appeared in the press release, the foundation's fascination with Johnson and his
work would continue for some time.

The Harmon Foundation's "Exhibit of Fine Arts," an annual show of works
by the awards applicants, was held in 1930 from the seventh until the nineteenth of January, at the International House on Manhattan's upper West Side.
Johnson's contributions, three landscapes (including his *Cagnes-sur-Mer*), two
portraits, and one *Self-Portrait*, were considered by many to be the most experimental works in the entire exhibition (see figs. 27,37).

Understandably, critical responses to Johnson's "modern" paintings ranged
from those that hailed Johnson's artistic efforts as "blazing a new trail" in Negro art to others that admonished Johnson for his "imitation" of "white painters" and his lack of "peculiar rhythm" and "directness of feeling." In particular,
the notion that the French moderns exerted "too much influence" over Johnson preoccupied the press and, thus, kept it from giving Johnson full praise.[13] That Johnson probably
did feel he had more in common with the proponents of *l'expressionisme français* than
with such Harlem Renaissance artists as Aaron Douglas, James Lesesne Wells, and Mi-
guel Covarrubias was hardly ever considered in the context of these reviews. Curiously,
coming to Johnson's defense in this flurry of criticism about European influences was an
editorial writer for the *New York Amsterdam News*, who noted that

. . . Negro artists are no more imitative than other American artists. Can we name one
eminent painter who is not saturated with European influences? Men like Sargent, Tan-
ner, and Whistler are Americans only in birth; they spend their lives in Europe and there
is nothing distinctively American in their work. This is as it should be, for a man is an
artist first and an American afterwards.[14]

This journalistic, critical discourse about black American artists, highly unusual for
1930, was viewed with much enthusiasm by the administrators of the Harmon Foundation. George Edmund Haynes, executive secretary of the Federal Council of Churches and
the chief administrator for the Harmon Awards, understood the importance of the annual
art exhibitions in promoting the values and goals of the foundation, as well as creating
public interest in black American culture. With the help of Mary Beattie Brady, the foundation's executive director, and her assistant Evelyn S. Brown, Haynes arranged for the

38. *Self-Portrait*, 1929. Oil on canvas, 23¼ x 18¼ in.

current exhibition to travel to sixteen U.S. cities in 1930 and 1931. As a result of the tour, the amount of publicity that Johnson received in New York was soon greatly multiplied, and news of his artistic merit appeared in the daily newspapers in Boston, Nashville, San Diego, Denver, Houston, Kansas City, and even in Johnson's hometown of Florence, South Carolina.[15]

As the dashing, circa 1927 photograph of William H. Johnson demonstrates, the once-insecure and withdrawn art student had evolved into a confident, almost cavalier, young painter, who took his new-found success and notoriety in the art world in stride (see fig. 33). Amid all the media attention and praise directed toward him, Johnson seemingly accepted his assigned role as a symbol of the "New Negro" arts movement with total grace. He did not, however, take this latest shift in his fortunes totally for granted. Instead of seeing his Harmon award and the accompanying money and acclaim as the ultimate fruits of his artistic labors, and possible inducements to complacency, Johnson continued to follow the humble, unconventional path of his existence prior to the awards: painting boldly expressive canvases, living and working modestly in his Harlem loft, and eschewing convention for the freewheeling life of an artist.

Although Johnson had not been in Florence since 1918, he frequently wrote to his mother, and she, in turn, regularly wrote to him, keeping him informed of various community events and family matters. Because of his recent successes in art and his share of media attention, Johnson decided in February to leave his Harlem studio, gather up his belongings (which consisted of a few clothes, some personal papers, and dozens of paintings) and make a special trip to visit his family in the Gate City.

Upon entering the Johnson household, William quickly realized that his siblings were no longer toddlers; with the exception of his twenty-year-old brother Lacy, the three younger children had only a vague memory of him. For the last five years, following a debilitating stroke suffered by Henry Johnson, Mom Alice and Lacy had been the principal breadwinners for the family. Willie's presence in Florence that spring and his contributions to the household budget no doubt helped the family considerably.

Conversely, Johnson hoped that his family, friends, and the town of Florence would inspire him, giving his art a little more of the "peculiar rhythm" and "directness of feeling" that some of his severest critics felt were wanting in his works. These expectations were alluded to in a letter to Dr. George E. Haynes, written by Johnson after one month in Florence. "I am feeling around at something," Johnson told Haynes, "as I am surrounded by little Negro boys and girls, hoping to abstract something of their [——] and putting it on canvas."[16] Although it is tempting to guess at what Johnson was suggesting in the empty space that followed his epistolary desire to "abstract something of" African-American youth, the answer perhaps rests in his Florence portraits. *Jim*, a portrait of Johnson's sixteen-year-old brother, encapsulates much of what was left unsaid in Johnson's half-voiced objective to paint Florence's young black citizens (fig. 39). A bifurcated back-

39. *Jim*, 1930. Oil on canvas, 21 x 18 in.

ground of black and ochre operates as a compositional anchor for the sitter, whose brown, russet, and light green colors create a dreamy and lucid effect. The figure's head and shoulders are not so much depictions of flesh and fabric as they are painted gestures of both the sitter's and Johnson's shared moods of anticipation and anxiety. Johnson willfully pushed and pulled the paint across his canvas—and while this accurately captured Jim's character, it also created a somewhat unsettling image.

Another painting by Johnson of a young black resident of Florence is reminiscent of the populist, multicultural concerns in portraiture of such American realists as Robert Henri and George Luks (fig. 40). But the awkward, naked stare and elongated, frontal position of Johnson's sitter in *Girl in a Green Dress* remove it from the standard light-hearted depictions of American types and, instead, place it among the stylized yet psychological portraits of Soutine, Modigliani, and other French antecedents in modern portraiture.

By using the pictorial devices—editing out background elements, for example, and exaggerating such physical characteristics as the eyes, necks, and torsos—of these modern portraitists, Johnson added to the emotional undercurrents already present within his sitters and, ultimately, made a convincing case for thinking of *Jim* and *Girl in a Green Dress* as visual evocations of the social and psychological complexities of growing up black in the American South. Given Johnson's own less than idyllic childhood, the vague and ineffable quality that he tried to describe to Haynes may very well refer to the *inner* self which, as these two portraits from Florence seem to suggest, was forever shaped in his art by a black *and* southern upbringing.

Minnie and *Jacobia Hotel*, unlike *Jim* and *Girl in a Green Dress*, are best understood in the context of Johnson's desire to document the local community (figs. 41, 42). The intense, highly energized *Minnie* succinctly records the features, as well as the legendary extroverted personality, of Minnie Kirkland, owner and principal chef of Florence's National Cafe.

Jacobia Hotel, on the other hand, depicts one of Florence's old landmarks, the Jacobi Hotel, which was named after one of the town's early merchant families. Although the hotel was considered an elegant and respectable place for visitors in the 1890s, by 1930 it was little more than a dilapidated old boardinghouse, frequented by transients and undesirables.

Jacobia Hotel features the same earthquakelike tremors as Johnson's landscapes from the south of France. The viewer's point of view, at some distance from the corner of the hotel, makes for dramatic spatial recessions and progressions. Although the building is in ruin, rhythms abound in the structure's multiple parallel supports and in its three projecting gables. Similarly, the colors in *Jacobia Hotel* cover the gamut, from the mostly pale blue sky and brown clapboards to the strong accents of blue-green and red-orange throughout.

40. *Girl in a Green Dress*, 1930. Oil on canvas, 24¼ x 19¼ in.

41. *Minnie*, 1930. Oil on canvas, 17½ x 12¼ in.

42. *Jacobia Hotel*, 1930. Oil on canvas, 19⅞ x 23¾ in.

43. *Landscape with Sun Setting, Florence, S.C.*, 1930. Oil on canvas, 23⅛ x 27 in.

Past biographers of Johnson have often relayed a thus-far unverified story about Johnson's arrest on the streets of Florence while painting *Jacobia Hotel*. As most accounts describe the incident, Johnson's indiscreet selection of the once-fashionable hotel-turned-brothel as an art subject irked local officials enough to cause the police to arrest him.[17] Family members say that Mom Alice's boss at the YMCA, Bill Covington, interceded for Johnson, who was *almost* arrested.[18] What *is* certain is that Johnson's outdoor public setting and lively animated act of painting *Jacobia Hotel* probably created an inordinate amount of attention and, possibly, a public nuisance, given the strange impression that an easel-toting, bobbing and weaving, black painter on Florence's streets would have conveyed in 1930.[19] For *Landscape with Sun Setting, Florence, S.C.*, Johnson chose a site in Florence's black community proper and, thus, was less likely to cause an "official" disturbance (fig. 43). *Jacobia Hotel*, with its collapsing architecture, swaying telephone poles, and barely perceptible powerlines, perhaps symbolizes Johnson's discomfort with old memories, former injustices, and the past and present social order of Florence.[20]

Then again, the local press coverage of Johnson's Harmon award, and a special one-day exhibition of his work while he was in Florence, suggested a genuine, though somewhat condescending, sense of pride on the part of the town's establishment in the achievements of this "humble Florence Negro youth." The description in the *Florence Morning News* of Johnson's mother (or "Aunt" Alice) as a "good old colored woman," a "good cook," and "faithful" in her twelve years of service to Florence's YMCA, situated the official praise of Johnson within a hierarchical, southern fantasy of loyal blacks and benevolent whites. Since segregation of the races was the traditional way of life, one can only assume that the newspaper announcements for the exhibition—with their invitations especially directed at "many of the town's ladies" and to "the public *generally*" (emphasis added)—indicated that the anticipated audience for the exhibition was probably not from Florence's black community. Still, the *Florence Morning News*'s closing statement from the announcement, which said that Johnson's "real genius may some day make the city of his birth famous," is a remarkable admission: one that paid an unqualified tribute to Johnson's accomplishments and their significance for his hometown.[21]

Johnson's exhibition of 135 paintings—an extraordinary number of works for such a limited showing—was held for one day only, on Tuesday, 15 April, from 3 P.M. until 6 P.M., in the Director's Room of Florence's YMCA. Bill Covington, the YMCA's secretary and Mom Alice's supervisor, made all of the arrangements for this unprecedented local art event.

Over the next several days, Johnson said farewell to his family and friends, quickly gathered up his paintings and, as he had done twelve years earlier, boarded a northbound train. But en route to New York, Johnson decided to stop in Washington, D.C., where he was a guest for a few days at the home of Alain Locke, Howard University professor of philosophy and the ex-officio spokesperson for the "New Negro" arts movement (fig. 44).

44. Alain Locke lecturing, on the occasion of a Harmon Foundation-sponsored exhibition, ca. 1942

Johnson probably had met Locke several months earlier at the presentation ceremonies for the Harmon Awards at New York's Mt. Olivet Baptist Church. Locke, who served as a consultant for the Harmon Foundation, prided himself on being *au courant* about the latest Negro authors, visual artists, and other creative people. His 1925 anthology of essays, short fiction, poetry, and reproductions of African and African-American art, *The New Negro*, was considered a kind of manifesto by all of the younger black artists. His reputation as an influential person in the art world and facilitator of contracts, fellowships, and other forms of support made him a much sought-after advocate by young, ambitious artists, among whom Johnson could certainly be counted.[22]

While Johnson was at Locke's home, he met the poet Langston Hughes, who had recently returned to the United States from a speaking engagement in Cuba. In a token of appreciation for Hughes's work, Johnson gave him one of his paintings.[23]

During their brief visit, Johnson informed Locke of his decision to leave the United States within the month and to settle in Europe. The two agreed to stay in touch, with Locke promising to work toward placing Johnson's paintings in museum collections, art galleries, and in the hands of a few private collectors.

Upon returning to New York, Johnson wasted no time in hiring himself out as a crew member on a freighter bound for Dunkirk, France. But unlike his first transatlantic crossing in 1926, this one carried expectations beyond those of a routine study trip abroad. With the confidence bestowed by the Harmon Award and cash prize, the knowledge that he could strongly compete with other painters, and the hopes of a loving reunion with Holcha Krake, the twenty-nine-year-old Johnson optimistically looked ahead to a life and career in Europe.

A Painter in the World
1930–1938

After docking in France around the middle of May 1930, William H. Johnson traveled by train, boat, and car along a northeastern route as he made his way through Belgium, the Netherlands, and Germany. Johnson's final destination was the Danish island of Funen, where he hoped to be reunited with his former European traveling companion, friend, and lover, the Danish artist Holcha Krake. He also hoped to marry her.

Holcha's family and friends, upon hearing of her impending marriage to Johnson, expressed surprise, but not only because William was black and sixteen years younger than she. Rather, they were more amazed that such a talented and fiercely independent woman would give up her freedom for something as conventional as marriage. Holcha, the product of a relatively enlightened upbringing, was considered by many to be a most unlikely candidate for matrimony. Her economic independence, unwavering commitment to her weaving, and lack of interest in such traditional "female" duties as keeping house and taking care of infants all suggested to her friends that she was destined to be the classic spinster. So when the well-traveled and sophisticated Holcha announced that she was going to be married—albeit to a twenty-nine-year-old Negro artist—her inner circle was in shock.[1]

In spite of the couple's determination to be wed, the forty-five-year-old Holcha did have some reservations about entering into such an arrangement, especially with a young, handsome foreigner whom she had known for only a little more than a year. With the warnings of her family ever present in her mind, Holcha convinced William that a prenuptial agreement was in order, so that in case of a divorce, she would be assured of getting back what she brought to the marriage. Apart from the traditional Danish heirlooms (furniture, glassware, books, and jewelry) Holcha listed, piece by piece, a substantial art collection—with paintings and graphic arts by brother-in-law Christoph Voll, sister Erna Krake Voll, former Dresden Kunstakademie associates Oskar Kokoschka and Wilhelm Rudolph, and eleven paintings by William H. Johnson, her future husband. Signed and dated by both parties on 28 May 1930, this prenuptial agreement—uncommon for that era—gave Holcha and her family some sense of security on the eve of the wedding.[2]

William and Holcha were married several days later in a simple ceremony in the town of Kerteminde. Officiating at their wedding was Kerteminde's mayor, who had been an old friend of Holcha's father, Søren Martin Sørensen (1860–1910), one of Funen's most re-

45. Holcha Krake and William
H. Johnson in their studio,
Kerteminde, Denmark, ca. 1931

spected educators.[3] For some reason, Holcha's widowed mother, Thora, and unmarried middle sister, Nanna, did not attend the wedding, although they lived in the nearby city of Odense, best known as the birthplace of Hans Christian Andersen, the nineteenth-century author of dozens of classic fairy tales.

After the wedding, William and Holcha decided to make their home in Kerteminde, so they gathered up their belongings and moved into a small house at Gasværksvej 5. A photograph from that first year in Kerteminde shows the couple at home, with Holcha's loom and Johnson's paintings sharing the close, intimate quarters (fig. 45).

Johanne-Marie Esbjerg, a family friend from Odense, remembered the newlyweds as a perfectly matched couple, in spite of their differences in age, race, and culture. The cheerful and light-hearted Holcha, along with the more reserved but gracious William, occasionally hosted Johanne-Marie and her family on their visits to Kerteminde. Holcha, remembered by Esbjerg for her voluminous, loose-fitting "peasant" dresses, outgoing manner with people, and passion for the "picturesque, *folkloric* aspects of life," was perhaps the perfect foil to Johnson's exotic looks and driven, brooding nature. Yet "Willie" and "Søster Søren," as the two were affectionately known to their close friends and family, were very much a pair in the eyes of Funen's citizens. And because the two were so totally committed to one another and to their respective art forms, the Johnson household always had the aura of "creative chaos," with half-completed canvases, unraveled yarns, paint-covered palettes, and art books scattered about.[4]

Although Kerteminde had long been regarded as one of Denmark's most picturesque port towns and oldest fishing communities, at the time of Johnson's arrival it also enjoyed a reputation as one of Denmark's best summer vacation spots. Kerteminde's pleasant climate during the summer months began drawing throngs of tourists, artists, and "sun-seekers" as early as World War I. Though Kerteminde's primary industry was fishing, travel brochures mentioned the elegant and popular Tornøes Hotel, the small but adequate strip of bathing beach, and Kerteminde's unique "mother-of-pearl" sunlight. By the time William and Holcha had settled there, this small town had a summer population in excess of five thousand, making the prospects of art sales to vacationers one of the probable reasons Holcha had for moving there.[5]

Surprisingly, the prejudicial attitudes about mixed marriages that one would have expected from a small, insular community like Kerteminde were nowhere to be found. Perhaps this openness had its roots in Holcha's ties to the town and the region, or maybe it

56

46. *Landskab fra Kerteminde* [Landscape, Kerteminde], ca. 1930–32. Oil on burlap, 23½ x 28½ in.

47. *Sun Setting, Denmark,* ca. 1930. Oil on burlap, 20¾ x 28⅛ in.

48. Vincent van Gogh,
Landscape from San Remy, 1889.
Oil on canvas, 27¾ x 34¾ in.

49. *Study for Sun Setting,
Denmark*, ca. 1930. Watercolor on
paper, 15 x 18 in.

was simply part of the straightforward and accepting nature of the people there.[6] In any event, the newlyweds felt completely at home in Kerteminde, and soon Johnson, with his portable easel balanced on his head, his rolled-up canvas under his arm, and his pipe with clouds of tobacco smoke trailing him, became one of the town's most common sights.

As Johnson wrote in an August 1930 letter to Alain Locke, Kerteminde's "vast fields of farms," and "its gardens of vegetables and flowers and even fruits" were "just like Paradise" to him, as well as the primary subject matter for his easel painting over the next several years.[7] *Landskab fra Kerteminde*, typical of these first Danish subjects by Johnson, is nevertheless comprised of those persistent, painterly mannerisms that Johnson had acquired in the south of France (fig. 46). Caught between a delirious bird's-eye view of Kerteminde and an experiment in autographic brushwork, *Landskab fra Kerteminde* attests to Johnson's continued exploration of an altered, self-defined outer world.

For the first time, however, Johnson went beyond Soutine as a role model in his searching of the landscape for its undercurrents, its patterns, and even its animated qualities. In *Sun Setting, Denmark*, for example, Johnson's debt to the pivotal, post-impressionist work of Vincent van Gogh is all too apparent (figs. 47, 48). Again, Johnson describes this painting in a letter to Alain Locke:

Have just done a good picture . . . the old port in Kerteminde . . . with the sun setting along the waters over the horizon with a fishing boat in the water to balance the old port on the other side of the canvas—it is a much improved composition and color harmony of that one you have from Florence, S.C. with the sun setting over the street. I'm quite pleased with it.[8]

Regardless of the success of *Sun Setting, Denmark*, Johnson's borrowing of van Gogh's insistent brushstroke suggests that the young artist was still very much an art chameleon, adopting the methods and gestures of significant art and artists who were close at hand. In nearby Copenhagen, Johnson would have had access to van Gogh paintings, both from reproductions and from the city's well-known art museum, Ny Carlsberg Glyptotek, a collection rich in works by van Gogh, Gauguin, and other early European moderns.

An interview with one of Johnson's old friends from those first years in Kerteminde perhaps reveals why Johnson's own artistic identity in *Sun Setting, Denmark* was so unresolved. Niels Hansen, a retired fish exporter, recalled that on occasion Johnson would study a prospective town view through a concave looking-glass.[9] Hansen was apparently referring to a "fish-lens," an apparatus once used by artists to see areas of land wider than the human eye normally allows. Like the wide-angle lens in modern photography, the fish-lens tends to bend and curve one's view, making the view conform to the lens's concave shape and round perimeter. An ovoid-shaped watercolor study by Johnson of the sun setting over Kerteminde's old port confirms Hansen's observation of over fifty years ago (fig. 49).

Of course, the fishermen of Kerteminde, not the most discerning of art critics, were often reverential to Johnson, perhaps awed by his strange pictures of town landmarks and local citizens. One of those fishermen, Niels Due, remembered Johnson as someone who "was always down here with the fishermen, painting." "He dressed just as we did," Due recalled, apparently referring to Johnson's donning of the standard blue overshirts of most Danish workers, "but he was a fine, handsome man" (fig. 50). On Johnson's use of the palette knife to paint his subjects, Due recounted an amusing moment between the artist and the fishermen:

50. William H. Johnson, ca. 1931

All of the fishermen laughed a bit in the beginning. . . . Naturally, we'd never seen painters spread their colors on with a palette knife—it looked like a sort of pliable table knife. I remember an old fisherman who came along and said, "Well, now we can throw all our brushes away! Now [when we paint our boats] we have to put the paint on with a knife!" Johnson just looked at him with his dark eyes, and the fisherman quickly realized that he was unwanted.[10]

Apart from these first, perplexing encounters with one another, Johnson and the people of Kerteminde quickly developed a camaraderie and emotional empathy for one another

51. Johannes Larsen, *Red Roofs, Kerteminde*, 1896. Oil on canvas, 22 x 27⅝ in.

that, from Johnson's point of view, resulted in a body of work that he considered his best. The distant, sometimes antisocial persona of Johnson's youth had given way to a more jocular, relaxed personality. Johnson seemed quite at ease among Kerteminde's fishing folk. When he was not in his studio or painting outdoors, he could usually be found with the town's fishermen, helping them carry the day's catch onto dry land or joking with them in the town's local pub. When asked by a Danish newspaper reporter if it was possible for a man of his race to paint Danish landscapes and Danish portraits, he replied, "Why not? On the contrary, I say that I have never worked as well in any place as in Kerteminde. In no place have I had greater peace in which to work, nor better motifs than right here in Denmark."[11]

Danish art critics, who were first introduced to Johnson and his paintings during this period, did notice, however, that he tended to lean a little too much on the methods of the modern European painters. "There is much in these pictures," wrote one art critic on the occasion of a joint William H. Johnson/Holcha Krake exhibition, "that reminds one of van Gogh and Cesanne [*sic*], two artistic geniuses, whose great art purified and made immortal a perspective which, when imitated, only becomes empty mannerism."[12] Another critic, writing about one of Johnson's first exhibitions in Denmark, observed that

Johnson . . . shows us pictures laden with nature and character, which one infrequently sees in these parts. He is a devotee of the most extreme form of modernism which . . . was at the height of popularity not more than a decade ago. There is merit in this art form but, for most northerners, it is just too difficult to embrace. With justification, one can argue about its merits, but not with Johnson, as he is definitely the master of it.[13]

The promise of an independent, latter-day expressionist vision in Johnson's Danish work did eventually manifest itself, as seen in *Tiled Roof Tops, Denmark* (fig. 52). Though van Gogh-like brushwork and other aspects of the post-impressionist legacy still linger in this painting, by now, through his fervent experimentation, Johnson has made these elements his own. Johnson's awareness of his artistic ancestors, coupled with an erudite management of the perceived lines and shapes in this townscape, basically worked in his favor. That this quest for a singular identity in a proven painterly tradition may have

52. *Tiled Roof Tops, Denmark,* ca. 1931. Oil on burlap, 22⅛ x 28⅛ in.

placed Johnson too close to van Gogh was evidently a perception Johnson was willing to risk.

Nevertheless, Danish critics were quick to point out that Johnson's artistic sensibilities stood in sharp opposition to the attitudes of many of Denmark's contemporary painters. In contrast to the pastel-colored, impressionist landscapes of such older, established Funen artists as Johannes Larsen, Johnson's Danish landscapes, one critic noted, "may appear a little strange upon first viewing them" (fig. 51). "In reality," the critic continued, "it is rather surprising that this foreigner has been able to capture the Danish character of our air and light on a summer day."[14]

Critiques of this kind, which appeared in Danish newspapers in Kerteminde, Odense, Aarhus, and Copenhagen, collectively document Johnson's career from his arrival in 1930 to his later status as one of the more familiar figures in Denmark's contemporary arts scene. Thanks to these newspaper reviews, a fairly complete picture of Johnson's Danish exhibition roster is known. In Johnson's first four years in Denmark, for example, he held about two exhibitions per year, in traditional art galleries, hotel lobbies, libraries, and department stores, often in tandem with Holcha and her weavings. Although Johnson's work never sold well in Depression-era Denmark, many of the reviews indicate that several paintings usually sold from each exhibition and that Johnson's prices were comparable to most of his Danish contemporaries. We also know from a close reading of these local reviews that in spite of his "foreign" status, Johnson was aware of, and often interactive with, several Danish painters. Frequently mentioning such painters as Johannes Larsen, Axel Salto, Olaf Rude, Vilhelm Lundstrøm, and Regnar Lange, Johnson showed a real desire to connect with the people and images that were equated with modern Danish art and culture.[15]

Danish interviewers also made note of Johnson's overtures to their culture and were often impressed by his ability to speak their language. Although some of his first newspaper interviews were probably collaborations between Danish-speaking reporters, an English-speaking Johnson, and a multilingual Holcha, by 1932 several interviewers commented on Johnson's "excellent Danish."[16]

Not every one, however, remembered Johnson as such a fluent Danish speaker. Helga Ejsing, Holcha's cousin, recalled almost fifty years later how Johnson, whenever rain clouds appeared, would always say (in what he thought was his best Danish), "it will *water* today!"[17]

Former acquaintances of the artist registered other instances of Johnson's discomfort with "Danish ways." Another Kerteminde fisherman, Niels Juhl Andersen, recounted one day when Johnson, while out on one of the big fishing boats, became extremely seasick:

I laid him down behind the wheelhouse and tucked him in a tarpaulin so that he couldn't fall out if the waves came on board. "Thanks Tjuller, thanks Tjuller," that was all he could say. . . . Well, we got the nets on board, and then sailed towards the land and the waves began to subside. Then he woke up, and I untied him and got him on his feet again. He wasn't completely all right, but he could begin to talk again. By the time we were just at Kerteminde, he'd completely come to himself again. When we tied up alongside, he said, "Do you know what I'm going to do now, Tjuller? I'm going home to my wife to get warmed right through—that's what I need. . . . " The day after that, when I met him, he shouted, "Tjuller—never going catching herrings again!"[18]

Johnson, usually reserved and aloof in the presence of strangers, was also capable of letting down his guard and being quite sociable. He was a participant in the lively discussions among Kerteminde's fishermen at the harbor and in the local café. Among family members and very close friends, he told jokes (usually revolving around his difficulties with the Danish language) and played parlor games with the children. Athletically inclined, Johnson was also a jogger, a gymnast of sorts, and an early convert to calisthenics (fig. 53).

Several women, reminiscing on their youth in Kerteminde in the early 1930s, remembered Johnson as a sensual, physically impressive man, who would often go barechested and wear cut-off pants on his summer painting excursions around Kerteminde. Standing about five feet, nine inches tall, with a solid muscular build, glistening bronze complexion, unruly, thick black hair, and dark, penetrating eyes, "Johnson was perhaps the closest thing to a Greek god that we had ever seen," recalled longtime Kerteminde resident Gunvor Jeppsen. "All the girls just swooned over him," said Helga Ejsing about his dramatic appearances on the beach at their family gatherings, "because he was so handsome." Not only women, but men, too, had lasting impressions of him and his athletic, physical bearing. Walking down Kerteminde's cobblestone streets, he moved with a rhythmic elegance uncharacteristic of most Danes. "And when he painted," recalled

53. Doing a handstand on the beach, probably on Jutland, ca. 1934

54. *Lilies*, ca. 1931. Oil on canvas, 23¼ x 14¼ in.

55. *Still Life (with Book and Fruit)*, ca. 1931. Oil on canvas, 20 x 24½ in.

56. Oskar Kokoschka, *The Friends*, ca. 1917–18. Oil on canvas, 40 x 59 in.

Kerteminde elder Frantzen Sennett, "he moved in a special way: graceful, self-assured, like an animal."[19]

Although Johnson's physical magnetism made him a prime candidate for any number of affairs—and there is some indication that several women were willing to meet him halfway—he apparently was not interested in this at all. Holcha, it seemed, was truly his primary object of affection. Sexual compatibility aside, Holcha gave William total support in his chosen aesthetic paths. Not only did she provide basic female companionship and the creature comforts, but she advised him on his direction in painting, often serving as his personal critic and counsel. "Holcha *believed* in Johnson," was the most oft-repeated assessment of their relationship, which perhaps explains why Johnson, in spite of his widely acknowledged sex appeal, was emotionally attuned and exclusively devoted to her.[20]

Along with these personal recollections of Johnson were other accounts that portray him a bit differently. In a 1930–31 interview for a Danish women's magazine, for instance, the portrait of Johnson that emerged was of a well-read, articulate, but often smug person, who nevertheless shrugged off an overly intellectual orientation to the world. When asked if he read many books, Johnson replied

Yes, I have. . . . But now, I will try to live my own life. Words, unfortunately, are often only a smoke-screen which life hides behind. Frequently, I exhaust myself quite ludicrously when I express myself in words. . . . In all these artistic circles, they constantly speak about various matters. I believe that it is simply hazardous for one's inner life, all of this chatter. All of these many ideas and points-of-view, . . . one eventually forgets when one lives *[emphasis added].*[21]

While this casual and anti-intellectual stance no doubt annoyed some people, there were many critics who welcomed this fresh, seemingly unaffected viewpoint, particularly when Johnson applied it to Danish subject matter. In his Danish landscapes, as well as in his still lifes and portraits of people, Johnson strove to record not only likenesses, but the inner life and specific character of places, people, and things (figs. 54, 55, 58, 59).

Some Kerteminde subjects, such as *Portrait of an Elderly Dane*, function both as actual portraits (in this case, of the town elder, Rasmus Christensen) and as images aligned with Continental artists who subscribed to the late expressionist agenda. Johnson's decision to layer this portrait with densely packed, crosshatched lines and a chromatically expansive palette recalls the painted linearities and high-key colors of the Austrian-born expressionist, Oskar Kokoschka. Johnson's familiarity with Kokoschka perhaps surpassed even his knowledge of van Gogh and Soutine, since his in-laws, Christoph and Erna Voll, as well as Holcha, all had firsthand experiences with this modern artist during the time they lived in Dresden in the early 1920s. In Kokoschka's painting *The Friends*, as in Johnson's *Portrait of an Elderly Dane*, the colorful and calligraphic wielding of the brush effectively fuses the exterior characteristics of the sitters with their inner, spiritual dimensions (fig. 59). That Johnson did in fact closely scrutinize Kokoschka's art is suggested in one of Johnson's still lifes, which includes, among other elements, the partially discernable name of the German Expressionist painter on the front of a book (see fig. 55).[22]

57. William H. Johnson, in north African attire, with Holcha Krake (ca. 1932), in a photo-collage documenting their tour of Tunisia, assembled by the Harmon Foundation, 1957.

And like Kokoschka (as well as other German Expressionists), Johnson made concrete plans to travel to Africa, where he expected to find, in his own words, "the real me." Reflecting on his travel plans with a Danish reporter, Johnson concluded:

I will go to Africa in order to crystalize all of these impressions. In reality, colored folk are so different from the white race. Europe is so very superficial. Modern European art strives to be primitive, but it is too complicated. Now Modigliani believed he was "in Africa," but just look at his pictures: Raphael permeates them! All of the darker races are far more primitive—these are the people who are closer to the sun . . . [the sun] is closer to us dark people. . . . We are closer to the sun [emphasis added].[23]

Contained in Johnson's stream-of-consciousness statement was, of course, a romantic view of Africa and Africans which, in spite of his conscious self-identification with the darker races, linked him nonetheless to the European moderns whom he denigrated. Continuing in this idealized, romantic vein with yet another interviewer, Johnson boldly asserted that "Gauguin painted Negro portraits, but only with brown [pigments]. I, with my primitive nature, think that only I am in a position to perfectly describe the light effects on brown skin coloring, something that white people, as it is, can see, but cannot effectively translate."[24] As these two statements illustrate, Johnson unabashedly took on a range of European moderns, from the original *sauvage*, Paul Gauguin, to the School of Paris's legendary *enfant terrible*, Amedeo Modigliani, in service to what he thought was his own premium relationship to an Africa still unknown to him.

After spending Christmas 1931 with Thora and Nanna Krake in Odense, William and

58. *Danish Youth*, ca. 1930. Oil on burlap, 25¼ x 21¼ in.

59. *Portrait of an Elderly Dane*, ca. 1931. Oil on burlap, 30 x 21¼ in.

Holcha commenced their African sojourn by traveling to Germany. In Hamburg, their first stop, they visited one of Holcha's old friends and spent many days in the city's historic Kunsthalle and in the progressive Museum für Kunst und Gewerbe (Museum for Art and Crafts). Years later, Johnson recalled that it was in Hamburg that he first became aware of "The Man," Adolf Hitler. From Hamburg, they traveled west into the Netherlands, and on to Amsterdam, where they saw many examples of van Gogh's work. After a period in Amsterdam, they crossed back into Germany and down the Rhine toward Cologne. While in that city, they visited its magnificent cathedral, as well as the famous Wallraf-Richartz Museum. From Cologne, the couple passed through Belgium and stopped in Paris for a few weeks. After returning to all of their former Parisian haunts, visiting museums and galleries, and unsuccessfully trying to contact prospective art dealers, William and Holcha traveled by train down to Marseille, where they boarded one of the many passenger ships that regularly crisscrossed the Mediterranean. In the spring of 1932, they arrived in the city of Tunis, finally reaching their destination: the continent of Africa.

A photo-collage from their stay in Tunisia includes a photograph of Johnson dressed in the traditional turban and hooded cloak of the north Africans (fig. 57). As seen in this impromptu snapshot, Johnson's physical features, along with the north African clothing, allowed him to blend in with Tunisia's indigenous peoples. Thus, he was able to closely observe many of the local ceremonies and religious rituals (including a seven-day Bedouin wedding) without drawing too much attention to himself.[25] Although blond, blue-eyed Holcha did not have these same options, with Johnson at her side and "the help of a smile, some tobacco, and French francs," she too was allowed to join these forays into the local culture.[26]

Still, Johnson and Holcha must have known that Tunisia had already been "discovered" by the previous generation of European artists and intellectuals. From the French novelist André Gide to the Swiss painter Paul Klee, scores of European moderns had already combed Tunisia's ancient ruins, explored its many *suqs* and *medinas*, and pondered the mysteries of Islam in Kairouan, Tunisia's famous religious center. And like their artistic predecessors, the Johnsons did similar things, like plein-air painting in Tunisia's countryside, sunbathing on Hammamet's four-mile stretch of beach, and engaging in idle conversations, over mint tea, with other tourists at the café in Sidi-Bou-Said (fig. 60).

But throughout William and Holcha's three-month stay in Tunisia, the study of local art traditions and the making of their own art were their principal catalysts for travels within the country. "In Hammamet," Johnson wrote some years afterwards, "a native woman took Holcha and I into her home . . . and showed us the family treasures of hand-woven wools, silks, tapestries, and clothing, their potteries and metal crafts and all the rest."[27] Holcha, an accomplished weaver and expert on Scandinavian textiles, found this visit equally fascinating, since scholars in the textile arts have long remarked on the striking

60. *Poppy Fields, Africa*, 1932. Watercolor and pencil on paper, 19¹¹⁄₁₆ x 25⅝ in.

61. William H. Johnson &
Holcha Krake Johnson, *Bowl*, ca.
1932. Glazed ceramic, 10 in.
(diam.)

design similarities between Tunisian weavings and those found, oddly enough, among traditional Norwegian weavers![28]

In the town of Nabeul, William and Holcha spent several weeks working with the local craftspeople at their celebrated ceramic center. Nabeul, known since biblical times for its excellent clay deposits and thriving pottery industry, introduced the Johnsons to working with clay. William and Holcha's ceramics, while never reaching the technical or artistic heights of their work in painting and weaving, provided them with opportunities for artistic collaboration, as seen in several surviving clay pieces from this period (fig. 61).

From Hammamet and, later, from Sousse, William and Holcha traveled inland to the holy city of Kairouan (fig. 62). There Johnson painted a series of watercolors of the city's crowded bazaars, towering minarets, and world-famous Great Mosque. He blended an improvisational, sketchy approach to the watercolor medium with a sharp, uncompromising eye for such architectural details as crenelated and arched gates, balconied towers, and single-storied vernacular structures (fig. 63). Johnson's interior views of the Great Mosque, though architecturally accurate, take the ninth-century colonnades and entablatures through his very own, earthquakelike sense of order (fig. 64).

After their stay in Tunisia and on their way back to Denmark that summer, William and Holcha spent several weeks in the south of France, primarily in Martigues, where they rested and reflected on their African journey. After Martigues, they continued north, via Paris, where they stopped and visited with black American artist Henry Ossawa Tanner, then seventy-three years old. By the summer's end, they had returned to Kerteminde, moved into another house, and were making plans for their upcoming two-person exhibition in Odense that autumn.

In September 1932, the couple received a surprise visit from Johnson's former National Academy of Design classmate, Ilya Bolotowsky. Bolotowsky, who had been traveling in Europe for the entire year, decided to make a special detour to see his old friend. Bolotowsky's arrival, though welcomed, was a sad reminder of the death, on 29 November 1930, of Johnson's former teacher and longtime mentor, Charles Webster Hawthorne. Upon first hearing of Hawthorne's death, Johnson probably grieved in his own, private way, but in the midst of the professional readjustments and personal changes that followed on the heels of the Hawthorne obituary, Johnson had essentially put the memories of Hawthorne and the N.A.D. behind him. Now, Johnson and Bolotowsky reminisced about the old N.A.D., drank a toast to the memory of Charles Hawthorne, and posed for photographs (fig. 65).

But during a joint painting excursion, Bolotowsky and Johnson began to argue, one perceiving the other as an artistic rival of sorts. Soon, the two friends were quarreling over painting techniques, art theories, and personal matters. Bolotowsky said that Johnson warned him that he would "never be an artist because, 'You're a white man and you are so tangled up in all kinds of encumbrances, ideas and responsibilities . . . that you'll never get out of them. One must be a simple guy of the jungle, free like an animal.'" Looking back on that ill-fated visit some three decades later, Bolotowsky recalled that "it was really pretty ridiculous," attributing Johnson's tirade against him as partially Johnson's artistic temperament gone haywire, partially Johnson's frustration over his dire economic circumstances, and partially a kind of emerging ethnic one-upmanship.[29] Unfortunately, the years of artistic growth and personal changes for both men since their student days had driven a wedge between them that ultimately ended their friendship. As a result of their argument, Bolotowsky left for England the next day.

38 KAIROUAN. – LA GRANDE RUE ET LES MOSQUÉES. – I.L.

62. Postcard, Kairouan, Tunisia, ca. 1930

As Bolotowsky said, some of Johnson's anger and frustration did, in fact, stem from his depressed economic situation. Although Kerteminde's cost of living was low, money was still required for the basic necessities as well as art supplies. Holcha provided most of these necessities with money from her savings and sales of some of her woven items. With the continued decline of the American art market throughout the early 1930s, Johnson's hopes for American art sales had, by 1932, plummeted. Letters during this period from Johnson's friend and unofficial agent Alain Locke and the Harmon Foundation gave the all-too-familiar Depression-era reply of "sorry, but we have no buyers."[30]

Regarding Bolotowsky's suggestion that Johnson felt artistically superior to him because of Johnson's sense of racial and cultural difference, one should again be reminded that Johnson's attitude was rooted in the concept of primitivism, which was based not on black culture itself, but rather on emotional and psychological interpretations of that culture. One might also look at this instance of brash, seemingly reverse racism in light of Johnson's recent trip to Africa. In Tunisia, Johnson encountered people who were engaged in various artistic enterprises that were closely connected to the local people's basic existence. From ceramic bowls to tile-covered mosques, the arts in Tunisia were inextricably linked to the physical and spiritual lives of its inhabitants. This symbiotic relationship was in sharp contrast to modern European art that, in an industrialized and secularized world, lacked this basic connection to the common people.[31] In his heated debate with Bolotowsky, Johnson tried, though without much success, to differentiate between the lofty ambitions of most western artists and the more earth-bound, seemingly relaxed attitudes of many nonwestern artisans.

Apparently, it did not matter to Johnson that his own life and career contradicted his claims to a primitive heritage. "And even if I have studied for many years in New York,

63. *City Gates, Kairouan,* 1932. Watercolor and pencil on paper, 19¾ x 25⅝ in.

64. *Arcade, Tunisia,* 1932. Watercolor and pencil on paper, 19¾ x 25⅝ in.

and all over the world," he told an interviewer in November 1932, "and know more about Scandinavian literature and classical music than my wife does, I have still been able to preserve the primitive in me." When pressed by the interviewer to sum up his particular philosophy, Johnson responded: "My aim is to express in a natural way what I feel, what is in me, both rhythmically and spiritually, all that which in time has been saved up in my family of primitiveness and tradition, and which is now concentrated in me."[32]

Although Johnson would have denied it, his philosophical stance echoed similar opinions by other European moderns, especially many of the German Expressionist artists. The painter Wassily Kandinsky, for example, wrote that "the philosophy of the future, besides studying the nature of things, will also study their spirit."[33] Like Kandinsky, Johnson placed a high premium on the spiritual in art. But with Johnson, this spirituality took the form of realistic subject matter, rather than, as in Kandinsky's case, abstractions.

The equivalencies between Johnson's comments concerning primitivism and his modernist paintings are also comparable to the analogies in words and deeds of another German Expressionist, Emil Nolde. In Nolde's art and thinking, he too interconnected the vital qualities of preindustrial cultures with an expressionist view of the world. The observation by one writer that Nolde perceived modern man as someone who "experiences himself through . . . [an] intuitive grasp" of nature echoes Johnson's statement about his own aesthetic ties to an animistic tradition. Johnson's expressed desire, in one of his Danish interviews, to visit "the famous German painter Nolde," leads one to believe that he was familiar with Nolde's position among the varying discourses surrounding primitivism in modern art.[34]

The contradictions contained in being both a "primitive" and "cultivated" man may have, in fact, implied that Johnson was himself grappling with that dialectic. Though he felt a real kinship with folk culture and sensed a superficiality in modern life, his statements—which stressed his participation in the contemporary art world and his interest in European culture—obviously pegged him as a cosmopolitan and intellectual. By willfully separating himself from those European artists who strove to be primitive, Johnson may have been articulating his own very unique position as *living* dialectic: the artistic equivalent to what W. E. B. DuBois referred to as the "double-consciousness" of the Negro American.[35] Johnson was a fascinating synthesis—African-American-born, European-American-trained; primitive/traditional in lineage, yet a product of the post-impressionist art schism.

Johnson's notion of the primitive was not entirely limited to people of color. When asked in an interview about his impressions of the Tunisians, he replied that they were "a wonderful, primitive people." "But for that matter," he added, "primitives can be found all over the world, even in Kerteminde, where the fishermen, as human beings, have preserved the [essential] characteristics of their nature, people in whom there is an element of tradition."[36]

This quality of being emphatically Danish, or having what was often referred to as *danskhed*, was frequently depicted by modern Danish artists and writers in images of old fishermen, net-menders, and other cultural prototypes. For example, the cover of a 1930 travel brochure for Kerteminde, entitled "A Summer in Kerteminde is a Summer Near (and Dear) to Denmark's Heart," shows Kerteminde's old harbor and the head and shoulders of an old fisherman (fig. 66). The brochure represents Kerteminde, or rather "Denmark's heart," using the image of a fisherman: a recurring symbol in Danish art and literature of the older, preindustrialized culture that was often presented as an idyllic alternative to the "overcivilized" sectors of modern Scandinavian society.

65. Receiving visitors in Kerteminde, ca. 1932. From left to right: Martha Mikelsen, unidentified man, Ilya Bolotowsky, Holcha Krake, and William H. Johnson.

Like the mythic associations with Danish folk culture on the cover of the brochure, Johnson's painting *Old Salt, Denmark* explores the mythic, primitive aspects of his adopted homeland (fig. 67).[37] Johnson's subject, bereft of any background elements, relays his saga by means of exaggerated physical characteristics. A red nose, ruddy cheeks, bearded chin, and irascible countenance seemingly unfurl from the fisherman's pedestal-like body, clothed in a classic Danish worker's pullover and undersweater. The malleability of perceived physical form, which was Johnson's primary means of capturing something as intractable as spirit, moved *Old Salt, Denmark* and other post-1931 portraits into the modern realm.

The thin line that separated pure caricature from modern portraiture was stretched by Johnson, just as it was brought into question by such expressionists as Kokoschka, Soutine, and others. Johnson's preoccupation with caricature in Denmark came into sharp focus with a series of portraits done between 1931 and 1933, many of which were exhibited in his first Copenhagen exhibition, held in April 1933 at the prestigious Christian Larsen Gallery.

Johnson and his exhibition were the subject of quite a few reviews, announcements, and features in Copenhagen's newspapers. A rather lengthy interview with Johnson in the Copenhagen tabloid *Ekstrabladet* carried the equally long and provocative headline

When One is Close to the Sun: Artistic Crossbreeding Culminates in Copenhagen. What the Fishermen of Kerteminde and North Africa's Arabs Have in Common. A Negro-Indian and His Danish Wife Exhibit at Højbroplads. William H. Johnson Speaks.[38]

Johnson, perhaps playing "the primitive" to the extreme here, often manipulated the Danish press with accounts of his interracial marriage to Holcha and his mixed parentage.

66. Tourist brochure, Kerteminde, Denmark, ca. 1930

But instead of publicly speculating about being the product of a black mother and white father—which was, in fact, quite possibly the case—Johnson consistently told interviewers that he was *Chinos*: the offspring of a Negro father and an Indian mother.[39]

Johnson extended this inquiry into ancestry and self to his art, as seen in several fascinating self-portraits from this period. In one of these works, which was actually reproduced on the cover of the Christian Larsen Gallery exhibition checklist, Johnson allowed the raw, expressive power of the relief print medium to boldly assert itself, though not to the detriment of his likeness (fig. 68). Similarly, in a *Self-Portrait* in charcoal from the same time period, an unadorned introspective quality permeates Johnson's facial features and expression (fig. 69). This latter *Self-Portrait* (inscribed in the lower right hand corner to friends of the artist) bears a striking resemblance in composition and overall form to a well-known Kokoschka *Self-Portrait from Two Sides as Painter* from 1923 (fig. 70).

In many of Johnson's watercolor portraits, the physical features of his sitters are also rendered in a loose, yet remarkably accurate, manner. With broad, pigment-loaded sweeps of the paintbrush, Kerteminde's fishermen and schoolboys alike are invested with a vitality that spoke not only to Johnson's primitivist agenda, but to a growing social concern in his art (figs. 71, 72). In *Young Dane*—certainly one of Johnson's finest watercolor portraits—the artist successfully bridges realism, classic expressionist imagery, and psychological reality. Concurrent works by Johnson's brother-in-law Christoph Voll and others suggest that this tendency toward social and psychological realism—known in German art circles as *Neue Sachlichkeit* (New Objectivity)—was indeed the next logical step in the expressionist quest for the spiritual (fig. 73).

In another portrait from the Copenhagen exhibition, *The Poet Olaf Gynt*, Johnson consciously tries to convey—through color, distortion, and placement—the many moods of this Funen-born, modern Danish poet (fig. 74). Several years after the sitting, Johnson talked about the

67. *Old Salt, Denmark*, ca. 1931–32. Oil on burlap, 31 x 25⅜ in.

68. *Self-Portrait*, ca. 1933.
Woodcut, 5 x 4 in.

69. *Self-Portrait*, ca. 1934.
Charcoal on paper, 33½ x 15½ in.

process of painting the temperamental Olaf Gynt to an interviewer, who then wrote up the following impressions from their conversation:

He painted the portrait of a young Danish poet, a man who had his ups and downs from being a child prodigy. For other painters, painting a portrait is the equivalent of a camera photograph, showing his physical characteristics at one particular moment. But in painting this picture of the poet, Johnson tried to show his conception of all his varying moods and genius, to paint all the different things that make him as we know him, the whole atmosphere, life and experience that make him so. [This] is what interested Johnson.[40]

Money, or the lack of it, was still a thorny issue for Johnson, although the few sales that came from his Copenhagen show and his last two exhibitions (in Kerteminde and Odense late in 1932) helped considerably. Ironically, he and Holcha were more successful at selling his work in Denmark than Alain Locke and the Harmon Foundation were in their efforts to find buyers in the United States. Yet Johnson continued to ship his paintings to Locke and the foundation, in hopes of placing them either with American collectors or museums.

Emotions over his art and finances, however, reached a boiling point in December 1932, following his rejection by one of the juried art exhibitions at the Corcoran Gallery of Art in Washington, D.C. Venting his anger at Harmon Foundation director Mary Beattie Brady, Johnson wrote:

I am beginning to wonder, did it ever occur to you that I need money to live and to carry on my work? I am beginning to doubt what I did believe about the Harmon Foundation; that [they] did all they can to foster the Negro['s] creative encouragements [sic], and by that I think of a body . . . of people with money . . . enough to go to that trouble to meet the creators half way. . . . I don't see where that is too much of me to expect of you. . . . Hope you don't misunderstand. . . . I am not beging [sic] you at all but am just saying what I feel is no more than right.

As you said in your letter that you are keeping my case in mind at all times, etc. Hope all friends don't think so slow; if they did I wouldn't be able to live very long.

I did understand from one of your past letters that my painting was not subjected [sic] to your judges . . . and . . . that you will enter some of my paintings in your exhibition of the coming February if your judges feel than they are suitable.

Note what I feel about my painting and your judges: . . . I need some profit that will help me along financially and not that cheap publicity, so I don't care very much if your judges feel that my painting[s] are not suitable if [they] continue in the old manner.

Your[s] sincerely

William H. Johnson

Enggade
Kerteminde Denmark

P.S. Happy New Year[41]

70. Oskar Kokoschka, *Self-Portrait from Two Sides as Painter*, 1923. Color lithograph poster, 50 x 32¼ in.

The "old manner," which the Harmon Foundation had mentioned in its previous letter to Johnson, referred to his painterly appropriations from van Gogh and Soutine, most evident in paintings like *Jim, Jacobia Hotel,* and *Sun Setting, Denmark,* all of which the Harmon Foundation had in its possession. Although Johnson had, more or less, abandoned "the old manner" by the time of his letter, there always seemed to be a significant lag in time—resulting in a significant leap in style—between the paintings he shipped to the Harmon Foundation and those he was currently working on.[42]

Port in Gray Weather, Kerteminde, painted late in 1933 or early in 1934, represented a stylistic departure for Johnson (fig. 75). While still a part of the expressionist art lexicon, this work pointed in the direction of a more individualized sense of vision. As with many of the paintings from this time period, *Port in Gray Weather* is made up of oils—straight from the tube and hand-mixed—applied on the canvas with the brush and palette knife.

71. *Portrait of Jesper Anderson,* ca. 1931–32. Watercolor, pen and ink with pencil on paper, 18¹³⁄₁₆ x 14⅞ in.

72. *Young Dane*, ca. 1931–32. Watercolor and pencil on paper, 18¹³⁄₁₆ x 15 in.

As with his Tunisian watercolors, Johnson supplies viewers with just enough visual information about the subject matter—here, Kerteminde's Lillestranden—to help them identify it correctly. Yet the fast, gestural, and intuitive rendering of the port collides with orthodox perceptions, presenting the old landmark and its dark, somber setting as something vivid, experiential, yet nonillusionistic.

These seemingly contradictory impulses in Johnson's post-1933 Danish works attracted the attention of several reviewers of his November 1934 exhibition in Aarhus, Denmark. One critic, commenting on Johnson's painting of an old Danish church, warned his readers that "the inclination to create a 'rhythmic' art has turned into an affected and obvious misunderstanding [of the church] which might be called pathologic."[43]

Another reviewer, voicing fewer objections to Johnson's artistic license, succinctly labeled his art "a form of Expressionism, a *dynamic* form, which has never really flowered here in Denmark." The reviewer went on to say, "For [Johnson] and all those who can master this art form, the sensations of life—most evident in lines and colors—maintain an importance which make the motifs live in one's consciousness."[44]

According to Danish family and friends, William and Holcha's orientation to the world was colored by a celebratory, life-affirming attitude. These "sensations of life"—often taking the form of family gatherings, visits to the old Krake/Sørensen homestead, and holiday retreats by the sea—complemented Johnson's artistic efforts and gave his paintings an unprecedented, emotional depth.

At the annual family gatherings for the Krakes, usually on a cousin's farm in Jutland (in western Denmark), in the town of Ebeltoft, William fit in comfortably, although the arrival of the Volls from Germany often meant that he and his brother-in-law, Christoph Voll, were bound to get into friendly—though, at times, heated—"art talks." Holcha's cousin, Helge Nilausen, remembered from those gatherings how William thoroughly enjoyed the "country life" and, in true country fashion, would fetch pails of water from a nearby stream, carrying them on his head all the way back to the farm. Then again, Helge recounted, William often showed his true artistic side, when he would milk the cows and then pour the milk into a tub to bathe his feet![45]

But family gatherings like those in Ebeltoft would soon become a memory for William and Holcha as, in 1934, they made concrete plans to take an extended trip outside Denmark. Following Johnson's moderate success with his Copenhagen exhibition, Holcha contacted friends connected with the art world in Oslo, Norway, who shortly thereafter arranged an exhibition for William in the spring of 1935.

Another compelling reason for their trip to Norway was Holcha's need to spend some time with her "other family." As a teenager, she had lived on and off for several years in western Norway with a family to whom she remained very close. Her marriage to William, the ensuing period of adjustment, and the worldwide economic depression, however, prevented her from visiting her Norwegian friends for almost eight years. Though the initial catalyst for the trip was Johnson's Oslo exhibition, the chance to see old friends and relive old times further fueled Holcha's desire to go.

That Johnson was ready for his debut in Norway is apparent in one of the self-portraits from this period (fig. 76). Johnson's will to self-imaging, which previously competed with other artistic role models, is the literal core of this latest *Self-Portrait*. Gone are the Soutinesque ambiguities of form and the Modiglianilike stylizations of his French, South Carolina, and early Danish portraiture. Also left behind are the overt quotations from the German Expressionists. Posed in the traditional quarter profile of most self-portraits, Johnson directs an all-knowing gaze squarely into the eyes of his audience. Painted intimations of a shirt, scarf, and a wide-brimmed hat carry free-form, colorful shapes across the squared burlap support, while the artist's head is realized from roughly drawn geometries. In what could be both a door in the distant background and a rectilinear abstraction extending beyond the right edge of the painting, Johnson has created a fitting emblem for this new self: a kind of symbolic "box," placed there to hold all of his past mannerisms and romantic gestures, leaving behind a layered reconstruction of nature and art.

73. Christoph Voll, *Joseph's Brother*, ca. 1924. Woodcut, 11⁹⁄₁₆ x 5½ in.

Just prior to their late January departure for Oslo, William and Holcha spent about a month in Copenhagen. Along with making some last-minute preparations for their departure, they attended the opening of the "Grønningen" exhibition, one of Copenhagen's most celebrated art invitationals. An illustrated newspaper article about the opening festivities mentioned Johnson in passing and included a caricature of him, shown among other gallery-goers intently looking at the paintings on exhibit (fig. 77).[46] The newspaper's description of Johnson as a "Sambo-painter" was, for that era in Denmark, not a derogatory one, although the designation perhaps contained a degree of sarcasm. In addition to attending this opening, William and Holcha made the acquaintance that month of the famous singer and actor Paul Robeson and his wife Eslanda, who had just returned from a two-week tour of the Soviet Union. During the Robesons' brief stopover in Copenhagen, William and Holcha took them to the home of Carl Kjersmeier, one of the world's leading collectors of African art.

Upon arrival in Oslo, the couple checked into Pension Ro, which was a block away from the Kunstnernes Hus, Oslo's recently opened exhibition hall for new, experimental art works. Oslo's other major meeting place for the visual arts—and the site for Johnson's upcoming exhibition—was the Blomqvist Gallery. Unlike the Kunstnernes Hus, Blomqvist was an older, very established gallery that catered to Oslo's wealthier collectors. Blomqvist also had the distinctive honor of being the principal dealer and gallery for Ed-

74. *The Poet Olaf Gynt,* ca. 1931–33. Oil on canvas, 25⅜ x 20½ in.

75. *Port in Gray Weather, Kerteminde,* ca. 1933–34. Oil on canvas, 21 x 26 in.

76. *Self-Portrait*, ca. 1934–35. Oil on burlap, 26⅛ x 26⅛ in.

vard Munch (1863–1944), the internationally renowned Norwegian artist, whose dramatic, symbol-ridden paintings provoked much debate in the European art world. Besides Munch, Blomqvist also sponsored other artists and exhibitions, both from Scandinavian countries and beyond.

Johnson's March 1935 exhibition at Blomqvist was comprised of recent landscapes, portraits, and still lifes, all hung in one room. Another artist, the Norwegian painter Olaf Holwech, had a simultaneous exhibition in another part of the building. Several reviewers immediately picked up on this paired, yet contrasting, display at Blomqvist, as is evident in such headlines as "Black and White at Blomqvist," or "Stark Contrast at Blomqvist: Norwegian Nature and African Primitives."[47]

Surprisingly, several of the local newspaper accounts of Johnson's exhibition report him retreating from his standard recitation on his alleged exotic lineage. Redirecting one reporter's barrage of personal questions, Johnson quickly and ironically interjected, "but it is not *I* who is on exhibition; my *pictures* are." Further into the interview, when asked how Negro art was looked upon in America, Johnson answered:

Sambo-Maleren Johnsson, Dir. Børresen og Louis Levy studerer Naurs Portræt af Inge Lise Bock.

Of course, it is not yet as cultivated as European art—with its infinitely longer development—but in its own limited way, it is growing up. The strong instincts of the Negroes cut through tradition, and for that reason one may say, with good conscience, that the best of Negro art has become a valuable part of modern American art.[48]

77. Caricature from *Dagens Nyheder*, 20 January 1935

In his fleeting but noteworthy reply to the reporter, Johnson seems to be saying that the "strong instincts" of the Negroes are, in fact, the barometer that will test whether or not Negro art (e.g., his own work) will be a valuable part of modern American art as a whole. Here, "tradition" isn't used with the same folkloristic meaning that Johnson had formerly assigned to the term. Rather, this "tradition" seems to be more akin to the artistic status quo, which the Negro's inner, cultural truths must somehow overcome.

Leif Østby, the chief curator at Oslo's Nasjonalgalleriet and an art critic for *Aftenposten*, found Johnson's line of thinking and manner of painting "challenging," to say the

least. After first describing Johnson's painting technique as "perhaps a bluff of giant dimensions," Østby then wrote the following assessment:

[Johnson] does not handle his motifs with silken gloves. . . . If he paints a peaceful village street, he jumps at it with a giant fist that makes the houses dance a wild can-can. Personally, I don't care for knocking a man unconscious in order to convince him, provided one has other arguments that can be used, and Mr. Johnson does not quite convince me that he has other arguments.[49]

In contrast to Østby, Pola Gauguin, Oslo's other widely read art critic, found purpose and "great original charm" in Johnson's "primitive expressiveness":

In spite of a very obvious French influence there is something in the nature of his forms and lines which has great original charm and is the expression of a viewpoint and perception which is very different from the European, even when the latter strives to give a primitive impression. Johnson is a primitive, with a marked sense of simplicity in colors, whose appeal to the eye is chiefly decorative.

This effect is brought about, as it is in Negro songs, through the infectious rising and subsiding in rhythmic movement, which nevertheless maintains a strange balance on the whole.[50]

Doubtlessly, Pola Gauguin's response to Johnson's work was greatly influenced by the post-impressionist legacies and the primitivist trappings of his famous father, Paul Gauguin. Yet, as Pola Gauguin astutely surmised in his review, Johnson's non-European cultural heritage, as well as his affinities for black music and rhythms, must have accounted, in a significant way, for his very different viewpoint.

During Johnson's spring residency in Oslo, he painted several cityscapes of the old, elegant town. Johnson's

Bazaars behind Church, Oslo, which documents Oslo's towering cathedral and surrounding shopping areas, illustrates his continued interest in painting various architectural settings (fig. 78). In another painting of Oslo, *A View Down Akersgate, Oslo*, Johnson again pays tribute to urban planning and man-made edifices: in this case, the copper-domed Trinity Church and (in the distant central background of the painting) Saint Olav's Church (fig. 79). In both paintings, Johnson combined absolute visual truths with inalienable, personal responses to the sites, resulting in renderings of Oslo that spoke not only to its architectural history, but also to its pace, tempo, and atmosphere.[51]

While in Oslo, Johnson was introduced to Rolf Stenersen, a collector of modern art, who ended up buying several of Johnson's paintings from the exhibition. In turn, Stenersen introduced Johnson to the legendary artist Edvard Munch, then age seventy-one and virtually a recluse.[52]

Munch's block prints—images of angst-ridden and often estranged subjects, conceived from undulating lines and odd combinations of colors—certainly expanded Johnson's sense of the medium's expressive potentiality (fig. 80). *Willie and Holcha*, a woodcut that he made sometime after 1935, illustrates—through its graphic technique and male/female subject matter—Johnson's awareness of Munch's prints (fig. 81). Johnson's double-portrait—with its allusions to African sculpture and its focus on a primal, one-on-one relationship—was, however, stylistically and emotionally distinct from Munch's art, which derived much of its form and meaning from symbolist ideas.

In spite of these ventures into Oslo's contemporary art scene, Johnson felt a real need to escape the city, in order to experience a more authentic—or, in his words, "primitive"—Scandinavia. Although he had already absorbed aspects of this "raw" side of the north through Kerteminde's fishermen, both he and Holcha grew increasingly restless and dissatisfied with life there. Holcha's frequent admission that she and William "traveled in order to feel renewed," became a self-fulfilling prophecy whenever their lives seemed a little too mundane and settled.[53] Holcha's descriptions of Norway, with its majestic mountains, fjord-lined coasts, grove-filled pastures, and breathtaking vistas, fed into Johnson's fantasy of an expressive, uncultivated landscape that would inspire him even more than previous ones. So when a reporter asked him what his immediate plans were following his Oslo exhibition, Johnson replied, "to experience the *real* Norway. . . . Not Oslo, but Norway's Northern, Western and Gudbrandsdal regions."[54]

William and Holcha left Oslo in May 1935 and gradually worked their way north that summer, through Norway's scenic Gudbrandsdal area. Known for its medieval churches, picturesque lakes, and eighteenth-century farmhouses, the Gudbrandsdal region has long been one of Norway's most popular destinations for tourists.

A retired Norwegian educator, Turid Riste, whose family knew Holcha, recounted an amusing anecdote about the couple's visit to the area. For a few weeks, William and Holcha stayed at a hotel in the town of Lillehammer. One evening, after a full day of sightsee-

78. *Bazaars behind Church, Oslo,* ca. 1935. Oil on burlap, 28¼ x 34¼ in.

79. *A View Down Akersgate, Oslo,* ca. 1935. Oil on burlap, 25¼ x 31¼ in.

80. Edvard Munch, *Man and Woman Kissing*, 1905. Color woodcut, 19 x 25½ in.

ing and outdoor sketching, they made the long trek back to the hotel. Johnson had on a loose-fitting shirt, wide cotton pants, string sandals, with his hair a little longer than usual. As he approached the hotel, with the evening sky ablaze with golds, reds, and lavenders behind him, the elderly (and nearsighted) hotel manager looked at the apparition before him, gasped, then cried out, "Jesus Christ is coming! Jesus Christ is coming! Look! Look!"[55]

After a summer of rest and recreation in the Gudbrandsdal, the couple continued their northwestward migration, eventually reaching Holcha's Norwegian "home," the town of Volda. Volda, one of several small communities lying along western Norway's coastal fringe of small islands, was well known throughout the country as the site of a nineteenth-century language revolt. This linguistic rebellion, which was led by a local intellectual and cultural activist named Ivard Aasen, resulted in the creation of what was considered to be a purer form of the Norwegian language, called *Nynorsk*. Besides being the place of origin for Nynorsk, Volda was also known for its excellent teachers' college and small, but vital, community of scholars.[55]

Holcha's "family" in Volda were the Kaarstads and Ristes who, as teachers in the community, represented Volda's educated elite. Holcha and the Kaarstad's daughter, Kjellaug, had spent summers together when they were girls and remained close friends. In the intervening years, Kjellaug had married a widowed clergyman, Lars Tjensvoll, whose brood of seven children expanded the already extended family to even greater proportions. For Holcha, the return to Volda was a family reunion in the truest sense, since she perhaps felt just as close to the Kaarstads and Ristes as to her own relatives in Denmark. In fact, for the duration of their stay in Volda, William and Holcha lived on property owned by Kjellaug and Lars (referred to as "the Dean") and were considered full-fledged members of the Tjensvoll clan (fig. 82).[57]

Writing in December of that year about Johnson and his art, one local newspaper reporter noted that, although the artist had only lived in Volda since the late summer, he had already shown in his first paintings of the region a genuine appreciation for Volda's flora and fauna, as well as its colors and seasonal changes.[58] The commentator may have had in mind, among several other works, Johnson's *Still Life—Wild Fowl*: a death study of a large gray heron (fig. 83). Upon seeing a photograph of the painting, Svanhild Øvrelid, one of Volda's longtime residents, immediately recalled how the dead bird was brought into town in the net of one of Volda's fishermen and how Johnson insisted upon painting it, much to Holcha's horror and dismay.[59]

Yet more than its animal life, Volda's distinct northern vegetation and geological characteristics captivated Johnson. As with many Scandinavian painters, Johnson's thematic identification with this remote and less urbanized area of the country symbolized an initiation into Scandinavia's true character. Analogous to Gauguin's escape from civilization, Johnson's journey into the Scandinavian hinterland offered the artist a chance to

81. *Willie and Holcha,* ca. 1935. Hand-colored woodcut, 13¾ x 17 in.

82. With friends in Volda, Norway, ca. 1935–37. From left to right: William H. Johnson, the Reverend Lars Tjensvoll, Kjellaug Kaarstad Tjensvoll, and Holcha Krake

celebrate his primitivist affinities for the north via his paintings of regional views and folk types. Like Johnson's sojourn to Africa, this expedition into the "real" Norway evoked previous journeys by other painters who also made an artistic altar out of the Norwegian wilderness. Evocative canvases depicting uninhabitable mountain ranges, mirror-crisp lakes, jutting fjords, and star-lit evenings came out of the open-air studios and sketchbooks of Jens Ferdinand Willumsen, Harald Sohlberg, Henrik Sørensen, and countless other Scandinavian landscape painters of the modern period.[60]

In his painting of an unidentified Norwegian landscape, Johnson shows traces of human industry, in the form of a roughly built, vernacular structure (fig. 84). Alive with color as well as brushwork, this painting and its subject matter elicit comparisons with contemporaneous Norwegian landscapes, such as Henrik Sørensen's *From Bøverdalen* (fig. 85). Though Johnson's painting is certainly the more anthropomorphic of the two, in both works Norway's mountainous terrain and the primitive, ancestral dwelling are central. Yet Johnson's painting gives far greater attention to color, texture, and "vital exaggeration," which propelled his art further along the path toward abstraction.[61]

Just as Kerteminde was reduced to several selected town and harbor views by Johnson, so too was Volda compressed into a couple of specific landscapes, painted repeatedly during Johnson's two-year residency there. Rotsethornet, a solitary and mammoth elevation standing at Volda's eastern edge, was one of the landmarks that Johnson painted, in different seasons and from varying angles. In his *Farmhouse at the Foot of Rotsethornet*, Johnson accurately observed, then painted the mountain's massive proportions, in relation to a seemingly dwarfed peripheral community (fig. 86). But unlike the previously painted landscapes—the terra-cotta-tiled rooftops of Kerteminde, for example—upon which Johnson freely superimposed his own rhythms, gestures, and interpretations, Rotsethornet challenged his license to alter reality. Rotsethornet's monumental components caused Johnson to acquiesce to the landscape's natural and spiritual presence.

In another depiction of Rotsethornet, this one painted during the winter months, Johnson avoided his characteristic painterly quirks (fig. 87). Monumentality and stoicism are achieved here, but with much less painted bravura. Interestingly, it was through his affirmation of Rotsethornet's physical reality that Johnson was able to address equally the mountain's metaphoric spiritual presence. Perhaps recalling the old African-American saying, "Lord, please don't move my mountain, but give me the strength to climb it," Johnson tackled the primordial forms of western Norway not as an aggressive conqueror,

83. *Still Life—Wild Fowl*, ca. 1935–37. Oil on burlap, 27⅝ x 21⅞ in.

84. *Untitled (Norwegian Landscape)*, ca. 1935–36. Oil on burlap, 25 x 28¾ in.

but rather as an attuned spirit. In the words of one enthusiastic critic, who saw examples of Johnson's *stemningsmaleri* (mood painting) several years later in Sweden, "[Johnson] lets his own vitality surge through the motif, which, in turn, can rise to its own power."[62]

In a series of canvases that look across the Voldafjord towards the Ulvestad mountains, Johnson continued to pay close attention to the topographical features and "spirits" along the Sunnmørsfjord. *Volda*, in spite of a seemingly exaggerated handling of materials and natural forms, is an authentic rendering of that site's ice-capped peaks, snow banks, and choppy waters (figs. 88, 89). Ironically, Johnson's expressive treatment of the Ulvestad's summits and vales coincided with the local, folkloric nomenclature for these same formations (from left to right in these images of the Voldafjord, "the cow," "Velsvik's bowl," and "the quilt").[63] These topographical features, immediately identifiable to those who know the region, functioned as unassailable natural landmarks that Johnson found essential to his artistic interpretations of Volda. Unlike the bird's-eye views and fish-lens vistas of earlier landscapes, Johnson's relatively uncomplicated perspectives on Volda established a simple background/middleground/foreground format that ultimately flattened his landscapes, pushing them into a two-dimensional, abstracted realm, where color, shape, and mood reign over pure emotion and realism.

Overtures to abstracted form and two-dimensionality are also present in Johnson's portraits from Volda. In the circa 1936 portrait, *Girl in a Red Dress*, Johnson employs brilliant colors, anatomical distortions, and a few enigmatic pictorial elements (e.g., the window in the upper-right corner and the wisp of a flower in the girl's hand), all of which foster an image more wooden and doll-like than flesh-and-blood (fig. 90). Yet these same abstracting devices by Johnson work toward making *Girl in a Red Dress* a more psychological and, essentially, a more expressive portrait.[64]

As with his landscapes of Volda, Johnson increasingly sought to synthesize the physical and spiritual aspects of his subjects. This synthesis was achieved in several ways. First (and as always), Johnson worked directly from the landscape and the sitter, an approach that forced him to come to immediate terms with his subjects. Second, Johnson often did multiple renderings of his subjects, a practice that afforded him numerous opportunities to see and understand them better (fig. 91). Finally, Johnson went after the essence of his subject rather than a photographic representation, thus letting the subject's primary characteristics define the nature of the work. Taken together, these techniques channeled his

85. Henrik Sørensen, *From Bøverdalen*, 1933. Oil on canvas, 24½ x 28⅜ in.

86. *Farmhouse at the Foot of Rotsethornet*, ca. 1935–36. Oil on burlap, 28¼ x 35¼ in.

87. *Rotsethornet, Winter,* ca. 1935–36. Oil on burlap, 20¼ x 24¼ in.

88. Voldafjord, Volda, Norway, February 1985

expressionism toward a depiction of the very nature of things: an objective that his Scandinavian critics often recognized. In the words of one of these commentators, works like *Girl in a Red Dress* conveyed "an earnestness tinged with melancholy that bears evidence of [Johnson's] personal entry into the spirituality of Nordicness."[65]

According to friends of the artist, Johnson was especially eager to paint the girl in the red dress, a pretty young resident of Volda. This portrait and related paintings show Johnson's career-long fascination with painting young people (see figs. 39, 40, 72). Although William and Holcha had no children of their own, several informants remembered that they were quite fond of children and very capable of empathizing with young people.

The Tjensvoll children, now adults, recalled how William commanded center stage during their holiday festivities in Volda, leading the children in regiment-style marching around the Christmas tree and playing geographic guessing games with them (which he always seemed to win).[66] Inngunn Steinnes, another resident of Volda, vividly remembers how, as a child, she and a girlfriend once ran up behind Johnson while he was painting alongside a road, and how he, pretending to be startled, cried out in mock surprise, "Oh, I thought I heard two wild horses coming towards me!"[67] According to Inngunn, the Tjensvolls, and others who grew up in Volda during the 1930s, Johnson was also an artistic mentor of sorts, constantly looking at their crude drawings and always praising their efforts.

On a few occasions, however, William and Holcha's worldly, artistic temperaments were a little too much for Volda's youth to appreciate and understand. Volda artist Nils Valnes remembered one winter day when a short-tempered Johnson, after being accidentally hit by a stray snowball, chased the unfortunate boy who threw it right into his classroom and then demanded an apology.[68] And in a somewhat related vein, Eivind Tjensvoll recalled his initial horror at seeing the "sweet" and "charming" Holcha puffing away on a large Cuban cigar! Kjellaug Tjensvoll, in an effort to assuage Eivind's youthful disillusionment, simply said "it's like that in Denmark."[69]

In June 1937, after almost two years in Volda, William and Holcha Johnson decided to continue their tour of Norway. Bidding farewell to their "family" and friends, they boarded a coastal steamer in the adjoining town, Aalesund, and headed north. From the steamer's observatory deck they saw Norway's legendary northern fjord country, which was especially picturesque and dramatic from their vantage point on the sea. Known as the "land of the midnight sun," the northernmost regions of Norway experienced con-

89. *Volda, Winter*, ca. 1935–36. Oil on burlap, 20½ x 25½ in.

90. *Girl in a Red Dress,* ca. 1936. Oil on burlap, 33¼ x 26¼ in.

stant daylight from early June until mid August. Through rain, mist, and sunshine, the Johnsons crossed the Arctic Circle and made stops in Bodø, the Lofoten Islands, and Narvik, going as far north as Tromsø (where they stayed briefly and held a small exhibition). After Tromsø, the couple reboarded the steamer and traveled south, down to Svolvær, the chief town in the Lofotens, where they lived in a rented flat for the remainder of that summer.

In a letter to the Tjensvolls, Holcha wrote enthusiastically about Svolvær. She described the mountains, sea, contours of the landscape, colors, and the whole atmosphere as "marvelously beautiful!" Concerning Johnson's progress in painting this particular landscape, she wrote:

Mr. Johnson has worked like a madman—night and day—some of his finest canvases and watercolors are painted up on the "Flojfjeld" (with the famous "Svolvær goat." "Flojen" rises sharply 2000 feet above the sea). The view from there—with the midnight sun shining all over the summits of the fjord—is among the most magnificent we have ever seen. [William] climbed up and down every day to paint that view at night—that is to say a higher and much more difficult way than up and down Rotsethornet every day for a month! But it was worth the trouble. [70]

Of the dozen or so known works from the Lofotens, *Harbor, Lofoten, Norway (III)* and *Harbor Under the Midnight Sun* stand out for their blazing colors and lively compositions (figs. 93, 94). In these images from Svolvær, Johnson returned to the subtle abstractions and reductive essays into nature that he first attempted in his paintings of Volda, but now with an even greater sense of empathy. In both of these paintings, Johnson clearly delineated the peculiar rock formations of the "Flojfjeld," including the double apex on one of the mountain peaks, which Holcha referred to as "the famous 'Svolvær goat'" (fig. 92). Johnson's impasto painting technique created a low relief surface across these canvases that mirrored the topographical facts about the environment.

This immersion in an expressive, yet controlled, painting technique is perhaps more readily seen in Johnson's *Midnight Sun, Lofoten* (fig. 95). Larger than any of his previous

91. *Study for Girl in a Red Dress,* ca. 1936. Pen and ink on paper, 3¼ x 2½ in.

landscapes and drenched in an array of heavily painted colors, *Midnight Sun, Lofoten* presents this northern Norwegian outpost as a surreal "land of dreams." Described by one critic as "brutal," with colors that "explode," and mountains that resemble "Cyclopean blocks on the verge of tumbling over," *Midnight Sun, Lofoten* also shows a painstaking orderliness, reflected in the landscape's carefully outlined and contained elements.[71] This fusion of a personal, artistic vision with the perceived dynamics of the land under observation fulfilled a central criterion for the expressionist landscape—that of bringing out "the great mystery that lies behind all events and objects of the environment."[72]

On first glance, the craggy mountains and rugged terrain of *Midnight Sun, Lofoten* bring to mind something old and prehistoric. Yet Johnson's vibrant colors, which range from a deep purple to a fire-engine red, also evoke the pulsations and energy of modern life. The blue-against-orange serrations of the sky and mountains across the top of the painting are countered by the similarly ragged, yet active, clawlike extensions of the sea on the right. Contrast is the operative concept here, and it is precisely from these juxtapositions that the painting derives much of its strength. "It seems," said one Swedish reviewer, "that the forceful power of this landscape has awakened to life something in [Johnson's] artistic soul; something that has to come out with an eruptive force."[73]

Midnight Sun, Lofoten and about sixty other oil paintings, watercolors, and woodcuts were exhibited in September 1937 in the northern Norwegian city of Trondheim.[74] In a letter to the Harmon Foundation that month, Johnson proudly told foundation director Mary Beattie Brady about the sale of one of his works to a local art society, his receipt of a portrait commission from a prominent citizen in Trondheim, and his improved outlook on his art work and career as a whole. In response to her last letter of 26 July, which informed him of the foundation's sale of *Port in Gray Weather*, Johnson conveyed his overall pleasure, but qualified this with his opinion that the sale price—$125.00 (or 507.25 Danish Crowns)—was rather low (see fig. 75). "I generally get around 600.Kr. and over for smaller landscapes," he wrote, "[and] 800.Kr. to 1000.Kr. for such size, etc."

92. Postcard, Flojfjeld, "Svolvær's Goat," Svolvær, Lofoten, Norway, ca. 1985

93. *Harbor, Lofoten, Norway (III)*, 1937. Oil on burlap, 27¼ x 35¼ in.

94. *Harbor Under the Midnight Sun*, 1937. Oil on burlap, 28 x 37½ in.

Continuing on the subject of prices for his paintings, Johnson admonished Brady to

demand a higher price for my paintings, for I am no ordinary American Negro painter, [nor am I an] ordinary American painter. I am recognized by known Americans and Europeans as a painter of value, so I must demand respect.

I see from your catalogue [that] so many of your Negro painter[s] have paintings in American Museums, colleges, etc. Why not . . . sell my paintings as well? Perhaps I am not [a] local enough Negro painter? [75]

Johnson's recent sales, his success with the critics, and his improved outlook prompted him to feel that his work had stature and rank on an international level. Johnson's self-assessment, though revealing a proud and perhaps somewhat inflated side of his character, nonetheless accurately reflected his wide experience in the art world. Far more seasoned than many of his fellow artists, both white and black, Johnson was a uniquely experienced painter whose work called into question the standard notions of both "Negro art" and "American art."[76]

One of the paintings that Johnson might have had in mind as worthy of a place in an American museum or university art collection was his *Self-Portrait with Pipe* (fig. 96). Like his earliest *Self-Portrait* (see fig. 8), this work, from circa 1937, presents the artist in the standard quarter profile, half-figure format of so many traditional self-portraits. But beyond their compositional similarities, Johnson's academic *Self-Portrait* and this recent *Self-Portrait* differ in numerous ways.

Unlike his first *Self-Portrait*, with its murky theatrical trappings, the later work is more closely aligned with the direct, vigorous paintings from Johnson's period in Volda and in the Lofotens. While the figure of the artist in this latest *Self-Portrait*—resplendent in a patterned smoking jacket and punctuated with pipe and paintbrush—revived a romantic image of the *artiste* from past art and literature, Johnson's intense colors and expressive painting technique catapult his self-image into a modern aesthetic, one riddled with formal dichotomies and underlying emotions. Light years ahead of those somber self-portraits that lined the halls of the National Academy of Design and other American institutions, this introspective view of the then thirty-six-year-old Johnson perfectly illustrates the talent behind the artist's demands for greater respect and recognition at home.

After Trondheim, the couple traveled by train to central Sweden where, in November and December, they mounted exhibitions in Västerås, Stockholm, and Gävle. Critics generally responded positively to the works in these exhibitions, one of them, for example, marveling at Johnson's "strong and fresh orientation to nature."[77] Perhaps an even greater compliment came from that same critic, who wrote, "I would believe that many of these

95. *Midnight Sun, Lofoten*, 1937.
Oil on burlap, 41⅝ x 59⅛ in.

96. *Self-Portrait with Pipe*, ca. 1937. Oil on canvas, 35 x 27 in.

works, although created by a stranger like Johnson, from another country and of another race, would be accepted by Norwegians as true interpretations of their exclusive mountain world."

Among the many visitors to Johnson's exhibition at Stockholm's Mässhallen in late November was the American ambassador to Sweden, Fred Morris Dearing (fig. 97). Ambassador Dearing, along with Allen Ebeling, Johnson's Swedish friend and fellow artist, helped facilitate a meeting between Johnson and curators at Sweden's National Gallery, which ultimately resulted in that museum's spring 1938 acquisition of *Girl in a Red Dress* (see fig. 90). Now in the permanent collection of Stockholm's Moderna Museet, *Girl in a Red Dress* was Johnson's first and only painting acquired by a major museum during his active years as an artist.

In January 1938, the Johnsons crossed back into Norway and, again, visited Oslo. While there, they saw a widely acclaimed traveling exhibition of French art (with works by Matisse, Picasso, Braque, and Laurens) that had been organized by Paul Rosenberg for galleries in Oslo, Copenhagen, Stockholm, and Göteborg. The centerpiece of the exhibition, Picasso's recently completed *Guernica* (1937), took up a major part of Oslo's Kunstnernes Hus, where the exhibition was on view. The Johnsons, who were again staying at the nearby Pension Ro, made numerous visits to the exhibition during its installment in Oslo.

William and Holcha's ultimate objective, however, was to stay in Oslo until May, whereupon they would travel westward, into the Hardangerfjord region. While in this majestic part of Norway, Johnson intended to paint the blossoming cherry and apple orchards along the shores of the fjord.

Actually, Johnson's encounter with western Norway's fabled blossoming fruit trees began during his two-year residency in Volda, which resulted in several semi-abstractions of apple trees in full bloom (fig. 98). The paintings from Hardanger, however, with their larger scale and tendency to fuse western Norway's rugged terrain with an impasto frieze of swirling white petals, suggest a broader, more enveloping eye for this particular phenomenon in nature (fig. 99).

Chalet in the Mountains, another Hardanger subject, surpasses Johnson's previous experiments in color (fig. 100). Aquamarine, cobalt blue, pink, canary yellow, and terra cotta red flash across this landscape in a supernatural, yet engaging, fashion. Comparing Johnson's color sense with "the clear air of the Norwegian mountains," one keen observer noted that Johnson found "colors in nature which Nordic painters have been forced to go to France to find."[78]

Finally, in the summer of 1938, William and Holcha returned to Denmark, after a very productive three and a half years spent mostly in western Norway. Upon their arrival in

97. With the American Ambassador to Sweden, Fred Morris Dearing, on the occasion of Johnson's exhibition at Mässhallen, Stockholm, Sweden, November 1937.

98. *Mountain Blossoms, Volda*, ca. 1936–37. Oil on burlap, 25 x 29 in.

Funen, Holcha learned of the frightening turn of events in the lives of Erna, her husband Christoph Voll, and the Voll's young daughter. The shifting tides of recent German politics, which had brought Adolf Hitler and his National Socialist German Workers' Party to power, had also touched the German art world. The results of the new order were ominous: severe economic cutbacks to the state-run art institutions; the firings and forced resignations of curators, teachers, and other arts professionals; and government-sanctioned persecution of artists and intellectuals who, because of their ties to international and/or leftist schools of thought, were deemed "degenerate." Not only had Christoph been fired from his teaching position at the Kunstakademie in Karlsruhe, but his art and career had been publicly ridiculed through the inclusion of several of his early expressionist pieces in the infamous and satirical "Degenerate Art" exhibition, organized in July 1937 by Hitler's cultural henchmen and seen by thousands of Germans for the next two years.[79]

These real, life-threatening trials for Erna and Christoph, coupled with the rumors that Hitler's war-bound fascist forces were only biding their time before invading and occupying Denmark, doubtlessly figured into William and Holcha's decision that summer to flee Europe and seek asylum back in the United States. But appended to these war-related motives for a return to America was Johnson's realization that one period of his career was coming to a close and, very soon, another phase would replace it. Writing to Mary Beattie Brady that summer, Johnson explained, "I am feeling . . . that I would like my own homeland next, as I know of no better country to inspire me at this period of my artistic development."[80]

Intimations of what this new "period of . . . artistic development" would yield were previewed in an October 1938 exhibition by Johnson, held in one of Odense's exhibition halls. Included among the paintings of Oslo, Volda, the Lofotens, and the Hardangerfjord region were several new landscapes of Kerteminde, none of them painted earlier than January of that year. In sharp contrast to Johnson's "fish-lens" views of the old harbor of eight years prior, these new Kerteminde landscapes, like their Norwegian counterparts, present the town's architecture, harbor, boats, water, and even sky as concrete, tangible entities (fig. 101). As opposed to the loose, almost baroque qualities of his earlier works, the palette knife's build-up of oil paint in these recent works substantiates the visual information about Kerteminde without sacrificing its atmospheric, spiritual side. Observations on this subtle, but decided shift in Johnson's perspective on Kerteminde were made by at least one critic, who, while reviewing the October exhibition, noted that

individuality, composing with color, and intense contrasting effects are standard, though never tedious, for Johnson and his art. [But] most interesting perhaps are his Kerteminde pictures which, while not completely suffering from exaggerated likenesses, nevertheless look good with these radiant colors and interesting perspectives.[81]

99. *Apple Blossoms, Norheimsund, Hardanger,* ca. 1938. Oil on burlap, 33⅛ x 39¼ in.

100. *Chalet in the Mountains*, ca. 1938. Oil on burlap, 28⅛ x 35 in.

101. *Kerteminde Harbor*, ca. 1938. Oil on burlap, 38 x 29⅛ in.

Each of the reviews for this final Odense exhibition commented on the couple's upcoming trip to America. Perhaps with an element of veiled optimism, one of the reviews carried the wistful headline, "Johnson Returns Home—but Only for a Visit."[82]

Sometime after the first of November, William and Holcha, with their belongings in used trunks and makeshift boxes, boarded an already crowded Polish steamer destined for New York's harbor. Although it was William's fourth transatlantic crossing, he and the other passengers, many of whom were from central Europe, all felt an overwhelming nervousness and anxiety as they made their way through the North Sea. Arguments over the prospects of war and reminiscences of loved ones left behind dominated everyone's thoughts. Holcha, who prior to embarking on any trip could always be counted on to announce cheerfully "we travel in order to feel renewed," was herself glum, already homesick, and very worried about Erna and Christoph. Yet both William and Holcha seemed to accept the fact that Denmark, Norway, Germany, France, North Africa, and the rest of the world that they had once enjoyed and explored in their work would soon be embroiled in a war that they, as artists/refugees, now sought to avoid. New York City, Johnson's first "home away from home," at least promised firmer ground and a war-free, though still unpredictable, future.

Homecoming
1938–1946

William and Holcha Johnson arrived in New York Harbor on Thanksgiving Day, 1938. Meeting them at customs were their American friends Helen and David Harriton, whom they had met almost a year earlier while traveling by coastal steamer from Aalesund to Tromsø in Norway. David Harriton, a glass designer by profession, shared William and Holcha's love for the arts; he and his wife also had a keen understanding of the personal and economic difficulties that creative people, like the Johnsons, often faced.

After that initial meeting along Norway's glorious northwest coast, the couples exchanged addresses and promised to write one another. "The next we heard from them," recalled Helen Harriton many years later, "was a letter, saying that they intended to come to the U.S. that fall—written by him. We wrote back trying to discourage them, reminding him of the discrimination the negro suffers in the U.S., and . . . what it would mean to his gentle wife. Nevertheless, he wrote again that they were coming—that they feared there would be a war in Europe soon . . . and also because he felt the need to come back to his own country and paint his own people."[1]

Johnson's need to "paint his own people," while a normal expectation on his anticipated return to the United States, was also very much related to his wife and her influence on his thinking. Holcha's lifelong involvement in the study of textile arts made her conscious of the important role that traditional arts and crafts play in contemporary culture. Her own education, which had started in Denmark's populist *folkhøjskole* movement, channeled her artistic interests away from elitist notions of "high" art versus "low" art and, instead, toward a more egalitarian position, in which she saw the art of the common people as equal to the creations of "fine" artists. Her investigations into the lore, aesthetic traditions, and cultural mores of various European peoples, as well as her experiences living and working among traditional artisans throughout Scandinavia, ultimately forced Johnson to reconsider his own professed relationship with traditional culture. Although Johnson often joined Holcha in her research (as was the case in Tunisia), it was not long before he realized that, in order to truthfully call himself "a modern primitive," he would have to interact with and artistically embrace his own African-American "folk."

But before this encounter between the artist and the folk could take place, William and Holcha had to address more immediate concerns, such as finding a place to live in New York. After several weeks as the Harritons' house guests, the Johnsons eventually found a

102. Helen and David Harriton, New York, ca. 1944

103. Christmas in New York City, ca. 1939

small, inexpensive apartment at 27 West 15th Street. Although an ocean apart from Kerteminde, family, and familiar surroundings, Holcha made the most of their new life in New York, as gleaned from a photograph of their place at Christmas, showing their tree gaily decorated with traditional, handmade Danish ornaments (fig. 103).

But adjusting to New York in those first few months did take its toll on the couple. Evelyn S. Brown, Assistant Director of the Harmon Foundation, remembered receiving dozens of telephone calls from both William and Holcha in those early days in New York, pleading with the foundation to help William get on the Works Progress Administration's local Federal Art Project (WPA/FAP).[2] Although Johnson's opportunities to show his work had greatly improved since moving to New York, sales had actually decreased from their low-to-moderate European level, forcing him to dramatically slash prices and aggressively investigate any possible leads for sales (fig. 105). Writing to Mary Beattie Brady after her visit to his studio/apartment, Johnson noted, "I thought I would have asked you to take that picture that the foundation would buy . . . as it would be very helpfull [sic] for us just right now. . . . I know you understand how serious it is for me—this difficult situation."[3] Not limiting his solicitations to the Harmon Foundation, Johnson made the rounds of several contemporary art galleries, all in hopes of making a sale or, at least, placing some of his work on consignment. Yet it eventually became clear to Johnson that, regardless of the encouraging words concerning his paintings from such "old world" art dealers as Curt Valentin and Karl Nierendorf, the New York art market simply could not sustain him, nor most living American artists, at this juncture. His best bet, in light of the available options in 1939 for American artists, black *and* white, was getting an assignment with the Federal Art Project.

After Mary Brady made a few calls to the local WPA administrators, Johnson was finally assigned to the WPA/FAP on 26 May 1939.[4] This much-needed boost to Johnson's economic situation was also a chance for him to try his hand at teaching, since he was assigned to the Harlem Community Art Center. There, Johnson joined artists/teachers Henry Bannarn, Elton Fax, Ronald Joseph, Norman Lewis, and Art Center Director Gwendolyn Bennett in providing art instructions to almost six hundred students per week.[5]

Another aspect of Johnson's Art Center assignment that played a major part in his artistic development was the opportunity it gave him to interact with the black community. In Johnson's first week at the Art Center, he not only met his fellow teachers, but encountered many important Harlem artists and personalities. As seen in a photograph from the Art Center's annual exhibition opening, Johnson was flanked on both sides by a virtual "who's who" of African-American artists: a youthful Jacob Lawrence, Selma Burke wearing a floral patterned dress, a preoccupied Henry Bannarn, a radiant Gwendolyn Knight, and many others (fig. 104). Johnson, not the most friendly or outgoing person among the artists, nonetheless benefited from being in their midst and witnessing firsthand their works and artistic choices.[6]

Johnson's daily subway rides from the downtown studio/apartment to his uptown classroom at 290 Lenox Avenue typified the cultural transitions going on in his life. Gradually, his work began to reflect these journeys into Harlem. Woodcuts made just prior to these uptown trips, while suggestive of New York's frenetic and, at times, impersonal character, actually differ very little from their Scandinavian antecedents (fig. 106). Real changes in Johnson's overall artistic approach began in 1939 with a series of drawings, numbering over a hundred, mostly executed during and after classes at the Art Center. These studies—of African sculptures and flesh-and-blood African-American models—not only demonstrate Johnson's first artistic efforts to focus on the full human figure, but his first attempts to re-comprehend a racially and culturally distinct figure (figs. 107, 108).

104. At the Harlem Community Art Center, 6 June 1939. Jacob Lawrence (far left); William H. Johnson (front, left center); Gwendolyn Knight (rear center)

Johnson's drawing of a Bamana sculpture, made after an illustration in the Museum of Modern Art's exhibition catalogue *African Negro Art* (1935), fuses his standard embellishments to a perceived reality with a sharp eye for capturing his subject's bare essentials—the end result being an anthropomorphic rendering of an inanimate wooden figure (fig. 109).[7] Considered in light of Johnson's previous encounters with the Danish collector Carl Kjersmeier and his world-renowned collection of western Sudanic art, these and other drawings of African sculpture by Johnson take on an even greater resonance.

Figure studies made at the same time also juggle close observations from life with inspired flights of anatomical hyperbole. In one nude study, for example, Johnson reduces the figure to an abstracted form, while retaining a position—arms akimbo and body contraposto—very much based in reality (see fig. 108). Through this editing process, Johnson indelibly fixes a culturally charged stance—as in this classically African-American, hands-on-hips gesture—in the minds and eyes of his viewers.[8]

In gesture, color, and attitude, these studies from African art and living African-American models celebrate a new racial aesthetic, circa 1939, that must have seemed exotic even to Johnson, especially after twelve years of living among Europeans. Unquestionably, the varieties of African-American body sizes, shapes, colors, and auras that daily presented themselves to Johnson inspired him to begin painting black people in ways that stood apart from strict, naturalistic representations. At first glance, Johnson's reductive approach to the human figure suggests the use of cubist formulas for his reinterpretation of nature. Certainly during Johnson's first year back in the United States, he would have seen how the New York art world had all but crowned Picasso, Cubism's leading propo-

105. Announcement for exhibition at the Artist's Gallery, New York City, 1939

106. *Street People*, ca. 1939.
Hand-colored block print,
15 x 13¼ in.

107. *Nude Study*, ca. 1939.
Tempera on paperboard,
28 x 22 in.

nent, as king, with countless exhibitions of his work regularly on view.[9] But the multitude of figure studies from Johnson's initial "artist-in-residency" in Harlem, coupled with his affinity for the "rhythmic and spiritual" in life, suggest that the community itself was Johnson's foremost source: a human landscape that, more than Norway's mountains or Picasso's cubist armatures, promised even more idiosyncratic works of art.

Away in the Valley by Myself, a painting known today only from photographs, also documents this new-found fascination with the distinctly black figure (fig. 110). With its depiction of the snow-capped mountains and icy fjords of Norway, this painting is also indicative of the transitions taking place in Johnson's oeuvre. Like the figures in Johnson's studies of African sculptures and Harlem models, the black figure in *Away in the Valley by Myself*, with its enormous hands and feet, borders on caricature. Yet Johnson's sense of caricature had less to do with satire than it did with recording and amplifying the essentials of a subject, as a way of documenting physical *and* cultural truths. By making his black subject's hands and feet appear larger than life, Johnson underscores the manual, blue-collar drudgery that defined the lives of most African-Americans during this era. For audiences already attuned to such racially grounded pop refrains as "Your Feet's Too Big" (sung by jazz musician Thomas "Fats" Waller), figures such as the one in *Away in the Valley by Myself* become stand-ins for an entire race and class of people.

In *Away in the Valley by Myself*, Johnson shows an anonymous, yet ecstatic black man, alone in nature. With arms flung upward and hands seemingly reaching out to the heavens, the man recalls the image of spirit-possessed worshippers in countless churches throughout black America. The difference, of course, is that this house of worship is an other-worldly, mountainous place, with jagged rocks, a heavenly orb, and a rainbow all within easy reach. Beyond the autobiographical aspects of *Away in the Valley by Myself*, Johnson's double image of abandonment and spiritual connectedness to the universe introduces a thematic dimension to his work that was previously submerged. In this painting, one of Johnson's first figure-dominated landscapes, the overriding sentiments of isolation and animism mesh with a lucid, non-illusionistic world of nature and black spirituality.

Another early figure painting that grew out of Johnson's work at the Art Center explores more earth-bound, corporeal issues (fig. 111). In a real stylistic departure for Johnson, the figure takes up the entire length of this horizontal painting. The expressionless face of the reclining female figure, along with the painting's vague title, *Nude*, suggests that Johnson's objective was to create a generic image, rather than a portrait of a specific person. Given the figure's voluptuous body, the opulent setting, and the compositional centrality of the genitalia (by way of a directional, phalluslike bottle), Johnson's impulse here is certainly of a sexual nature.

Yet far from creating a pornographic or sentimental image of a love object, Johnson confronts sexuality in this painting in a stark, matter-of-fact manner. The unmodulated colors, simplification of form, and direct, yet constrained, imagery in *Nude* create a visual metaphor for female allurement and male desire that, despite the potential for sensationalism, remains level-headed and clear.

Johnson's choice of a large, dark-skinned woman of unquestionable African ancestry to embody the sensuous and the beautiful was a radical step in 1939. A more conventional choice would have been a blonde pin-up type, or even a caucasian-featured black like the then-popular Lena Horne. That Johnson himself was married to Holcha Krake, a white woman, might have also raised questions in people's minds as to why Johnson would paint this sensual image of a black woman. Certainly there were viewers in 1939 who were repelled by the nudity and perhaps embarrassed by Johnson's focus on a figure they would have regarded as an "unattractive" Negro woman. Still, there must have also been a significant number of people, black *and* white, who welcomed Johnson's artistic realignment of the ideals of feminine beauty, and who were able to understand how his marriage to Holcha and his recent artistic overtures to Afro-America could harmoniously coexist.

Interestingly, Johnson signed this painting twice: first, with his standard "W H Johnson," and again with the pseudonym "Mahlinda." Appearing infrequently on his paintings and derived from unknown origins, "Mahlinda" perhaps personified, through its folksy and non-western sounding cadence, a different and more decidedly ethnic artistic presence.[10]

Johnson's rediscovery of the black figure also involved its placement within a popular and/or folk setting. As Johnson began to seriously employ these African-American subjects in his art, he was no doubt aware that many American artists of his day celebrated "the American scene." Perhaps encouraged by the WPA's call to artists to visualize America in all its regional diversity, Johnson created works in this early period, such as *Man with Plow*, that re-fashioned his Art Center figure studies into content-laden, socio-economic, artistic statements (fig. 112).

Johnson's previous notions of "Negro" culture certainly changed during this first year back home. While he had been living a somewhat rarified—though still poverty-stricken—existence in Scandinavia for much of the 1930s, black America as a whole underwent major social, political, and economic changes. A number of forces—including the Depression, continuing racial discrimination and violence, and a sense of entitlement installed by the New Deal—combined to break up, at least in part, the African-American cultural monolith. This new eclecticism was reflected in racial viewpoints ranging from

108. (above) *Study of Bamana Figure*, ca. 1939. Watercolor and pencil on paper, 10 x 3⅛ in. **109.** (below). Charles Sheeler, photograph of a standing female figure, 1918. Gelatin silver print.

110. *Away in the Valley by Myself*, ca. 1939. Oil on burlap, dimensions and whereabouts unknown

activist Angelo Herndon's Marxist politics to the more mainstream stand of Roosevelt-confidante Mary McLeod Bethune.

Nineteen thirty-nine—the year Johnson started working at the Harlem Community Art Center—marked an auspicious moment in African-American cultural history. African-American churches, schools, and newspapers busied themselves with Negro history pageants, large-scale expositions, and other educational activities to commemorate the upcoming seventy-fifth anniversary of the Thirteenth Amendment to the U.S. Constitution. Social scientists ranging from E. Franklin Frazier to Melville J. Herskovits were studying the social patterns and cultural mores of African-Americans. Artists followed suit with what seemed to be a new-found appreciation for black American language, imagery, and culture in all of its manifestations.

In literature, three important novels dealing with various aspects of black life were published in 1939: William Attaway's *Let Me Breathe Thunder*, Arna Bontemps's *Drums at Dusk*, and Zora Neale Hurston's *Moses, Man of the Mountain*. Richard Wright received a Guggenheim fellowship that year for *Uncle Tom's Children*, a riveting collection of short stories that was first published in 1938. In jazz and popular music, band leaders such as Duke Ellington, Count Basie, Andy Kirk, Jimmy Lunceford, and Cab Calloway performed for audiences throughout the country, while popular singers like Billie Holiday and Ella Fitzgerald were featured soloists on radio and in nightclubs. In classical music, both Roland Hayes and Dorothy Maynor presented critically acclaimed concerts at Town Hall that year, and Paul Robeson's CBS-Radio performance of "Ballad for Americans" was heard and appreciated by millions. In the New York theater world, two black versions of Gilbert and Sullivan's *The Mikado* competed with one another, and Ethel Waters received much praise for her starring role in the Broadway production *Mamba's Daughter*. In motion pictures, not only were several black actors featured in major roles in 1939 (Hattie McDaniel in *Gone with the Wind*, Paul Robeson in *Big Fella*, Leigh Whipper in *Of Mice and Men*, and Rex Ingram in *The Thief of Bagdad*), but black, independent filmmakers were reaching large numbers of African-Americans with "All-Colored" westerns, musicals, and melodramas. And finally, in the visual arts, the Baltimore Museum of Art mounted the exhibition "Contemporary Negro Art," one of the very first surveys of African-American art to appear in a major U.S.

111. *Nude*, ca. 1939. Oil on burlap, 29¾ x 38¼ in.

112. *Man with Plow,* ca. 1939.
Tempera on paperboard,
28 x 22 in.

museum. Realizing that black art and culture were alive and thriving in 1939, William H. Johnson had little choice but to come to terms in his own art with what he had once called (but perhaps never really fathomed) his "family of primitiveness and tradition."

Probably the two "artists" who best epitomized the ideals and aspirations of black Americans at the end of the 1930s were concert singer Marian Anderson and world heavyweight boxing champion Joe Louis. Their widely recounted struggles against the forces of racism gave their work potent social value and clear political implications. The press coverage surrounding the refusal of the Daughters of the American Revolution to permit Marian Anderson to sing in Washington, D.C.'s Constitution Hall brought the ugly realities of racial discrimination into sharp focus for all Americans in the first few months of 1939. At about the same time, Joe Louis, black America's antidote to fascist claims of Aryan superiority, was preparing to defend his world championship against a rather vocal white challenger named "Two Ton" Tony Galento. Vindication for the two—for Anderson in an Easter Sunday concert on the steps of the Lincoln Memorial with over seventy-five thousand well-wishers on hand, and for Louis in his knock-out victory over Galento on 28 June after four dramatic rounds—was a vindication for *all* black Americans in 1939.

Johnson joined his fellow blacks in celebrating the professional and personal triumphs of these two "beacons of the race" (fig. 113). Using newspaper photographs as his source, Johnson painted these two at their respective moments of truth—Anderson, singing under the benevolent marble image of Abraham Lincoln, and Louis, boxing a red-faced, beleaguered white opponent. (For Johnson's image of Marian Anderson, see *Marian Anderson,* circa 1939, in the collection of the National Museum of American Art. The painting is, unfortunately, in very poor condition.)

In a similarly conceived painting, but one executed on a far grander scale, Johnson paid homage to the people and environment that inspired this new stage in his artistic development. *Street Life—Harlem* depicts a stylishly dressed couple standing on an urban street corner (fig. 114). The couple's clothing—hats topped with bright plumage, shoes with big platforms and open-toes, spats, a vest, long gloves—serves as a kind of urban

113. *Joe Louis and Unidentified Boxer*, ca. 1939–42. Tempera, pen and ink with pencil on paper, 18 x 12 in.

insignia that, along with the multicolored buildings around them, suggests that the city, or rather Harlem, was indeed a colorful, throbbing organism.

That Johnson's view of Harlem was neither overstated nor fabricated can be seen in the following excerpt from an April 1939 article in the *New York Amsterdam News*, reporting on clothes and lifestyles at Harlem's famous dancehall, the Savoy Ballroom:

Women young and old began packing into the Savoy at 10 P.M., all decked out in their Sunday best. They were breaking-in Palm Sunday and Easter clothes last Thursday— tiny veiled, cock-eyed hats, perched at crazy angles on their freshly shampooed, shiny hair; and swing skirts a tantalizing fraction of an inch below their knees.[11]

The Savoy Ballroom, minutes away from the Harlem Community Art Center, provided Johnson with vast amounts of visual information and inspiration.

Another painting that reveals Johnson's close observations of Harlem's fads and fashions is *Cafe* (fig. 115). The scene in *Cafe* is the interior of a bistro, where a man and woman sit at a round table. Like *Street Life—Harlem*, *Cafe* features the latest in urban apparel: broad-shouldered dresses and suits, stylishly angled women's hats, platform shoes, and vividly colored textiles. Yet Johnson also interjects a dash of oddball visual humor into this scene—a collection of indecipherable, intertwined legs (both human and wooden) under the table and the deadpan facial expressions of the couple.

Johnson's couple in *Cafe*—communicating a mood that suggests either boredom or allurement—resembles another famous male/female pairing in a bistro scene from modern art: Picasso's 1904 etching, *The Frugal Repast* (fig. 116). While not replicating exactly the gaunt couple in Picasso's work, *Cafe* appropriates their gestures, reverses them, and then superimposes the scene on a stylized and abstracted African-American couple.

Actually, *Cafe* and *Street Life—Harlem* bear closer comparisons to Johnson's studies of African sculpture—as evidenced in each couple's angular, almost figurinelike appearance—than to Picasso's work. Johnson's exaggerated, high-fashion men and women perfectly illustrate what novelist Ralph Ellison described in *Invisible Man* as a kind of clashing, expressive formalism found in African-American fashions of the period. Ellison's image of three zoot-suit-wearing Harlem youths, looking like "African sculptures, distorted in the interest of design," aptly describes the harnessed energy and emphasis on design in *Cafe* and *Street Life—Harlem*.[12]

Study for Playground Scene, a drawing originally intended as a mural study for the Federal Art Project, reveals another side of Johnson's homage to Harlem and urbanity: children's culture in the inner city (fig. 118). Johnson's outlined and geometric treatment of the children and their urban environment transforms this drawing into an animated scene of shifting circles, parallel bands, and other linear configurations. Though incom-

114. *Street Life—Harlem*, ca. 1939–40. Oil on wood, 45¾ x 38⅝ in.

115. *Cafe*, ca. 1939–40. Oil on fiberboard, 36½ x 28⅜ in.

plete, *Playground Scene* and other works by Johnson that examine urban child's play convey an almost conceptual sense of city children and their activities (fig. 117).

Although Johnson had long been an avid supporter of encouraging children in the visual arts, his tenure at the Harlem Community Art Center formalized this advocacy, as it regularly exposed him to the direct, colorful statements of these budding artists (fig. 119). Child artists, like the one shown kneeling and drawing in the lower left corner of *Playground Scene*, fueled Johnson's imagination and inspired him to continue pursuing a two-dimensional, non-illusionistic approach to painting.

Another painting of city life that confirms Johnson's position as an astute observer in and about Harlem is *Street Musicians* (fig. 120). This painting, apart from the now familiar male/female pairings in many of these circa 1939 works, also includes an active narrative: musicians in open-air performance.

The angularity, pictorial flatness, intense color scheme, and overall visual economy of *Street Musicians* mirror the sparse, plaintive harmonies and modest, threadbare appearance of real-life street musicians. Wandering songsters like Blind Boy Fuller, Sister Rosetta Tharpe, and the Reverend Gary Davis, who made their living by singing ballads and spirituals on pedestrian-clogged street corners, were a common sight in black communities. And Johnson, who would have certainly remembered these and other black troubadours from his South Carolina youth, may have sensed a real need and desire to not only "paint his people," but to selectively re-collect these and other folk images from his past.

Johnson's South Carolina origins, although long overshadowed by subsequent travels and experiences, nevertheless conditioned him to be more conscious of the African-American folk tradition and, as seen in works like *Street Musicians*, the manifestations of that tradition in the urban North. In a gouache painting of a two-man "string band," Johnson also places two folk musicians—a fiddler and guitarist—in an inner-city, urban environment, continuing his celebration of the basic folk roots of Afro-America (fig. 121).

Prior to 1938, Johnson's forte was the landscape. After 1938, however, it is his figural works—filled with urgency and energy—that dominate. Johnson's swift transition from landscape painter to figure painter was, as amazing as it may seem, an established pattern for this intuitive, keenly observant artist. Johnson, who had been trained by Hawthorne earlier in his career first, to paint what was around him, and second, to commit quickly

116. Pablo Picasso, *The Frugal Repast*, 1904. Etching on zinc, 18⅛ x 15 in.

Children Playing at Dockside

117. *Children Playing at Dockside*, ca. 1939–42. Tempera, pen and ink with pencil on paper, 16½ x 13⅞ in.

to paper or canvas the visual essentials of a given subject, was merely continuing in this manner with these latest works from Harlem.

His change, however, to a more simplified, colorful, and geometric painting technique was, in fact, a more gradual phenomenon, indicative of his steady movement toward what he long considered an inevitable "return to the primitive." His notions of primitivism had, more or less, been voiced from the very beginning of his Scandinavian stay, yet it was understandably difficult for Danish critics to pinpoint exactly how these ideas manifested themselves in his expressionistic harbor views, portraits of old fishermen, and still lifes. Beginning with many of his Norwegian paintings—with their flattened perspectives, strong colors, selective distortions, and spiritual dimension—Johnson's earlier pronouncements on his own movement toward primitivism finally began to make sense. And, as seen in these works from his first year back in the United States, the fusion of these formal devices with selected African-American themes makes an even stronger case for seeing his artistic development as a steady, linear progression. This progression, how-

118. *Study for Playground Scene*, ca. 1939–42. Pen and ink with pencil on paper, squared for transfer, 12½ x 22⁹⁄₁₆ in.

137

119. Anonymous child artist, *Untitled (Airplane in the Sky)*, ca. 1942–43. Tempera on paper, 16⅝ x 16⅜ in.

ever, is an evolution away from ostensible sophistication and toward art's primal, folkloric beginnings.

Upon seeing these expressionistic, colorful, yet seemingly crude and folkloric-looking new paintings, Johnson's American critics were, at first, perplexed. Again, the critical expectations for someone of Johnson's background—with his tenure at the National Academy of Design and his years spent in France—were for works that reflected either a consummate realism or a readily identifiable school of European modernism. But even Johnson's former "agent" and confidant, Alain Locke, could only write that Johnson, in these new works, had moved "somewhat extremely to the artistic left of disorganized expressionism."[13]

On the other hand, when several of these new works were shown in the summer of 1940 at the "Exhibition of the Art of the American Negro (1851–1940)," for the American Negro Exposition in Chicago, one local critic immediately responded with enthusiasm:

The heavy paint, the free drawing of figures and the discarding of nonessentials might at first glance make us think he is naive. But each color mass holds its own as a color and yet is related to every other mass, without getting lost or sweet. This proves that Johnson, as an artist with a mind and emotion, knows what the great modern masters have contributed to the clarification and progress of color.[14]

For both the reviewer in Chicago and Alain Locke, Johnson's flirtation with images and forms that suggested naiveté was symptomatic of the art world's then-current fascination with self-trained "daubers," "scribblers," and "whittlers," whose creative lives had been spent (for the most part) outside of the art world proper. One of the most celebrated of these folk artists, black American painter Horace Pippin, worked in a somewhat similar manner to Johnson, with oil paints applied in a thick, impasto consistency, and visual narratives punctuated by strong, solid areas of pure color. Schooled and dedicated artists like Johnson must have felt a little envious of these self-taught painters such as Pippin who, in only a matter of a few years, had several museum and gallery exhibitions to their credit.

As Johnson's past comments about primitivism and folk culture demonstrate, he acknowledged the innate power and spirituality that emanated from the art of common people and had decided to allow that part of his own folk heritage to assert itself in his work. Although no less eager to have his own work seen and appreciated, Johnson no doubt accepted the broad appeal of those folk artists then deservedly enjoying the art world's spotlight.

Johnson was not alone in his perception that black folk culture presented numerous opportunities for the visual artist. Alain Locke, although perhaps not entirely convinced of Johnson's close relationship to the folk, was nevertheless a strong advocate himself of

120. *Street Musicians,* ca. 1940. Oil on wood, 36⅜ x 28¼ in.

121. *String Band*, ca. 1940. Gouache, pen and ink with pencil on paper, 17 x 12⅞ in.

the creative potential that folk culture could provide the fine artist. Discussing this point in his foreword for the Baltimore Museum of Art's *Contemporary Negro Art* exhibition catalogue, Locke wrote:

Recently in strategic places in the South, the [Federal Art Project has] sponsored public art centers which may serve not only to carry art to the people but to carry the artist, too long isolated from the folk, back to a vital source of his materials. It may be impossible under modern American conditions to revive folk art effectively, but surely a people's art is possible. In this drive toward democracy in art, the Negro artist and the Negro people have an unusual stake, for the very term "Negro art" implies in addition to a blossoming of Negro artists the flowering of an art of folk expression and interpretation.[15]

122. *Cotton Pickers*, ca. 1940. Watercolor and pencil on paper, 10¾ x 11½ in.

Locke's idea of "an art of folk expression and interpretation" could cover a lot of ground. Locke thought highly, for example, of the "intuitive genius" of the young Jacob Lawrence, as evidenced in his widely seen exhibition of forty-one paintings documenting the life of Toussaint L'Overture and the course of the Haitian Revolution. In a more naturalistic and academic vein, Locke was also enamored of what he termed the "racial to the core" subject matter of sculptor Richmond Barthé. And perhaps stylistically wedged in between Lawrence's mosaiclike narratives and the literal, socially relevant bronzes of Barthé were the paintings of Johnson's former N.A.D. colleague, the late Malvin Gray Johnson, whose sentimental yet unaffected scenes of rural blacks inspired Locke to call his direct and sincere approach an "object lesson" for the younger generation of African-American artists.[16]

Around 1940, keenly aware of his own motives and of what was happening around him, Johnson embarked on a visual return to a rural, folkloric South. Johnson's aesthetic journey took him through an invented panorama of the South, comprised of people, places, and activities engendered in reality, but born in his imagination (fig. 122). The many years that had passed since Johnson's upbringing in the South seemed to bring an almost timeless and ethereal quality to these new works. Held together by intriguing color relationships, a strong rhythmic sensibility, and selective bits and pieces of the African-American folk experience, Johnson's depictions of the South transcended romanticism.

Johnson's sketches and studies for these rural paintings concentrated on such common activities as drawing well water, picking farm produce, husking ears of corn, and operating

an animal-engineered plow (fig. 123). But in his often painstaking focus on mundane work rituals, Johnson conceptually re-positioned the standard folk narratives about rural people and the South along thoroughly modern lines. In Johnson's *Farm Couple at Work*, for example, the sharply delineated bands of cultivated ground, the iconographically conceived farm equipment, and the raw physicality of his farm couple raise this "pastoral" subject to the level of a calculated, boldly expressive discourse on black labor (fig. 124).

In *Chain Gang*, modernist vision and rural subject are again synthesized (fig. 125). Johnson's unreal chromatics and anatomical distortions seem to transform conscripted labor, the theme of this work, into something positive and almost redemptive in nature.

The visual linkage of prisoners, tools, trees, and terrain in *Chain Gang* forces a perception of the painting's context as one total entity, transfiguring an otherwise commonplace situation into something emblematic. Form and content fuse here as Johnson takes the sordid reality of work in a southern, rural, discriminatory penal system and redefines it as a rhythmized, ennobled, and intrinsically creative act.

Chain Gang has much in common with the musical/aural aspects of actual chain-gang life. Alan Lomax's field recordings of African-American work songs from southern penitentiaries and prison farms capture a sense of affirmation and expressive conceptualizing similar to that in *Chain Gang*. In Lomax's 1934 recording of "Long John," for example, the constant repetition of staccato phrases from leader to chorus, punctuated by unisonal chops from the chorus of conscripted axmen, functions in the same way as the black and white stripes and other color components of *Chain Gang*: in service to an aesthetically affecting and emotionally sustaining rhythm.[17]

Johnson's *Chain Gang* was not a denial of the atrocities perpetuated against blacks by this infamous system of punishment, but rather an affirmation of an old African-American maxim to "make a way out of no way." The horrors of the southern chain gang notwithstanding, Johnson's prisoners, as well as those on the Lomax recordings, redeem a bad situation through collective hard work, self-awareness, and the solace of their culture.

This process, with Johnson recollecting a southern past and then refashioning it to conform to his aesthetic needs, is also evident in several other paintings with rural sub-

123. *Study for Rural Subject,* ca. 1939. Pen and ink with pencil on paper, 12 × 9 in.

124. *Farm Couple at Work,* ca. 1940. Oil on wood, 34¾ x 31½ in.

125. *Chain Gang*, ca. 1939. Oil on wood, 45¾ x 38½ in.

126. *Folk Family*, ca. 1939–40. Oil on wood, 50⅜ x 35⅝ in.

127. Pablo Picasso, *Portrait of Dora Maar*, 1937. Oil on canvas, 36½ x 25½ in.

128. *Detail of Standing Figure* (Dogon People, Mali, West Africa)

jects. In *Folk Family*, Johnson underscores the cyclical patterns in African-American traditions by using contrasting colors and a preponderance of abstracting formal devices (fig. 126). Everything that Johnson presents in *Folk Family*—the farm, tools, family, mule, even the land itself—conforms to a striped pattern or a bandlike shape.

Several factors help explain Johnson's almost manic use of stripes and bands of color during this period. One source of inspiration for this new emphasis on the decorative may have been the paintings of Picasso, especially those executed between 1937 and 1942, when he was preoccupied with a highly decorative, pattern-oriented art (fig. 127).

But Johnson's friendship in the early 1940s with the artist, connoisseur, and theorist John D. Graham may have been the major factor in his use of stripes. Graham's Primitive Arts Gallery (which opened in New York's Greenwich Village in 1940), as well as his modern art primer, *System and Dialectics of Art* (1937), would have been familiar to Johnson as visual and literary sources for his new work.[18]

Graham's book, which included a section on the pervasive formal elements of African and African-American art, inadvertently addressed Johnson's use of stripes. In Graham's typically declamatory—yet engaging and inimitable—way, he begins the section in question by drawing a parallel between "Negro spirituals" and the "horizontal stripes in a painting": two examples of what he describes as the "creative articulation of rhetoric." Later, Graham concludes a six-point list of the African artist's "method of aesthetic argumentation" with the following: "drama of *stripes*: insistency, eternity through endlessness, origins of waves, threatening growth, inevitability, tenderness of caress, formality of poise."[19]

The important insights of Graham's poetic musings and theories on "Negro Art," based on his own highly imaginative "system and dialectics," had significant implications for works such as Johnson's *Folk Family*. Graham's philosophical grasp of the hypnotic, eternal, and dynamic qualities of stripes in African art is echoed in the way Johnson uses stripes. The confluence of stripes in *Folk Family*—from the tiniest ones on the horizon to the biggest stripes of the roadways, hills, and vales—operates in a rhythmic and interpolated fashion that recalls Graham's black-music metaphor.

Graham's phrase, "formality of poise," though meant to characterize the geometric elegance and severity of African art, describes the figures in Johnson's paintings (fig. 128). In another rural subject, *Early Morning Work*, the large hands, spindly limbs, and stoic, oblong heads of Johnson's three black farmers echo similar anatomical treatments and perceived moods in wooden figurines within the Dogon, Bamana, and other western Sudanic sculptural traditions (fig. 129).

A visual component that plays a symbolic role in *Early Morning Work* and in other paintings with rural themes is the mule (figs. 130, 131). Harnessed to plows or wagons, mules become emblems of the agricultural life. The mule in *Sowing*, though based on an earlier, more naturalistic study, assumes the abstracted and distorted forms of its keepers

129. *Early Morning Work*, ca. 1940. Oil on burlap, 38½ x 45⅝ in.

130. *Going to Market*, ca. 1940. Oil on wood, 33⅛ x 37⅞ in.

131. *Sowing*, ca. 1940. Oil on burlap, 38½ x 48¾ in.

and the surrounding environment (see fig. 123). And just as the large hands and feet of Johnson's black farmers in *Sowing* suggest a life of hard work, so are the mules' knobby knees, broad hooves, and blinders emblems of a harsh existence entirely consumed with bearing burdens and pulling weights. That all the cultivators in *Sowing*—man, woman, and mule—perform their duties under a waxing, crescent moon insinuates the almost instinctual, ritualistic aspect of their endeavor. With an obvious appreciation for the mule's essential role in a pre-tractor, agrarian culture, Johnson's mule imagery assumes a centrality in these paintings.

Johnson's interest in black folk culture was the subject of his January 1941 fellowship application to the Julius Rosenwald Fund. Although he had already completed a number of paintings that were derived from an imaginary, re-created South, in his application he asked for support to actually travel south so that he could "paint Negro people in their *natural* environment" [emphasis added]. By "natural environment," what Johnson and most African-Americans meant was the South. Further on in his application, he explained:

On returning to the U.S.A. from 13 years successfull [sic] *spent in Europe and Africa, I came back with the burning desire to commence where I left off. . . . This development shall continue for the rest of my life, and* [it] *is the painting of my people. My travels taught me that to create an artist must live and paint in his own environment. The completion of such a project cannot be stated in time. The freedom from economic cares for a time would be a great aid in the development of my art.*[20]

Although Johnson's application was not funded, it nevertheless forced him to articulate, for himself and others, what he had been doing in his art for the last year and a half. From the lofty perspectives of Lenox Avenue uptown and West 15th Street downtown, Johnson *was* painting his people, literally piecing together, as in quilting, the "natural," or rather, the southern, folkloric aspects of Afro-America.

As alluded to above, his friendship with Graham was but one of many relationships that Johnson had with artists in New York in the early 1940s. Since the New York art community in those days was much smaller and, perhaps, less competitive, relative newcomers such as Johnson could easily meet fellow painters in the surrounding neighborhoods, "talk shop" with them in their studios, and freely mingle with the art crowd at openings, in galleries, and over coffee in cafés and bars.

William and Holcha's studio/apartment in New York's Chelsea section was practically in Greenwich Village, whose tiny family restaurants, antiquarian bookstores, curio shops, and other cultural establishments were a constant attraction. Although Johnson's initial WPA/FAP assignment placed him among Harlem's artists, he and Holcha felt most comfortable *downtown*, in "the Village," among a middle-aged, artistic, and mostly foreign-born crowd.

Their inner circle of friends were a motley crew of painters, sculptors, collectors, and other "culture brokers," who accepted William and Holcha's racially mixed marriage and shared the couple's international perspective on life and art. Among the members of this inner circle were: Onya La Tour, collector and gallery director; Selma Burke, sculptor and one of the few black American women active in the downtown art scene in that period; David Burliuk, Russian-born constructivist-turned-expressionist painter; Sidney Janis, well-known collector—and later, dealer—in folk, modern, and contemporary art; Ivan Goll, the German Expressionist poet and playwright; John Graham, the painter and all-around aesthete, and many others. From small, Danish-style dinners hosted at their apartment, to lively lunchtime gatherings at the ever-popular Jumble Shop on West 8th Street, William and Holcha Johnson figured prominently in the social lives of one segment of the Village's odd cast of characters. [21]

132. At Johnson's solo exhibition at the Alma Reed Galleries, New York City, May 1941. Joseph Hawthorne (second from left); William H. Johnson (third from left); Holcha Krake (second from right)

Many of these same people attended Johnson's first major solo exhibition in New York in May 1941 (fig. 132). Held at the Alma Reed Galleries on 57th Street, this exhibition was the first public display of many of these African-American, folk-inspired paintings. It was also Johnson's first solo exhibition to be covered by the two major art journals, *Art Digest* and *Art News*, as well as *all* of the big daily newspapers in New York City.

Along with *Nude, Street Life—Harlem, Cafe, Early Morning Work, Chain Gang* and others, Johnson showed the painting that best summarizes all his sentiments concerning the folk and African-American rural life—*Going to Church* (fig. 133). *Going to Church* presents a fairly straightforward scenario: four country people going to church in an ox-drawn wagon. But beyond this narrative is a self-conscious, two-dimensional concept at work, underscored by horizontal and vertical bands of color and an overall exploration of color contrasts and juxtapositions.

Also present in *Going to Church* is an almost mesmeric scheme of visual parallels and imagedoubling—two crosses on the green-and-brown-striped plateau, two fir trees on a canary yellow area of land, two pairs of people riding in the wagon, two visible wagon wheels, and two blue buildings at opposite ends of the composition. Aside from the obvious, rhythmic effects, the double imagery implies a built-in dialectic of opposing and complementary elements in this depiction of "the Negro's natural environment." These visual dualities and pairings of opposites (e.g., male/female, child/adult, sacred building/secular building, animal power/mechanical power) all contribute to an environment of

balance and counterbalance. With all of its dialectical questions and posed alternatives, Johnson's painting provides a complete, self-contained universe in a highly ordered, spiritually enveloped setting.

As with Johnson's other works inspired by folk themes, his use of bandlike forms and contrasting colored stripes in *Going to Church* evokes the two-dimensional design systems of African-influenced textile artists. The principle of a "deliberate clashing of 'high-affect' colors" via an improvisational assembly of striplike design units—evident in everything from West African examples of woven, multi-striped cloth to African-American examples of pieced, freehand quilt work—was a natural choice for Johnson in his attempt to compose "Negro" paintings (fig. 134).[22] The *Herald Tribune*'s art critic, Carlyle Burrows, though mistakenly attributing Johnson's stripes and "strong patterns" to "French Modernism," nevertheless sensed that these paintings contained "some of the Negro's sense of the *primitive* and the lyrical" [emphasis added].[23]

Howard Devree, writing for the *New York Times*, was perhaps more in tune, sensing the combined ingredients of "the formal influence of African art with a . . . Scandinavian color sense. . . . In a somewhat brash modern idiom," Devree continued, "[Johnson] nevertheless expresses himself with queer rhythmic force."[24]

Johnson's exhibition at the Alma Reed Galleries—a rare instance of a black American artist being given a solo exhibition—was perhaps one of the shows that fueled a trend toward "all-Negro" art exhibitions in the New York art world, circa 1941. Months after Johnson's show, two other much-talked-about exhibitions featuring the works of black artists were presented in New York: in October, the "Contemporary Negro Art"

134. Daisy Wiley (Lithia Springs, Georgia), *Quilt*, ca. 1970. Cotton, wool, 74½ x 83 in.

133. *Going to Church*, ca. 1940–41. Oil on burlap, 38⅛ x 44½ in.

135. *Ten Miles to J Camp*, ca. 1942. Gouache, pen and ink with pencil on paper, 13½ x 17¾ in.

exhibition (organized by the interior design firm, Mc-Millen, Inc.) and in December, "American Negro Art: 19th and 20th Centuries" (organized by The Downtown Gallery). Of the two exhibitions, "American Negro Art" seemed to be the most celebrated, because of its historical/stylistic breadth (artists from Henry Ossawa Tanner to Horace Pippin were included) and because it showcased Jacob Lawrence's recently completed Migration series.

Johnson, who had paintings in both exhibitions, hoped to build on these shows with another solo venture. Suddenly, however, everyone's plans and hopes changed in the face of a shattering world event: the Japanese sneak attack on Pearl Harbor, on 7 December 1941. For Johnson, this act of military aggression was only the latest in a series of incidents that would forever alter his professional and personal spheres.

136. Soldiers at attention before moving out the bivouac, Fort Huachuca, Arizona, ca. 1942

The first incident that signaled a change for the worse in William and Holcha's world was the death of their brother-in-law, Christoph Voll, on 16 June 1939, after he had been repeatedly harassed and interrogated by local Nazi officials in Karlsruhe, Germany. Holcha's sister Erna had to quickly make funeral arrangements, close up their house in Karlsruhe, and travel (with their young daughter Karen) through Nazi Germany to the family homestead in Odense, Denmark.

The second event that alerted the couple to hard times ahead was Denmark's occupation by German troops, which began on 9 April 1940. Because of Denmark's proximity to Germany, as well as its complete lack of military readiness, the takeover was accomplished by the Germans in just two hours and lasted for five years. Like the rest of the Danish population, Holcha's mother, her two sisters, a brother, and their families coped with the occupation to the best of their abilities, though the rationing of goods, cut-backs in public services, and the threatening presence of the German troops created widespread hardship.

As Americans prepared to go to war in December 1941, Johnson began to investigate the ways in which he could participate in the struggle against fascism. He had first become aware of Adolf Hitler during his brief stay in Hamburg and years later in Norway had heard about the atrocities the Nazis and their allies were perpetrating against Jews, artists, people on the political left, and others. Although men up to his age (forty), and some even older, were enlisting in the armed services, Johnson could not bring himself to leave Holcha or interrupt an American career that was finally beginning to receive some long-overdue critical attention. And now, with family members whose lives had been profoundly altered by the Nazi presence in Europe, and fellow Americans planning scrap-

137. *Lessons in a Soldier's Life,* ca. 1942. Tempera, pen and ink with pencil on paper, 15 x 18⅛ in.

metal drives, mock air-raids, food rationing programs, and other forms of support, Johnson looked for a way he could take part in the war effort.

That opportunity came in the week that followed Pearl Harbor, with the announcement of a national open art competition for the purpose of mounting a traveling exhibition to "inform the public about war and defense activities." Organized by the Office of Emergency Management (OEM), in collaboration with the Section of Fine Arts of the Public Buildings Administration, this national art competition drew over 2,500 art entries from 1,189 artists nationwide in just one month alone.

The resulting exhibition, "American Artists' Record of War and Defense," opened on 7 February 1942 at the National Gallery of Art in Washington, D.C., and from there traveled for the remainder of the year to museums in New York, Chicago, and Milwaukee. The exhibition itself—narrowed down to 125 works by 74 artists—was neither artistically innovative nor particularly beautiful. It served a good purpose, however, in that it gave American artists and the art-viewing public some sense of how art could be an effective tool in the mobilization of the country in time of war.

Johnson's watercolor entry for the exhibition, *Training Camp,* has long since disappeared, but numerous other works inspired by the war effort have survived, revealing much about Johnson's perspectives on World War II and related activities on the home front. Typical works in this vein, such as *10 Miles to J Camp,* differ very little from Johnson's colorful, quiltlike paintings of the rural South (fig. 135). In these military-inspired works, Johnson's conscious depictions of the soldiers, commanding officers, and other military personnel as African-Americans transform these paintings into social statements, given the real-life controversies and debates that surrounded the issue of black participation in World War II.[25]

Dorie Miller—a black navy messman who, without any training, manned a machine gun and shot down four Japanese planes at Pearl Harbor—was often cited as an example of African-American heroism by black leaders questioning the racist policies of the U.S. military: the segregation of enlisted men and discrimination in the training and promotion of soldiers (fig. 136). Although Johnson did not create blatant, propagandistic pictures with overt racial connotations to protest the U.S. Government's double standard, his World War II paintings, taken as a whole, are compelling visual arguments against racism in the armed services. Apart from his painting, *K.P.* (or *Kitchen Patrol*), which makes a subtle social comment on the demeaning chores that were often assigned to black en-

138. *K.P.*, ca. 1942. Tempera, pen and ink with pencil on paper, 17 x 21 in.

139. *Killed in Action*, ca. 1942. Tempera, pen and ink on paper, 15 x 20½ in.

listed men, the majority of his war paintings feature black soldiers in such standard military activities as infantry training, ammunition drilling, and actual battle (figs. 137, 138).

The violent and deadly side of war also appears in this body of work, as seen in *Killed in Action* (fig. 139). In this painting of six dead Japanese soldiers, piled one on top of the other and alongside an American-made machine gun, the dual message—war's ultimate human toll along with its relationship to marketing and business—again shows an ironic aspect to Johnson's visual commentaries on World War II.

Johnson's painting of eight underwear-clad soldiers walking single file into a makeshift bathing facility shows that he was also capable of capturing the more humorous aspects of war (fig. 141). In the hands of another artist, this scene might have been broad caricature, the humor of racial slurs and scatological references. But Johnson opts instead to make honest fun out of the army's compulsion for regimentation. Robert Beverly Hale, a curator at the Metropolitan Museum of Art and a critic for *Art News* magazine, was perhaps thinking of *Soldiers' Morning Bath* when he made the following statement about Johnson's war paintings: "[Johnson] is the only artist we have so far encountered who has been able to cope with the war. His secret: understatement, humor, and a deep human understanding."[26]

Another OEM-sponsored art competition that year—focusing on the activities of the American Red Cross—was the impetus for yet another series of gouache paintings by Johnson on the combined subjects of World War II, public service, and African-American participation in the war effort. Unlike the paintings that specifically deal with soldiers and battle, Johnson's Red Cross works neither celebrate militarism nor endorse America's bid for victory but, rather, concentrate on black volunteerism and cooperative labor for the common good (fig. 140).

From paintings of wounded soldiers and military nurses to pictures of hospital interiors and health-care workers, Johnson created provocative images of a committed black presence in the Red Cross (figs. 142, 143). Yet even with these images, the real-life subtext—an organizational policy that segregated black health professionals from their white counterparts and "Negro" blood from "white" blood—transforms Johnson's pictures into subtle, though pointed, commentaries on racism in the public-health sector.

In *Red Cross Nurses Handing Out Wool for Knitting*, which shows one of the Red

140. Red Cross volunteer serving an enlisted man, ca. 1945

141. *Soldiers' Morning Bath*, ca. 1942. Tempera, pen and ink with pencil on paper, 16 x 20⅜ in.

142. *Station Stop, Red Cross Ambulance*, ca. 1942. Tempera, pen and ink on paper, 18¾ x 22⅜ in.

143. *Operating Room*, ca. 1942. Tempera, pen and ink on paper, 16¾ x 11½ in.

144. *Red Cross Nurses Handing Out Wool for Knitting,* ca. 1942. Tempera, pen and ink on paper, 17⁷⁄₁₆ x 21⁷⁄₈ in.

145. *Convalescents from Somewhere,* ca. 1942. Tempera, pen and ink on paper, 14⅛ x 18⁵⁄₁₆ in.

Cross's basic public services, Johnson places the Red Cross "Gray Ladies" and their patrons in one of his typical rural-folk settings (fig. 144). *Red Cross Nurses Handing Out Wool for Knitting*—with its stark landscape and sculptural, transfixed women and children—could easily be interpreted as depicting some time-honored African ritual, involving an "offering" by three cross-wearing priestesses.

In another Red Cross painting, *Convalescents from Somewhere*, Johnson's uncanny composition and abstract treatment of the figures again contribute to a mood of otherworldliness and spirituality (fig. 145). Johnson's evocative image of a woman in white, flanked on both sides by altarlike, wooden ceiling supports, takes the painting's hospice narrative to another, more symbolic level, one that suggests spiritual as much as physical healing.

Johnson's paintings of black soldiers, Red Cross volunteers, and other war-related subjects were appreciated by people not only for their documentary aspects, but for their ethical/religious dimension as well. On "National Negro Achievement Day," 27 June 1942, for example, Johnson was awarded a certificate of honor by a Harlem-based committee for his "distinguished service to America in Art."

In addition to Johnson's images of the war, the committee may have also been responding to his concurrent paintings of black families and couples. In the dozen or so paintings identified as the Breakdown and the Honeymooner series, the primary motif is a malfunctioning automobile or mobile home, surrounded by a black family (figs. 146–148). In the paintings collectively called *Jitterbugs*, the basic image is a black couple dancing, sometimes surrounded by musical instruments (figs. 149–154).

The Breakdown series is comprised of brilliantly composed pictures showing roadside car repairs and families camping out. The "breakdown" in these works not only refers to what has happened to the old cars, but to how *people*—from nuclear families to newlyweds—cope with life's hardships. In black English, the term "to break down" means to suffer utter despair and discontinuity, as in the following stanza from a blues composition:

I have rambled and I have rambled
Until I have broke my poor self down,
I believe to my soul
That the little girl is out of town.[27]

Johnson's Breakdown and Honeymooner series—colorful, simple, and straightforward—tell the stories of black families who are "broke down," stranded, but coping in the world. If mechanical malfunction is emblematic of the soul's dysfunction, then repair suggests spiritual healing. Subliminal elements, such as crosses (in the form of automobile hood

146. *The Breakdown*, ca. 1940–41. Oil on wood, 33⅞ x 37 in.

147. *Breakdown with Flat Tire*, ca. 1940–41. Oil on wood, 34⅛ x 37½ in.

148. *Honeymooners (I)*, ca. 1940–41. Gouache, pen and ink with pencil on paper, 14 x 18 in.

149. *Jitterbugs (I)*, ca. 1940–41. Oil on wood, 39¾ x 31 in.

ornaments and outdoor fencing) and genuflection (the kneeling and reclining figures), further develop this overall theme of faith and spiritual repair.

On a more literal level, Johnson's Jitterbugs series scrutinizes the fads of young, black New Yorkers, as epitomized by the 1940s dance craze. In the earliest of the Jitterbugs paintings, Johnson makes no attempt at all to capture the frenetic, acrobatic pace of the dancers (see fig. 149). Instead, he stops the action, which allows his viewers to conceptualize the dance, dissect the subtle gestures, and note the latest fashions.

In four subsequent *Jitterbugs*, however, Johnson's approach progressively gives way to more abstracted, reconstructive analyses. One painting records a broad, choreographed dip by a female Jitterbug while her male partner dramatically supports her (see fig. 150). Their anatomies, made up of jigsawlike torsos, arms, and legs, rhythmically interlock with a perspectiveless floor, background, and fractured musical instruments. Even more geometric and angular is a second *Jitterbugs*, where the dancing couple, musical instruments, and implied "floor" and "background" literally collapse (see fig. 151). The third painting presents the Jitterbugs as shattered, cubistic figures with hardly any naturalistic elements left at all (see fig. 153). In a kind of painted (and choreographed) finale, a circa 1942 *Jitterbugs* (see fig. 154) completes the dance cycle with the characteristic "throwing" of the female partner through the air (fig. 152). But in contrast to the first *Jitterbugs* and the other three in gouache, the heads, bodies, and appendages on this latest set of dancers—along with a double-belled trumpet, snare drum, and cymbals—evoke movement, creating an almost whirling, gestural pattern against the solid background. As overtures to a palpable, *living* Cubism, the three *Jitterbugs* on paper and two in oil on plywood indicate that Johnson fully understood that the hyperkinetic dances and fashion extremes of contemporary black culture were appropriate inspirations for a modern African-American art.

Toward the end of 1942, Johnson's life suddenly shifted into high gear. In November, he left the New York City Art Project and took another WPA assignment as a lab assistant. No longer earning his WPA salary by making art, he now had to find additional time in his day for painting. An upcoming solo exhibition (in the spring of 1943) created even greater pressure on him to find not only additional time for painting, but studio space as well. By early December, William and Holcha had finally moved to Greenwich Village proper, into a more spacious, studio loft. Within one week of their move, however, their new building caught fire, forcing William, Holcha, and the other residents into the streets. After the fire was extinguished and it was safe for the residents to return, the couple discovered that many of their belongings—paintings, drawings, weavings, valuable papers, and clothing—had been burned beyond recognition, and the remaining things that had not burned were either water-damaged, trampled, or broken. William and Holcha spent the better part of the Christmas and New Year holidays securing what little was salvageable from the fire and finding another place to live. In order to help the already

150. *Jitterbugs (II)*, ca. 1941. Tempera, pen and ink with pencil on paper, 17¹⁵⁄₁₆ x 12³⁄₁₆ in.

151. *Jitterbugs (III)*, ca. 1941. Tempera, pen and ink on paper, 14 x 9 in.

overstressed Holcha with the ordeal of repacking their belongings and searching for another loft, Johnson resigned from the WPA on 13 January 1943, a move that anticipated the eventual disbanding of the entire WPA program in the following weeks. Finally, toward the end of February, they moved into a loft "without conveniences," at 79 East 10th Street, not far from their close friend, sculptor Selma Burke.

Nineteen forty-three already had an ominous air about it for the Johnsons, evident in the foreboding, disquieting quality that seemed to inhabit many of his works. *Burned Out*, a circa 1943 painting, comes directly out of William and Holcha's own ordeal by fire (fig. 155). Painted in the high-key colored, flat, and unmodulated technique of Johnson's recent work, *Burned Out* nonetheless captures pathos and hopelessness, via a carefully laid-out composition depicting the contorted faces and gestures of the unfortunate folk couple.

152. Anonymous, *Jitterbugging at the Savoy,* ca. 1939

In *The Home Front* and *Fright*, two circa 1942 works, Johnson had already explored these oppressive, darker sides of African-American reality (figs. 156, 157). In both works, the uncompromising frontality, rough, textured surfaces, and big, questioning eyes and groping hands of the figures work in concert to fuel a vague, but persistent, thematic sense of anxiety. Johnson's spring 1943 show, where many of these recent tempera and gouache paintings were first exhibited, was held at the Wakefield Gallery and Bookshop on East 55th Street. The person at Wakefield responsible for Johnson's exhibition was Betty Parsons (1900–1982), soon to become known as a dealer and collector of Abstract Expressionist art. Like Johnson, Parsons had studied art in Paris in the 1920s. After returning to the United States, she continued her art studies on the West Coast. By the late 1930s, however, she had moved back to her native New York City, where she eventually became a gallery assistant at Wakefield.

Johnson's exhibition of about thirty works was widely and favorably reviewed. Almost all of the reviewers agreed with *New York Times* art critic Howard Devree, who felt that these outwardly "primitive" paintings revealed "a lot of keen observation and setting forth of ideas in what [seems to be] an authentic Negro idiom."[28]

The *New York World-Telegram*'s Emily Genauer gave this latest work by Johnson the most in-depth critique of all of the reviewers. Genauer, who was probably the most acerbic and unsympathetic of the New York art critics toward various "schools" of modernism, devoted several paragraphs to Johnson's exhibition, describing his work as "unpretentious, casual, but extremely imaginative." She continued her observations:

153. *Jitterbugs (IV)*, ca. 1941. Tempera, pen and ink with pencil on paper, 12⅞ x 10¾ in.

154. *Jitterbugs (V)*, ca. 1941–42. Oil on wood, 36½ x 28¾ in.

155. (above left). *Burned Out*, ca. 1943. Tempera, pen and ink with pencil on paper, 16¹¹⁄₁₆ x 12⅝ in.
156. (above right). *Fright*, ca. 1942–43. Tempera, pen and ink on paper, 17 x 12½ in

[Johnson] is a Negro, and his subjects are always Negroes. And yet, as depicted by him, they're devoid of any consciousness of race. They're not particularly emphasized as people . . . but rather as elements in his design. He distorts and stylizes them and then organizes them into flat, shadowless compositions built on a linear pattern. They're almost like cartoons, . . . but they're put together with an extremely original flair for design, with a pervading sense of movement and rhythm.[29]

Among the many sales that came from this exhibition, two were of special note, though for different reasons. One of the gouache paintings, *Children at the Ice Cream Stand* (also known as *Candy Man*) was sold before the exhibition opened to Ralph D. Paine, Jr., the managing editor of *Fortune* magazine and an avid art collector. In November 1941, *For-*

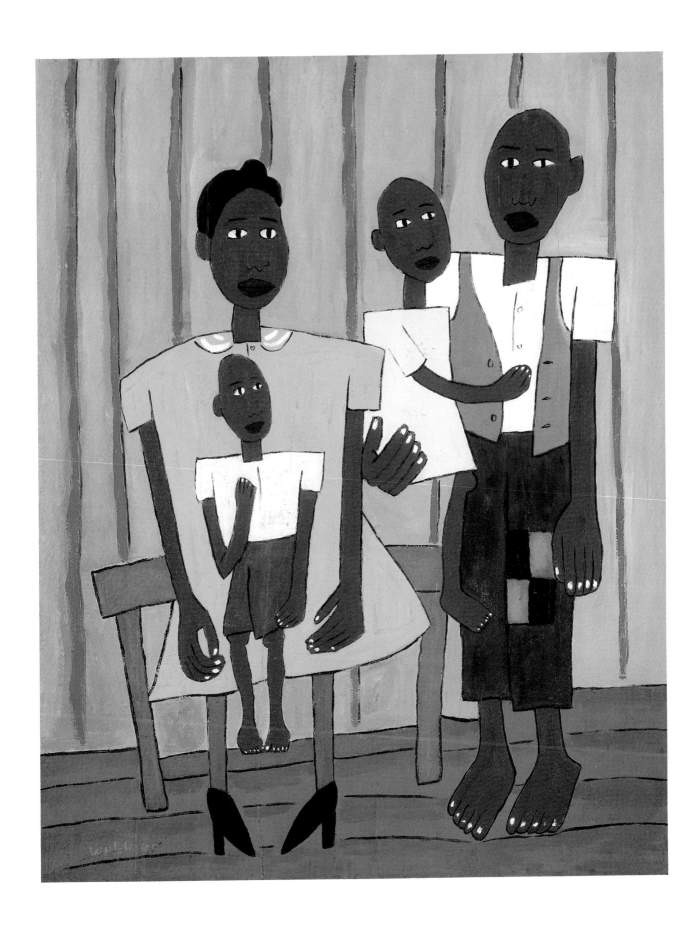

157. *The Home Front,* ca. 1942. Oil on wood, 39½ x 31¼ in.

tune had helped launch Jacob Lawrence's career by reproducing several paintings from his Migration series.

The other sale—to a Mrs. Hugh Knowlton of Syosset, Long Island—was more noteworthy for what Johnson had painted.[30] The circa 1942–43 gouache, *Lift Up Thy Voice and Sing* is a strange mixture of African-American folklore and political commentary (fig. 158). The scene, showing eight black children singing under the direction of a chorale leader, with all of them standing in front of an inverted American flag, posed innumerable questions. Why was this particular image given the same title as black composer James Weldon Johnson's famous "Negro National Anthem"? If this gathering is being held under a call of distress (as the flag's position indicates), then why are the children singing? Considering both the world situation and the plight of black Americans in the early 1940s, what exactly was Johnson's message?

The answers to these questions can be found in Johnson's evolving attitudes toward the contrasts between the conditions of African-American life and those of the rest of society. *Lift Up Thy Voice and Sing*, perhaps more than any other work by Johnson, challenged the sentimentalists and the cynics alike to examine America's democratic values and to reflect seriously on how the American system worked, and for whom. Johnson's use of the navy's distress sign was double-edged: it is a comment both on

158. *Lift Up Thy Voice and Sing*, ca. 1942–43. Gouache, pen and ink on paper, 15 x 12 in.

the desperate battlefront situation and on the signs of distress and dissatisfaction among blacks on the domestic front. That Johnson's black youth in this painting raise their voices and sing in the face of a crisis is, however, not so much absurd or satirical as a sign of hope, an affirmation of the human spirit. Although its potent message was missed by reviewers in 1943, *Lift Up Thy Voice and Sing* presaged a more philosophical and political William H. Johnson.[31]

This new philosophical and political sensibility of Johnson's emerged again after the summer of 1943, following one of New York's worst race riots. On the evening of 1 August, a heated exchange in a Harlem hotel between a white policeman and a black woman quickly escalated into a fistfight between the policeman and a black soldier, who had been standing nearby. During the scuffle, the soldier hit the policeman with his own nightstick and then, according to witnesses, ran. The policeman pulled out his revolver and shot the soldier, wounding him in the arm. As the policeman arrested the soldier and

159. *Moon Over Harlem,* ca. 1943–44. Oil on wood, 28½ x 35¾ in.

160. *New York Skyline at Night*, ca. 1943. Tempera, pen and ink on paper, 15⅞ x 18¾ in.

took him to a nearby hospital, a crowd gathered and followed them. While the soldier was being operated on, the crowd outside the hospital grew in numbers and emotional frenzy. After someone shouted "A white cop shot and killed a black soldier," angry people began streaming onto the adjoining avenues, demanding that justice be done, gathering momentum and soon, in their outrage, breaking windows, looting stores, turning over cars, setting fires, and turning Harlem into a chaotic hotbed of destruction. On Monday, after the city's police had restored some semblance of normalcy, the reports showed that six people had been killed, over one hundred people had been injured, several hundred had been arrested, with loss of property estimated in the millions of dollars.[32]

In *Moon Over Harlem*, his version of the 1943 Harlem riot, Johnson abandons the compositional structure based on bands of interlocking, high-keyed colors (fig. 159). Instead, he takes a flatter and more organic approach, with the figures, city pavement, urban skyline, and horizon all resembling the off-kilter pictures of an amateur artist's hand-painted shop sign. Johnson's ghostly silhouette of New York, recalling another work from around the same time, evokes an alien and remote image of the city that echoes the mood of estrangement and anger in Harlem that night (fig. 160).

Several of Johnson's figures in *Moon Over Harlem* were adapted from newspaper photographs of the rioters, showing beaten and bloodied suspects and underage offenders wearing stolen top hats and tuxedos (figs. 161, 162). These photojournalistic documents are stripped by Johnson of their melodramatic quality, as he creates in their place a kind of expressive distortion and calculated rawness. The central figure in *Moon Over Harlem*—a black female rioter, bloodied, with one breast exposed, and turned upside down by three uniformed men—is the very embodiment of the riot's victims: an oppressed and debased community, whose frustration and self-destruction prompted an authoritative abuse of power. Although many felt that the riot was a spontaneous, violent reaction to a perceived incident of police brutality, others saw it as a symptom of Harlem's deeper, festering problems: urban poverty, racial oppression, and economic exploitation. In *Moon Over Harlem*, Johnson uses a new visual language, joining those who felt indignation over the second-class status of Harlemites and all black Americans.

Not everyone appreciated this move by Johnson into the truly primal territories of art. James A. Porter, the renowned Howard University art historian and author of *Modern Negro Art*—one of the first books to seriously examine the art of Afro-America—commented that Johnson's "new style" suffered from a fascination with "pre-historic and primitive art." Continuing his assessment of Johnson's latest work, Porter wrote that

the slat-like, angular grotesques that he invents are hardly more than flat symbols for the human figure. . . . Even though we welcome the gain in bright, charming color to which this change of style opens the way, it is difficult to understand why any American artist in this day of confusion should elect to be unintelligible. The singular and cryptic nature of Johnson's work sets it apart from anything else in the studios of the Negro artists.[33]

In truth, Porter was equally intolerant of other black artists, like Aaron Douglas, Archibald J. Motley, Jr., and Palmer C. Hayden, who also avoided the easy route of merely painting black subject matter within the traditions of Western Europe. Yet Porter accurately assessed that what these artists were engaged in was a redefinition of art—one that, in the words of Aaron Douglas, would "drag forth material rough, crude, neglected" or, as Motley put it, would conjure up "the jazz aspects of the Negro" or, in Johnson's words, would "express . . . both rhythmically and spiritually . . . my family of primitiveness and tradition." Ralph Ellison, in a November 1943 review of Porter's *Modern Negro Art*, also sensed that it was precisely this interest in folk expression, grass-roots culture, popular music, and, in general, current African-American visual styles that made a work, in spite of Porter's disdain, a true manifestation of "modern Negro art."[34]

This latest transformation by Johnson—from "primitive" sophisticate to unbridled expressionist—might have also been brought on by emotional disruptions in his personal life. Less than a year after the devastating fire, Johnson had to face the revelation in September that Holcha was suffering from breast cancer. In the wobbly, barely readable handwriting of someone obviously distraught, Johnson wrote a postcard to Holcha's mother and sister in Denmark, telling them that Holcha had first noticed symptoms while still in Europe, though she did not give them much thought back then.[35] But as time passed, with the pressures of trying to make a comfortable life out of very little taking their toll on her, the disease worsened and soon Holcha was bedridden. The Johnsons' friends, the Harritons, first became aware of the problem in November, after sending an invitation to William and Holcha to join them for their annual Thanksgiving dinner. "I did not receive an answer till after Thanksgiving," Helen recalled, "then a note came saying she was sick, and the handwriting was so strained that I knew she must be very sick." Helen, continuing her recollection, said,

161 and **162.** Police arresting rioters during the 1943 Harlem riot

Dave and I went at once . . . to the loft, which we had not before visited, and found her bundled up on a cot, with him taking care of her, and she was very sick indeed. We had never seen cancer and didn't know what we were seeing, but we insisted that he must

*get her to a hospital, which he didn't want to do for he feared they would take her away
from him.*

By 12 December, William had checked Holcha into "a very poor city hospital," where she
was immediately placed in the cancer ward. "It was a tragic place," remembered Helen,
"and we hated to see her there as much as she hated to be there. At that time, her mind
was still clear . . . and she tried to arrange her affairs, realizing that she was dying. She was
not afraid to die, not even very unwilling."

With the Harritons' assistance, William moved Holcha shortly after the first of the year
to the House of Calvary, a less crowded, quieter hospital in the Bronx, operated by Roman
Catholic nuns. Helen, who was with Holcha one evening after she had been at the House
of Calvary for about a week, noticed that after receiving her regular injection of painkill-
ing drugs, Holcha started behaving a bit more agitated than usual:

*She was in an exalted, ecstatic state of mind. . . . She kept recalling all of the happiest
times of her life. . . . [She] told me about the wonderful days in Norway that she and
Billy had spent and of their friends there. She spoke of . . . her love for . . . [her family],
and her wish that she could have been with [them] once more. However, her speech was
disconnected. She was like a person who had just taken ether, and [was] about to float
away into unconsciousness . . . with sensitive, loosened speech.*

*When I left her, the nurse told me that she was near death. I phoned Billy immedi-
ately, but she was gone when he reached her.*

William, arriving at the hospital that cold January morning only to discover that Holcha
was dead, was at first absolutely inconsolable. But within a few hours he took hold of the
situation and proceeded to make all of the necessary arrangements. The next day, Holcha's remains were cremated and Johnson, clutching the funerary urn as if it were the
most precious object ever created, brought it back to the loft on East 10th Street. It was
after Holcha's death, Helen later remembered, that Johnson began to paint religious
themes.[36]

Johnson had already explored some religious ideas in his work, as seen in earlier subjects such as Harlem storefront churches, and rural, outdoor services in the deep South
(figs. 163, 164). Also by 1944, Johnson had painted *Jesus and the Three Marys*, a brilliant,
Afrocentric folk version of the Crucifixion (fig. 165). Drawing on source materials as far-
ranging as the northern Renaissance Crucifixion paintings of Matthias Grünewald and
the "crucifixions," or lynchings, of black men in the United States, *Jesus and the Three
Marys* demonstrates Johnson's first serious attempt at creating a black analogue for a standard biblical theme (figs. 166, 167).

Though also Afrocentric, the religious paintings mentioned by Helen Harriton evolved from an entirely different set of stylistic and compositional concerns. Unlike its predecessor *Jesus and the Three Marys*, the circa 1944 painting *Mount Calvary*, for example, is thinly painted on a primed sheet of paperboard paneling and comprised of simple compositional devices (fig. 168). What Johnson sacrifices in amounts of paint in *Mount Calvary*, he certainly makes up for in chromatic brilliance, as displayed in the polyphony of colors and patchwork patterns throughout the composition. Not contorted and angular as in *Jesus and the Three Marys*, the figures in *Mount Calvary* recall the rough, untutored, sticklike figures in *Moon Over Harlem*.

Other than unconscious appropriations from African sculpture and/or European modern art, Johnson's inspiration for works such as *Mount Calvary* was the intuitive, fundamentalist spirit of black religiosity. Perhaps even more than the works painted prior to 1943–44, *Mount Calvary* and its progeny seem especially tied to a black folk tradition, in which biblical imagery and an unconscious African mode of cultural articulation reign supreme.

In spite of the marked simplicity and crude treatment of form in this Crucifixion scene, numerous smaller paintings and studies on this theme suggest that seemingly spontaneous compositions like *Mount Calvary* were, in fact, carefully worked out beforehand. *Lamentation*, the painting that sequentially follows *Mount Calvary* in the "Passion cycle," is, for example, actually based on a tiny pen-and-ink drawing that describes in sparse outline the death of Christ and the lamenting of the Three Marys (figs. 169, 170). As in all of Johnson's black interpretations of Christian themes, the raised arms and genuflecting postures of his figures reenact an eloquent, spiritual gesture closely identified with black religious expression (fig. 171).

Johnson's sense that this gesture was emblematic of African-American religion is confirmed time and again in his art. In *Ezekiel Saw the Wheel*, Johnson uses the gesture to communicate both religious supplication and spiritual ecstacy, consciously linking his portrayal of the Old Testament character Ezekiel to the classic Negro spiritual:

'Zekiel saw de wheel, 'Way up in de middle of de air,
'Zekiel saw de wheel, 'Way in de middle of the air.

163. *Storefront Church*, ca. 1940–41. Pen and ink with gouache on paper, 18 x 14 in.

164. *I Baptize Thee*, ca. 1940. Oil on burlap, 38¼ x 44⅛ in.

165. *Jesus and the Three Marys*, ca. 1939–40. Oil on wood, 37¼ x 34¼ in.

166. Matthias Grünewald, *The Crucifixion of Christ*, ca. 1510–15. Varnished tempera on wood, 28¾ x 20¾ in.

167. *Lynch Mob Victim*, ca. 1939. Oil on burlap, dimensions and whereabouts unknown

De big wheel run by faith,
Little wheel run by de grace of God;   *(twice)*
Wheel widin a wheel, 'Way in de middle of de air,
Wheel, oh, wheel, Wheel in de middle of a wheel.[37]

While not a literal illustration of the spiritual's loosely structured narrative, *Ezekiel Saw the Wheel* does transmit the song's repetitive phrasing and mysterious feeling of religious observance (fig. 173).

Ezekiel, his body turned toward the wheel (similar to the figure in *Away in the Valley by Myself*) and posed in the gesture of a typical African-American worshipper, is a surrogate for the viewer in this work (see fig. 110). The wheel, which leaves linear traceries of its ascent, joins the heavens and the strange, anthropomorphic tree on the right in a sort of juggling, animated sense of airborne movement. This rhythmic, manipulative conceptualization in *Ezekiel Saw the Wheel*, like the similar dynamics of Johnson's Jitterbugs series, places it squarely within the traditions of African-American cultural expression and spirit.

Two paintings that continue this exploration of a spiritual space and time in Afro-America are *Swing Low, Sweet Chariot* and *Climbing Jacob's Ladder* (figs. 174, 175). Like *Ezekiel Saw the Wheel*, *Swing Low, Sweet Chariot* was inspired by a Negro spiritual of the same name:

Swing low sweet chariot, comin' for to carry me home,   *(twice)*
I look'd over Jordan an' what did I see,
Comin' for to carry me home,
A band of angels comin' after me,
Comin' for to carry me home.[38]

Floating over the river Jordan in Johnson's version of this spiritual are eleven black angels with magenta-colored wings, wearing an assortment of brightly colored dresses and, for a contemporary accent, anklet socks. As in his other religious paintings from the 1940s, Johnson recast fair-skinned and blue-eyed figures—Jesus, the three Marys, and the angels—into distinct, black American racial types. This racial alchemy was a revolutionary act, perhaps related to the common practice of "familialization," in which biblical figures became characters such as "Sister Mary" and "Brudder Moses." Such cultural transmutation was common in black sermons, gospel music, and in portrayals of black religious expression in the popular culture (e.g., the motion pictures *Green Pastures* and *Cabin in the Sky*).[39] Still, as art historian David C. Driskell has pointed out, at the time when Johnson painted these black versions of standard Christian imagery, they were more likely to be viewed as dispensable to most black congregations, if not totally rejected by them.[40]

168. *Mount Calvary*, ca. 1944. Oil on paperboard, 27¾ x 33⅜ in.

169. *Lamentation (Descent from the Cross)*, ca. 1944. Oil on fiberboard, 29⅛ x 33¼ in.

Given its nudity, a religious painting like *Climbing Jacob's Ladder* probably would have been considered too risqué for most black congregations. The lyrics of the Negro spiritual, however, suggest that Johnson's imagery may have captured the true spirit of the song:

We am clim'in' Jacob's ladder,
We am clim'in' Jacob's ladder,
We am clim'in' Jacob's ladder,
Soldiers of de cross.
Ev'ry roun' goes higher higher,
Ev'ry roun' goes higher higher,
Ev'ry roun' goes higher higher,
Soldiers of de cross.[41]

These lyrics, which conjure a dreamy image of an endless, spiraling ladder to Heaven, demanded a painted version that matched the cryptic language and otherworldly atmosphere of this Old Testament vision. Johnson accurately captures this illusion by superimposing the silhouette figures and other pictorial elements against a contrasting yellow field. The six nude figures—five of whom lunge toward the ladder while the sixth lies twisted and prone alongside a cross—revive a late Gothic sense of heavenly aspiration and sinful decline which, though fantastically conceived here, would have been well understood from a black, Christian, fundamentalist perspective.[42] Although Johnson's particular religious affiliation, if any, is unknown, these paintings and drawings clearly suggest that Johnson had a keen understanding of the black church, as well as a reverence for traditional African-American religious values and expression.

Although Holcha's death left a void in Johnson's life, these new religious paintings seemed to function as spiritual antidotes to his loss. In fact, the spring of 1944 proved to be one of Johnson's busiest seasons, with works in a number of exhibitions, including Atlanta University's Third Annual "Exhibition of Paintings, Sculpture, and Prints by Negro Artists" (March–April); the Newark Museum's "American Negro Art: Contemporary Painting and Sculpture" exhibition (April–May); the G Place Gallery's "New Names in American Art," in Washington, D.C. (May); and the Wakefield Gallery's "Small Oil Paintings" (May), which was a solo exhibition for Johnson. Among the scores of people who saw Johnson's latest work was Paul Robeson, an acquaintance from his time in Europe, who caught a glimpse of Johnson's Wakefield exhibition (and bought two paintings) between his appearances as Othello that season on Broadway. Another visitor to the gallery was Carl Van Vechten—author, literary critic, New York socialite, amateur photographer, and "Negro art" aficionado. On the occasion of Johnson's exhibition, the irrepressible Van

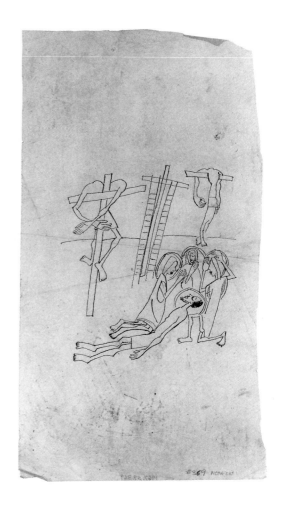

170. *Study for Lamentation (Descent from the Cross),* ca. 1944. Pen and ink on paper, 16½ x 9⅜ in.

171. Russell Lee, *Members of the Pentecostal Church Praising the Lord, Chicago, Illinois*, 1941

172. Carl Van Vechten, *William H. Johnson*, 1944

Vechten invited Johnson back to his mid-town apartment, where he took a series of portrait studies of him (fig. 172).

After a fourteen-year absence, William H. Johnson finally returned to Florence, South Carolina, in June 1944. While he had not visited his family in all those years, he had stayed in touch with them by mail, sending regular updates on his career, snapshots of him and Holcha, art works, elegant linen (handwoven by Holcha), and, occasionally, money. In the intervening years, his family had experienced their own losses (notably, the death of William's father Henry, in 1933). The loss of Holcha (ironically, on his mother's birthday) made Johnson want to see his family again.

James "Boots" Johnson, the eldest son of Lillian, William's youngest sister, recalled that day in June when his Uncle Willie walked up on the porch of their house.[43] James, who had only heard about his uncle in bits and pieces from his mother and grandmother, remembered seeing this medium-built, fair-complexioned, slick-haired man appear at their door with a lot of luggage. Taught never to let strangers into the house, the eight-year-old James asked through the screen door, "Can I help you, sir?" to which William replied, "Boy, I'm your uncle."

After the customary shrieks of surprise, the routine inspections for additional white hairs (and extra pounds), and the ceremonial introductions to previously unknown nephews, nieces, and their various mates, William soon settled into his role as the prodigal son. Although back on familiar turf, Johnson maintained a mysterious, artistic aura, at least in the eyes of his nephew James. "He had a real bad temper," remembered James, "whenever any of us kids got too close to his paints and personal things." Setting up his makeshift studio on the porch, in the back of the house, or wherever he could avoid the family traffic, Johnson continued with his work. Lillian remembered that during his summer there he bought a picture frame at the local Kress Department Store, and put one of his *Lamentation* paintings in it, as a gift for Mom Alice. "And when it rained," James recalled, "Uncle Willie would stop whatever he was doing, go to his room, undress, wrap a towel around himself, and go to a private part of backyard, where he would take outdoor rain baths!"

Aside from wanting to reconnect with his family, Johnson came to Florence hoping to capture forever an *image* of his people: one that would reflect his recent interest in direct, yet spiritual interpretations of African-American life. *Mom Alice*, one of many portraits of his mother, perfectly illustrates the degree to which Johnson totally abandoned the illusionistic, perspectival, and painterly techniques of the European-American art academy for the decorative, two-dimensional, and high-contrast African-American sensibility (fig. 176).

Characteristic of Johnson's art, and apparent in works ranging from his first portraits in France to this painting of his mother, was his ability to capture just enough of a likeness to make recognition of the sitter possible. Again, Johnson's lifelong affinity for caricature played a big part in his approach to subject matter. His selective use of a telling gesture, a marked expression, or a distinguishing facial feature allowed those who knew his mother, for example, to identify her immediately, even within the flat, abstracted context of *Mom Alice* and other portraits. In *Mom and Dad*, Johnson created an interesting double-portrait that for the first time addressed the issue of his questionable lineage (fig. 177). Mom Alice, again shown brown-skinned and seated in a rocking chair, is visually contrasted with her late husband, Henry Johnson, represented as a yellow-skinned man in a picture on the wall behind her. On the painting's periphery are two calico cats: an adult possibly nursing her kitten. The color variance in the complexions of Alice and Henry (inaccurate according to the family members' recollections) perhaps indicates an acknowledgment by Johnson that his ancestry, like that of the calico cats, was a piebald, heterogeneous affair.

In other portraits from his stay in Florence, Johnson painted his nephews and nieces, the older members of his family, and many anonymous black Florentines (figs. 178–181). Underlying these seemingly simple paintings of ordinary black folk are subtle evocations of their covenants with God and their travels along a spiritual path. The figure in *Woman in Calico*, Johnson's portrait of his Aunt Lillian, perfectly epitomizes the concept of complete obeisance to a greater power. The accretion of Christian symbols in this portrait (e.g., the red crosses on the dress and the crossed arms), coupled with the bifurcated background of darkness and light, is certainly a reference to human redemption through the Crucifixion. Like the popular gospel recording of the 1940s, "The Sun Didn't Shine"—which recounts, in an upbeat, a cappella arrangement, how absolute darkness fell over Mount Calvary when "my Lord was Dyin'" on the cross"—this painting's "good news" is that "God's children" are direct beneficiaries of this ultimate sacrifice.[44]

Returning to New York that fall, Johnson made preparations for his first retrospective exhibition, scheduled in December for the Marquié Gallery on 57th Street. He also faced some cold, economic realities (overdue rent on the loft and empty food cabinets among

173. *Ezekiel Saw the Wheel*, ca. 1942–43. Tempera, pen and ink with pencil on paper, 18 x 13½ in.

174. *Swing Low, Sweet Chariot,* ca. 1944. Oil on paperboard, 28⅝ x 26½ in.

175. *Climbing Jacob's Ladder,* ca. 1944. Oil on paperboard, 29 x 24 in.

176. *Mom Alice*, 1944. Oil on paperboard, 31 x 25⅛ in.

177. *Mom and Dad*, 1944. Oil on paperboard, 31 x 25⅜ in.

178. *Li'l Sis*, 1944. Oil on paperboard, 26 x 21¼ in.

them) that forced him to take a position as a laborer at the navy shipyards. Still, his rotating schedule allowed for plenty of time to paint, which he took advantage of whenever the opportunity arose.[45]

While visiting with the Harritons one Sunday morning, for example, Johnson painted their daughter, Carol Cartwright, and Helen's mother, Mrs. Carrie Smith (figs. 182, 183). Though these two portraits, like his Florence portraits, are painted in an unaffected, two-dimensional and, some might say, unflattering manner, both Dave and Helen liked their simple, truthful quality and immediately hung them.

Also during this period, Johnson painted another *Self-Portrait*, but this one showing the artist from three different sides (fig. 184). Reminiscent of the famous triple portrait *Charles I in Three Positions* (ca. 1635, Windsor Castle) by the Baroque painter Anthony Van Dyck, Johnson's *Self-Portrait* presents the figure as if it and a second variant were presenting yet a third variant. The stylized gestures of the two flanking figures, together with a strange quality of dissociation and pathos on all three faces, bear witness to Johnson's intensely interior, psychological self-image at this point in his life.

Just prior to the December retrospective at the Marquié Gallery, Betty Parsons, who had just started a new job at the Mortimer Brandt Gallery, selected one of Johnson's paintings for a big survey exhibition there called "Thirty Pictures, Thirty Artists." Besides Johnson, the other twenty-nine artists whose works were selected—including John Graham, Hedda Sterne, Adolph Gottlieb, Theodoros Stamos, Walter Murch, Richard Pousette-Dart, and others—represented an interesting mix of New York painting talent.

At the Marquié Gallery, however, Johnson was given the entire space, which he took advantage of by exhibiting everything from "explosively expressionist . . . landscapes of Scandinavia" to "flatly executed presentations of his people in the South and in Harlem," to quote Howard Devree of the *New York Times*.[46] Johnson also included numerous ceramics and textiles by Holcha, including her much-praised handwoven copy of the Baldishol Tapestry, a famous thirteenth-century woolen fragment owned by the Oslo Kunstindustrimuseet (fig. 185). Reviewing the exhibition for the *Brooklyn Eagle Sun*, one art critic traced Johnson's career from Europe to America, concluding that

179. *Little Girl in Green,* 1944. Oil on paperboard, 31⅞ x 22⅝ in.

180. *Woman in Calico*, 1944. Oil on paperboard, 26½ x 20½ in.

181. *Woman Ironing*, 1944. Oil on wood, 29 x 24⅜ in.

182. Painting Carol Cartwright, New York City, ca. 1944

now with a palette of no more than four or five colors and using primed cardboard panels, he produces with a naiveté all his own such diverse subjects as "The Nativity," "Li'l Sis" and "Moon Over Harlem." He is definitely an individual American modern.[47]

Else Hvistendahl, writing in January 1945 for the Brooklyn-based Norwegian-language newspaper *Nordisk Tidende*, gave readers an insightful, behind-the-scenes perspective on Johnson's life and art. Beginning her article by quoting her cab driver questioning whether *anybody* could really live in Johnson's soot-covered, ancient building on East 10th Street, Hvistendahl created an entertaining tale about a novice's entry into the sometimes strange world of artists:

In semi-darkness we ascended the rickety old stairs. . . . We wondered where he lived and optimistically shouted "Hello." At the top of the stairs a dark apparition was seen. It was the painter William H. Johnson who had invited us to see his paintings from Norway.

"Look, I have taken out a few flags for you," said the painter, and on the table we noticed the American, Danish, and Norwegian flags. The Danish flag was in honor of Mr. Johnson's Danish-born wife, who died last year.

Around the walls there were pictures with Negro motifs. . . . These are his works of the last few years. One can see the transition in his style—the gloriously rich colors in the Norwegian paintings have been transferred to these simple, primitive pictures.[48]

Not mentioned in *Nordisk Tidende*'s profile on Johnson was his current participation in "The Negro Artist Comes of Age: A National Survey of Contemporary American Artists," an exhibition at the Albany Institute of History and Art. As the title of the exhibition suggested, the thrust of this show was dual: to spotlight the works of contemporary black artists nationwide and to develop a frame of reference that, once and for all, would contextualize them in the larger picture of American art. Admittedly, the convening of these artists in yet another "all-Negro show" struck some of the participating artists as contradictory to this latter objective. Still, the diversity of art styles on view, in concert with the impressive credentials of many of the painters and sculptors, emphasized the fact that by 1945, African-American artists had indeed entered a new era.

Johnson's two exhibited paintings, *Mount Calvary* (see fig. 168) and an oil on cardboard painting, *Booker T. Washington Legend* (ca. 1944, whereabouts unknown), were a part of

183. *Portrait of Carrie Smith*, 1944. Oil on paperboard, 26½ x 20⅞ in.

184. *Self-Portrait*, 1944. Oil on paperboard, 25½ x 31 in.

a body of work described by Alain Locke in his catalogue essay as combining "warmly human" elements with "piercing social irony."[49] An earlier gouache version of *Booker T. Washington Legend* perhaps illustrates what Locke meant in his brief discussion about art "in the social commentary vein" (fig. 186). Johnson's image of Booker T. Washington shows the famous black leader educating a group of students in the industrial and agricultural arts. As a kind of illustrative backdrop for Washington and his "legend," Johnson not only renders miniature pictures of shovels, wheels, and plows—examples of the tools Washington felt symbolized advancement for post-Emancipation Afro-America—but also a few pens and books: "tools" for the intellect as well.

The backdrop of illustrative pictures in *Booker T. Washington Legend* became the overall mode of expression in Fighters for Freedom, Johnson's 1945 series of historical paintings. In this group of paintings, Johnson depicted famous men and women in African-American history—including Nat Turner, Frederick Douglass, Abraham Lincoln, John Brown, and Harriet Tubman—who were in the forefront of the struggle for racial equality in America.

Nat Turner, which pays homage to the leader of an 1831 slave revolt in Virginia, was Johnson's latest "crucifixion" painting among a number—e.g., *Lynch Mob Victim, Jesus and the Three Marys, Mount Calvary*, and *Lamentation*—that examine Christian and/or black American martyrdom (fig. 187). Even without some previous knowledge of the famous slave revolt, visual clues (the red horizon, a lynched black man, and a surplus of segregated "Caucasian" and "Negro" crosses/grave markers) relay a story of bloody insurrection and personal sacrifice. Also present in *Nat Turner* is a shade of self-portraiture, evident as well (for perhaps similar, self-martyrizing reasons) in *Mount Calvary* and *Lamentation*.

Let My People Free and *Three Great Freedom Fighters* also trumpet prominent figures in black history, but from an almost surreal, visionary standpoint (figs. 188, 189). In *Let My People Free*, Johnson has his own way with history,

185. Holcha Krake, *Study for a Copy of the Baldishol Tapestry*, ca. 1938. Watercolor on paper, yarn attachments, 15 x 19¾ in.

186. *Booker T. Washington Legend*, ca. 1942–43. Gouache, pen and ink with pencil on paper, 18⅛ x 15¼ in.

187. *Nat Turner*, ca. 1945. Oil on paperboard, 31⅜ x 25⅞ in.

188. *Let My People Free*, ca. 1945. Oil on paperboard, 38¼ x 30 in.

189. *Three Great Freedom Fighters*, ca. 1945. Oil on paperboard, 36 x 27⅛ in.

placing Abraham Lincoln and Frederick Douglass on opposite ends of a table, both facing nightmarish vignettes of fettered, lynched, and escaped slaves. In *Three Great Freedom Fighters*, Frederick Douglass is literally "joined" with abolitionist John Brown and Underground Railroad "conductor" Harriet Tubman. Their clasping of hands, all the more noticeable because of Johnson's deliberate contrasting of complexions, underscores the artist's sense of a shared mission among the three, regardless of whether they had actually convened in history as shown.

The Fighters for Freedom series also encompassed famous people from a larger pool of current world figures—politicians, military figures, opposition leaders, grass-roots activists—who were recognized for their roles in liberating various peoples from colonial rule. Inspired no doubt by the end of World War II and the international community's discussions about the creation of a United Nations Charter, Johnson saw his Fighters for Freedom series as one artist's contribution to postwar peace and understanding.[50]

Starting with earlier, historical paintings like *George Washington Signing the Declaration of Independence*, Johnson increasingly sought to document important political actions and their key players (fig. 190). By the end of 1945, these paintings were rather up-to-date, covering everything from Emperor Haile Selassie's triumphant return to Ethiopia after that country's five years under fascist Italian rule to Hindu leaders Nehru and Gandhi on the occasion of their "All India" Congress, which called for complete independence from Great Britain (figs. 191, 192).

World politics again appeared in several Fighters for Freedom paintings concerned with World War II's Allied powers. At least five of Johnson's paintings reenact the much-touted "world power conferences" (in Teheran and Cairo in 1943 and in Yalta and Potsdam in 1945) between U.S. representatives and leaders of the Allied forces. *Three Allies in Cairo* shows Chinese nationalist leader Chiang Kai-shek, U.S. President Franklin Delano Roosevelt, and British Prime Minister Winston Churchill at their 1943 history-making meeting in Cairo, where they discussed measures for defeating the Japanese (fig. 193). Johnson painted the Egyptian capital and the three world leaders as one would paint a shop sign: boldly, clearly, and with a definitive narrative.[51]

Many of these history paintings, however, are little more than actual signs themselves. *Underground Railroad*, a large, sprawling panel that documents the men and women who worked against slavery in the nineteenth century, has neither the thematic complexity nor the planar clarity of Johnson's previous works (fig. 194). Johnson's collection of historical vignettes and portrait busts in *Underground Railroad* are also similarly wanting in his once formidable ability to grasp—in a few brilliantly drawn lines—a subject's essential characteristics. Instead, *Underground Railroad* transmits a strained, awkward handling of materials and subject matter: a discomforting manner that, unfortunately, was becoming noticeable as well in Johnson's personal and professional dealings with people.

Johnson's increasingly erratic behavior was noticed even as early as 1943, though it was

190. *George Washington Signing the Declaration of Independence*, ca. 1942–43.
Tempera, pen and ink with pencil on paper, 16⅜ x 16⅝ in.

191. *Haile Selassie,* ca. 1945. Oil on paperboard, 32⅞ x 25½ in.

192. *Nehru and Gandhi*, ca. 1945. Oil on paperboard, 33⅞ x 27⅞ in.

193. *Three Allies in Cairo*, ca. 1945. Oil on paperboard, 28⅝ x 36½ in.

194. *Underground Railroad*, ca. 1945. Oil on paperboard, 33⅜ x 36⅜ in.

often explained away as typical of the "artistic" temperament. About a year before Holcha died, she had confided to Helen Harriton that William occasionally behaved "very hysterical" and was prone to get quite upset over minor matters. Helen herself had noticed that following Holcha's death Johnson acted a little more eccentric—but considering his emotional dependence upon Holcha, Helen felt that kind of behavior was to be expected.[52] As time passed, however, Johnson grew more moody and irritable, striking everybody who encountered him as a very intense person unusually driven by his own art, easily made indignant by a perceived lack of appreciation for his work, and almost pathologically caught up in undying adoration of his late wife (fig. 195).

195. William H. Johnson, ca. 1945

Nora Holt, the arts and entertainment editor for the *New York Amsterdam News*, picked up on these and a few other idiosyncrasies during her interview with Johnson on the occasion of his "Negro History Week" exhibition (of about twenty-five paintings) at the 135th Street Branch of the New York Public Library. Holt, choosing her words with evident care, wrote that "as [Johnson] talked, in a halting and carefully defined manner of intensity, you could not help but feel [that] the man has reached the highest degree of personal concept, shorn of all imitation and maudlin sentiment." Regarding his mother's portrait, Johnson was quoted as saying:

I am a Negro and proud. My mother was black, as I have shown in my portrait of her, sitting with folded hands and an expression of resignation in a simple polka dot dress. In Europe, they asked me if I was a Moor, an Indian, or North African. My answer has always been, "I am a Negro."

When asked by Holt why he had changed from more "traditional forms" of painting to his "recent primitives," Johnson answered:

It was not a change but a development. In all my years of painting, I have had one absorbing and inspiring idea, and have worked towards it with unyielding zeal: to give— in simple and stark form—the story of the Negro as he has existed.

According to Holt and the staff at the library, Johnson's biggest admirers during the run of his show were the children of Harlem, who were enthralled by his colors, his "freedom of expression," and his skillful recounting of "the Negro's story."[53]

Shortly before the exhibition closed, however, Johnson began to tell friends and fellow artists that, with the war now finished, he was going to return to Denmark. Writing to art critic Emily Genauer, Johnson announced, "I am returning to Denmark to my deceased wife's family. From there, I will start my European exhibitions."[54] To Holcha's mother, Thora, and middle sister, Nanna, Johnson wrote:

I did not answer your xmas letter. Neither did you answer mine. But I am still thinking of you all the time and also about coming to Denmark this summer.

I will have a lot of baggage with [me] and great work to pack in it.

I do want to continue where Holcha and I left off: exhibiting all over Europe this time. I have great pictures I did while over here, just for that purpose. And I am thinking and hoping that Musse [the nickname for Christoph Voll's widow, Erna] can take Holcha's place in this great journey. It's to start in Denmark. I'm thinking of a memorial exhibition of Holcha's things.

I have a Singer sewing machine. Holcha's. I want to know whether you all need it over there, [so that] I can bring it with me when I come over.

I can bring coffee, tea.

It wont be long now before I can see you all again.

My best love to you both

Willie Mar, 26, 1946 [55]

An eternal romantic, Johnson obviously fancied that he and Holcha's widowed sister, Erna Voll, would make an ideal couple. That illusion, coupled with his other fantasy of exhibiting his Fighters for Freedom series throughout a liberated Europe, were vivid enough in his mind that he not only talked about his plans, but actually began to implement them.

His first step was to save up enough money for passage on a European-bound ship. According to letters written to Thora and Nanna, it took Johnson only two months to save the required amount. It seemed that the only thing holding him back from leaving that summer was a reservation on a ship, which he eventually secured that spring, on the S.S. *Drottningholm*, for a departure on 18 October 1946.

His next move was to assemble all of his work—over a thousand paintings, drawings, prints, ceramics—and all of Holcha's work, from the loft space as well as from various other sites. In several letters to Evelyn Brown and Mary Beattie Brady of the Harmon Foundation, Johnson was quite adamant about the return of his work, though they felt that many of the paintings (which he had given to them as early as 1930) rightfully belonged to the foundation.[56] Johnson apparently was also asking those to whom he had given works in the past to return these gifts to him, at least for this proposed European exhibition tour. Langston Hughes, one of the recipients of a painting, half-jokingly replied to Johnson's request that "fifteen years is a long time for Negroes to keep anything, considering the unsettled conditions of our life . . . but if I am able to trace it, I will return it to you."[57]

On 20 August 1946, Johnson applied for a passport, since his last one (issued in 1935) had deteriorated beyond recognition. Under the section on the application headed "Purposes of visits," Johnson wrote, "Artist painter," which was crossed out and changed (in someone else's handwriting) to "Personal Business." Under the section inquiring as to the length of time the applicant intended to remain outside of the United States, Johnson wrote "Indef."[58]

Finally, on an unusually chilly October day, passengers and ship were ready to depart New York Harbor. Helen Harriton was there to see Johnson off, just as she had been there in 1938 to welcome "Bill" and Holcha to America. According to Helen, "he took everything [back that he and Holcha] had—no matter in what condition it was."[59] Johnson himself had written in September to Thora and Nanna that "I'm bringing all Holcha's clothes, hats, shoes, dresses, black thread, yarn . . . cigarettes, coffee, tea, other things, etc."[60] These items—not to mention the rolls of unstretched paintings on canvas and burlap, stacks of painted cardboard sheets and wooden paneling, portfolios of works on paper, and Holcha's art—were an unbelievable sight to behold in the ship's storage area. Recalling that cold, "raw" day, Helen said, "He stood erect and withdrawn on the deck after we parted, but was touched and happy that we came to see him off. "Will you write to us, Bill?" I asked, and he answered "Oh, no—but I will think of you, in my new life."[61] As it would turn out, Johnson's "new life," in postwar Denmark and beyond, promised much for the troubled artist to think about and to question.

196. *Min Minde fra Kerteminde Fyn 1930 (My Souvenir from Kerteminde, Fyn 1930),* ca. 1945. Oil on paperboard, 36⅜ x 33½ in.

Professional and Personal Decline
1946–1947

For William H. Johnson, returning to Denmark was a joyous occasion. Seeing Holcha's seventy-eight-year-old mother Thora and the rest of the family and friends vividly brought back to him all of the good memories of life in Denmark prior to the war. In his circa 1945 painting *Min Minde Fra Kerteminde Fyn 1930* (*My Souvenir from Kerteminde, Funen 1930*) Johnson had already created an enduring image of all of the people and places that, for him, made up the Danish side of his "family of primitiveness and tradition" (fig. 196).[1] His return to Denmark carried this painted homage to an idyllic Scandinavian existence a step further, putting him again in direct contact with a people and society that he considered free of the economic constraints and social conventions of modern civilization.

For Holcha's family, however, Johnson's return was bittersweet. While they genuinely enjoyed seeing him again and marveling at his new work, his constant talk of "nothing but 'Holcha'" was a painful reminder to them of their prolonged separation from "Lille Søren," especially during her last years of emotional and physical suffering. Still, they welcomed Johnson as a returning member of their family, with whom they shared their homes, meals, and stories of survival under four humiliating years of German occupation.[2]

The family quickly sensed, however, that "Willie" was not the same person he had been before the war and that Holcha's death (and, perhaps, the difficulties of life in general) had made him a peculiar, sometimes irrational person. "It started," family members recalled, "with the urn." "At first, Willie refused to give it to us so that we could give Holcha a proper burial. No matter how much we pleaded with him, he wouldn't bring it out. At one desperate moment, we even tried going through all his belongings while he was away, but we still couldn't find it."[3] Although Johnson did eventually surrender the funerary urn, the episode sent up signals that he was emotionally disturbed.

The next series of events suggesting that William was deeply troubled took place following his December 1946 move to Copenhagen, where Erna, Christoph Voll's widow, was now living. Johnson again proposed that she "take Holcha's place" as his wife. Though she soundly rejected this bizarre proposal, Erna still permitted William to share the family's living quarters in Copenhagen. But shortly after William moved in, the tiny apartment—which already housed Erna, her daughter Karen, Karen's husband Sven, and

Karen's infant son—simply became too crowded, and Erna then had to tell William that he could have his meals with them there, but would have to find someplace else to sleep.[4]

Johnson, who was hurt by Erna's decree (and probably a little angry at himself for not seeing what a strain he had put on her family), marched off that evening into the cold winter air, with his burlap sacks (filled with art and personal belongings) and wounded pride dragging behind him. For the next few months, he shuttled back and forth between Erna's place, cheap rooming houses in and around Copenhagen, and the city streets.

Johanne-Marie Esbjerg, whose family had come to Copenhagen during this period to see Erna and several other close friends, actually saw Johnson one night on the streets, not too far from Erna's apartment. "It was cold," Johanne-Marie remembered. "He was surrounded by bundles of clothing and art, and was wearing a pair of old worker's shoes, painted metallic gold." They stopped to talk with him, and later that evening they all congregated at Erna's place for refreshments.[5]

Johanne-Marie then discovered that although Johnson presented a poverty-stricken appearance, he had the economic resources—although apparently not the desire—to move into a hotel. At that time, Johnson had in his possession at least six thousand American dollars: money earned and scrupulously saved from art sales and his two-year stint at the navy yards. According to Johnson, he had been picked up several evenings earlier by the local authorities for vagrancy and brought to the police station. When asked by the arresting officer if he had any means of support, he pulled out a thousand-dollar bill and boldly waved it before the amazed policeman's eyes. They immediately released him.[6]

In spite of Johnson's increasingly erratic behavior, he was rational and knowledgeable enough to secure for himself an exhibition space in the spring at the Kunsthallen, a well-known art gallery and auction house in Copenhagen. Yet when the exhibition of seventy-eight works finally opened on 6 March a city-wide newspaper strike prevented any of the local art critics from reviewing it, with the exception of the art critic from *Land og Folk*, Copenhagen's communist newspaper.

"To William Johnson, social freedom is the greatest and most important need of mankind," wrote the critic from *Land og Folk*. "For this reason he considers his series of paintings, *Fighters for Freedom*, as some of the most important of his artistic production." Describing Johnson's religious paintings as "refreshing and topical," the critic said that they showed religious figures (such as Jesus) as they "exist in the minds of the Negroes; a far cry from ecclesiastical art which, in Europe, has become strained and vapid." In summation, the critic wrote: "The exhibition at Kunsthallen proves William Johnson to be a painter who has managed to completely put to use all of his artistic means, and a man in whom the working people and their problems awaken strong and true feelings."[7]

Following the exhibition at the Kunsthallen, Johnson left Copenhagen and traveled by ferry to Oslo, Norway. Friends of Erna Voll who were also on the ferryboat later reported to her that Johnson's behavior was outrageous and that he gave all of the other passengers much cause for anxiety and concern. One incident that several people later relayed to Erna took place in the ferry's fancy and somewhat pretentious dining café. William, to everyone's shock, spilled a bottle of red soda water over a pristine piece of white linen that covered his table. The sad truth is that Johnson's deteriorating mental condition and the erratic behavior it triggered prompted his Danish family and friends to view him increasingly as a stranger, outsider, and social outcast.

In Oslo, William began to roam the streets, retracing an earlier, happier time, carting his paintings and belongings around like a nomad and appearing to be an indigent, crazed person to everyone who encountered him. Both he and his baggage, constantly exposed to the elements, became covered with dirt and grime, so that an ordinary person would have had no inkling that he was an artist whose stash of cardboard boxes and rolls of burlap were actually prize-winning artworks.

Around Easter, Johnson took up residency in a workman's shed on Oslo's wharf. When the police discovered that he was living in this makeshift shelter and asked him to vacate it, Johnson refused, whereupon he was immediately escorted to Oslo's old police station. But unlike the authorities at his last encounter, Oslo's police were not impressed with his large sums of money; they locked him up and placed him under close observation.[8]

Before the night was out, however, Johnson was transferred to Oslo's Ullevål Hospital, where doctors ran a complete battery of psychological and physical tests on him. By sheer coincidence, while waiting for an x-ray in one of the hospital's hallways that evening, Johnson ran into Torbjørg, one of the Tjensvoll children, who was then a young student nurse at Ullevål. "We immediately recognized each other and embraced," Torbjørg recalled, "but Willie's attending nurse became angry with me, for fear that my talking to him might further upset him."[9]

Days later, after Johnson was officially diagnosed as suffering from an "advanced case of syphilis-induced paresis," he was transferred to the larger, better-equipped Gaustad Hospital, where doctors treated him for his immediate ailments. The disease, which he had presumably contracted earlier in his life, had already progressed, however, to the point where his motor skills and mental functions were severely impaired. The doctors saw little hope for recovery or even for significant, marked improvements.

Johnson's paresis explains, to a great extent, his gradual shift from carefully conceived, quiltlike compositions, such as *Going to Church* and *I Baptize Thee* (see figs. 133, 164), to stark insignialike pictures, such as *Underground Railroad* and *Min Minde Fra Kerteminde* (see figs. 194, 196). Another explanation for this formal transition could certainly be made from Johnson's oft-repeated forecast that art (including his own) "would eventually return to the primitive." Tempting as it may be to attribute the forms and themes of these later works by Johnson to his mental illness, studies of the artist and these paintings conclude that, despite their crude renderings and simple formats, the themes and ideas that Johnson presents in these last works are lucid and provocative, if also reflective of his

197. Central Islip State Hospital, 1972

impaired motor skills. Holcha's death and Johnson's subsequent feelings of extreme bereavement account for more of his antisocial behavior—as well as his delusions and utter sense of isolation—than his syphilis-induced paresis.[10]

Torbjørg, several of her sisters, and Holcha's sister Nanna—who traveled all the way from Denmark—visited Johnson periodically through the spring and summer of 1947 when he was well enough to receive guests. Nanna, recalling one of her visits with him, wrote that although "he was . . . glad to see me," he was also "in despair at being [hospitalized]," and exclaimed, in utter frustration, "I *will* live my own life in liberty!" When she suggested to Johnson that he might spend his time painting and drawing while hospitalized, he looked at her very surprised and said, "Look about you, and try to imagine *anyone* being artistically inspired here." She had to admit that this observation made absolute sense though spoken by someone diagnosed as "insane."[11]

By October 1947, the U.S. Embassy in Oslo stepped into the case and decided that Johnson and his belongings would have to be returned to the United States. Nanna's flurry of letters to the Norwegian authorities failed in their attempt to keep Johnson in Norway: his mental incompetence, American citizenship, and the absence of any fiscally responsible guardians necessitated that the U.S. Government become the official custodian of his "personal interests."[12] In November, Johnson, his property, and a caretaker boarded the S.S. *Stavangerfjord*, for the transatlantic journey to New York.

Within a week of Johnson's return to the United States, all of his books, personal effects, paintings, and works on paper—as well as Holcha's art, and assorted drawings and prints by Christoph Voll, Oskar Kokoschka, and Edvard Munch—were placed in a locked wooden storage bin in a warehouse on New York's Franklin Street. Johnson's court-appointed attorney paid the rent on the storage space out of Johnson's savings and assumed overall responsibility for Johnson's finances.

On 1 December 1947, Johnson was admitted to Long Island's Central Islip State Hospital—New York State's largest mental health facility and, at one point, the second-largest institution of its kind in the world (fig. 197). Ironically, the syphilis spirochete—the root cause of Johnson's mental impairment—was first isolated by scientists at this same institution in 1913. By the time of Johnson's arrival, the hospital's vast acreage accommodated a patient population of almost 9,000, a network of buildings, a farm, and 1,700-plus employees.[13]

In a letter to Helen Harriton, Nanna Krake said that the hospital had written to her to say that William "was getting better," beginning "to draw a little," and that there was "some hope of recovery." Helen's view—from the vantage point of Central Islip itself—was far less optimistic than Nanna's. As seen in her reply, Helen held out no hope that William H. Johnson, the artist, would ever reappear:

Willie . . . is physically very well, but his mental condition is not good, and not likely to get better. . . . He is well cared for, and seems content, imagining himself in telepathic communication with someone. He likes doing outside work, but will not attempt to paint. He asks for nothing.[14]

Resurrection
1955–The Present

I n a letter written in February 1955, Helen Harriton apologized for the five-year hiatus in her correspondance with Nanna Krake. In those intervening years, Helen explained, there had been very little for her to report regarding William H. Johnson's situation. "Willie," wrote Helen, "is still in an asylum or hospital in Central Islip. . . . He is in a hopeless condition. . . . He does no painting. He will not get well. It is very sad. . . . But his work we have tried to save."[1]

This last statement referred to Helen's efforts to reverse a decision by Johnson's court-appointed attorney to remove the artist's belongings from the Franklin Street warehouse and to "destroy everything." Johnson's savings (from which the attorney regularly drew to pay storage fees) were finally exhausted in 1955, explaining the decision to dispose of his things. But Helen Harriton's many inquiries to Johnson's attorney, and her eventual success at convincing the Harmon Foundation to act as the caretakers of Johnson's belongings, finally insured that his art and personal effects would not be lost.

To accept custody of Johnson's art in good faith, the foundation stipulated to the Surrogate's Court that it would have to have unconditional rights over the works. It was also agreed that there would be no profiting from his estate and that the foundation's use of his art would be for the dual purposes of advancing the cause of interracial understanding and promoting the achievements of African-Americans in the fine arts.[2] In her letter to Nanna, Helen explained how the foundation planned to accomplish this:

We have agreed to pay the expense of having the heavy stuff moved to a place held by the Harmon Foundation, where a selection of paintings can be made by a few interested negro institutions. The Harmon Foundation gave help to Willi at various times, both before and after he was in Europe. Miss Brady is very kind and has put a great deal of effort into interesting the Negro institutions. But they will only accept the paintings as gifts—there is no money or interest in purchasing them. At any rate, in this way his best work will be saved from destruction.[3]

Almost one year later, the court finally accepted Mary Beattie Brady's offer, and a date was set to deliver the art to the foundation's offices. "It came," wrote Brady about the Johnson estate to a friend, "and believe me, I have never seen such mishandled stuff in my life." The content of Johnson's storage space—paintings, watercolors, drawings, prints, textiles, books, papers, and personal photographs—had suffered through nine years of accumulated neglect. Many of Johnson's heavily painted oils on canvas (and burlap) were cracked and chipped beyond repair. Paintings on laminated wooden panels had buckled under countless temperature and humidity changes. And dozens of textiles and works on paper had been chewed down to shreds by vermin.

After discarding the absolutely unsalvageable material, the staff found that an expansive collection was miraculously left: approximately 1,300 objects. This voluminous body of work, as Mary Beattie Brady and her staff quickly discovered, documented Johnson's entire career: from his timid but facile student paintings at the National Academy of Design, through his various periods of art-making in Europe, Africa, and the United States, to the colorful and didactic Fighters for Freedom series of 1945. Upon discovering that the foundation had in its possession the lifetime work of an extremely talented, former Harmon award recipient, Brady and her assistant Evelyn S. Brown began, with almost missionary zeal, to develop exhibition plans that would bring Johnson's life and work to the public's attention. "I have learned to be a pretty good scrub-woman on canvases," Brady jokingly wrote in one of her letters, referring to the tremendous (and unanticipated) responsibility that lay ahead as "caretaker" of William H. Johnson's art.[4]

Although the foundation's original intention was to give selected works of art to black colleges as "handsome and exciting additions" to their dining halls and sitting rooms, the first task turned out to be a complete reorganization of the materials. With the invaluable assistance of Palmer C. Hayden (a Johnson colleague, longtime foundation employee and the first recipient of a Harmon Gold medal and cash award for artistic excellence), the staff sorted Johnson's work into what they deduced to be his different periods (French, Scandinavian, and American), and then into its respective media (paintings, watercolors, block prints, etc.). After figuring out chronologies and types of work, the staff began the long and arduous assignments of cleaning the paintings, performing minimal conservation work, placing wooden stretchers behind paintings on woven fabric, matting the works on paper, and framing as much as their budget would allow. This full-scale enterprise, which occupied a major portion of the foundation's space on Nassau Street (and used up a significant part of its dwindling budget), continued for the next year and a half.

The bulk of Johnson's estate, minus the few gifts of art to Holcha's family and the Harritons, was kept intact for exhibitions and donations to interested institutions. After consulting with Frederick Douglass Patterson, the founder and president of the United Negro College Fund, Mary Beattie Brady put into motion plans for several of the UNCF-affiliated colleges to accept some of the paintings, with the schools agreeing to pay for the matting, framing, and general care of the works.

Starting with a major retrospective of Johnson's art at the Countee Cullen branch of the New York Public Library in December 1956, the foundation embarked on an ambitious traveling exhibition program of selected paintings by the artist. For the next two years, "William H. Johnson: An Artist of the World Scene" toured colleges, secondary schools, libraries, and community centers in New York, Vermont, Massachusetts, Nebraska, Alabama, Tennessee, and the District of Columbia, among other places. Though none of these sites had the art-world cachet of a major museum, the foundation nevertheless felt that bringing Johnson's story to ordinary people was an honorable, as well as immediately attainable, goal.

But as the Harmon Foundation entered the 1960s and crept toward its own fortieth anniversary, promotional activities for William H. Johnson's work—traveling exhibitions, printed brochures, etc.—slowed down considerably. Depleted funds and shifts in the foundation's overall focus brought about a decline in programming of any kind. Finally, in 1966, its board of trustees announced that the foundation had to cease all operations within a year. Brady and Evelyn S. Brown were suddenly faced with a monumental task— quickly finding an appropriate permanent repository for more than one thousand art works by Johnson. They contacted several New York museums, but with no success.

On a trip to Washington, D.C., in the spring of 1966, however, Evelyn S. Brown met someone who could possibly assist them—David W. Scott, Director of the Smithsonian Institution's National Collection of Fine Arts (NCFA). Brown explained the urgent need to find a home not only for the "Johnson material," but for the foundation's collection of works by other black artists as well. Dr. Scott had already told Evelyn Brown of plans to expand and transfer the activities and collections of the NCFA (previously located in a hallway of the National Museum of Natural History) to the spacious, newly renovated Old Patent Office Building at 8th and G Streets, NW. "As the Foundation will close out its active program of experimental, stimulative work," wrote Brown shortly afterwards in a follow-up letter to Dr. Scott, "we would be pleased to know of your interest at a fairly early date." [5]

After inspecting the art and studying the research materials about Johnson, Scott concluded that Johnson's work certainly had an important place in any representative collection of American art, and he assured both Brown and Brady that the NCFA's acquisition of the entire Johnson collection would have "much merit." [6] Following mutual visits— first, by Scott and his staff to the Harmon Foundation's offices and, then, by Brown to the new, though still unfinished, headquarters for the NCFA—the parties involved came to this agreement: the title of ownership of the William H. Johnson collection, which the court had given to the Harmon Foundation in 1956, would be transferred to the Smithsonian Institution as of 19 April 1967. This transfer was contingent upon the NCFA carrying on—through future William H. Johnson exhibitions, loans, and publications—the Harmon Foundation's objectives: to reach out "to the masses of our people" and help them "raise their sights and . . . feeling for art at the *core* of life." Many art museums at that time recoiled at the thought of "grassroots outreach" and education within the museum proper. The NCFA, however, was sympathetic to the Harmon Foundation's general philosophy and agreed to these conditions for the transfer of title without hesitation.

Scott placed Adelyn Dohme Breeskin (1896–1986), the NCFA's twentieth-century art consultant, in charge of organizing the work and preparing Johnson's first museum retrospective. Breeskin, previously director of the Baltimore Museum of Art and of the Washington Gallery of Modern Art, was perhaps best known for her scholarly work on the nineteenth-century American expatriate painter Mary Cassatt, as well as for bringing the Cone collection, one of the most important collections of modern European art ever assembled, to the Baltimore Museum of Art. Recalling her first encounter with Johnson's work that spring, Breeskin said, "I was overwhelmed by it—the strength of it—the power—and the beautiful color—it's all there!" [7]

One of Breeskin's first duties was to help fulfill the NCFA's promise to donate selected works from the Johnson collection to several black colleges and universities. Starting with gifts to Hampton University and Fisk University in 1967, Breeskin continued the donations of selected works by Johnson to other universities—Atlanta, Howard, Morgan State, North Carolina Central, South Carolina State, and Tuskegee among them. Breeskin also arranged for the loan of several paintings by Johnson to one of the first major African-American art exhibitions organized since the 1945 show at the Albany Institute of History and Art. "The Evolution of the Afro-American Artists: 1800–1950," on view at New York's City College in October 1967, was Johnson's first featured appearance in a New York gallery in ten years.

Meanwhile, William H. Johnson, the man whose work was at the center of all this momentous activity, remained institutionalized and totally unaware of any of these undertakings on his behalf. His mental deterioration seemed complete: he could no more comprehend the clippings and brochures about his work that friends would sporadically send him than he could grasp the meaning of such family milestones as the deaths of his mother, Alice (in 1959), and brother, Lacy (in 1960). [8]

In preparation for the Johnson retrospective, now scheduled for the fall of 1971, Breeskin (with the assistance of Jan K. Muhlert and Florine Lyons) conducted extensive research into Johnson's productive years, contacting former acquaintances of the artist in this country and abroad. Among the many contacted were several of Johnson's contemporaries, who shared their memories of him and his times. Painter and collagist Romare Bearden (1914–1988), for example, cited his debt to Johnson, who introduced him to Caresse Crosby, the colorful art collector who gave Bearden one of his first solo shows at the G Place Gallery in 1944.

"Although I found him a rather serious man," Bearden told Breeskin, "his works come from a real emotional vision of life. . . . This intensity we see in all Johnson's work, from [the] first to the last things he did before his illness." Bearden also felt that Johnson, far from being an unconscious primitive, knowingly used "folk sources and a simplified style" so as to "best express what he was attempting to say about his subjects."[9] Bearden's own "signature" pieces from the mid to late 1960s—collages of urban and rural black folk life—were conceived with a sense of composition, spirituality, and understanding of black folk traditions that compare rather closely with Johnson's explorations of similar territory.

While Breeskin and her staff were immersed in the work of the retrospective—researching objects, conducting interviews, and preparing a chronology for the artist and his work—Johnson was admitted to Central Islip's medical infirmary, following complaints of abdominal pain and high fever. On 13 April 1970, less than a month after his sixtyninth birthday, William H. Johnson died in the infirmary from massive inflammation and hemorrhaging of the pancreas. Yet, apparently, no one—either in the art world or in his own family—knew of his passing until almost one year later, when Breeskin wrote Central Islip to see if there was any way Johnson could be informed of the Smithsonian's upcoming festivities. The one-sentence death notice she received in reply, perfunctorily typed on hospital stationary, was not so much shocking as sad—the widespread recognition and critical approval that Johnson so desperately wanted was now about to happen, but neither he nor his wife Holcha was alive to bask in any of the glory.

Johnson's immediate family, however, *were* willing and able to celebrate his art and life. Johnson's sister, Mrs. Lillian Cooper, learned of the upcoming exhibition in Washington and also, sadly enough, of her brother's death while reading her *Florence Morning News*. "The papers said that he had gone to visit God after twenty-three years in a mental institution," said Lillian. "We weren't even notified."[10] Lillian then called the Smithsonian and spoke to Adelyn Breeskin who, in turn, made certain that she got an invitation to the opening. Lillian and Johnson's other sister, Lucy, attended the November 1971 opening, as did Lillian's daughter Ernestine (subject of the 1944 Florence portrait, *Li'l Sis*). "Although I had to scrounge together all of my money to make the trip to Washington," Lillian remembered, "I was determined to see my brother's show." With similar resolve, Lillian, an amputee, refused to accept the NCFA's offer of the use of a wheelchair that evening. "I was too filled with pride to just sit back and roll around. I *had* to walk and stand in front of my brother's pictures" (fig. 198).[11]

Lillian Cooper's spirit of celebration at the opening was shared by the NCFA's new director, Joshua C. Taylor. In his brief but insightful foreword to Breeskin's exhibition catalogue, Taylor quickly recounted, but did not belabor, Johnson's tragic circumstances. Instead, his foreword largely explored the predominant themes in Johnson's art and life—primitivism, eclecticism, and spirituality—and suggested that these motifs were, in fact, what made Johnson such a "forceful and original" painter. "It is high time," wrote Taylor, "that Johnson be looked upon as a whole man who, in his relatively short career, recognized the complexity of his spiritual background and found solace rather than despair in the expression of its diverse promptings."[12]

In the succeeding years, the NCFA (now the National Museum of American Art) has utilized the William H. Johnson collection in a variety of exhibitions, museum programs, and publications. From world tours of the paintings (under the auspices of the United States Information Agency) to thematic exhibitions (such as "William H. Johnson: The Scandinavian Years" and "Homecoming: William H. Johnson and Afro-America, 1938–1946"), the Johnson collection has been seen and enjoyed by people the world over.

That the nation's capital and its national repository for native art treasures would end up as the latest haven for Johnson's works is, in one sense, divine justice. Washington, D.C.—a big, world-class city with small-town, southern ways—seems an appropriate place for Johnson's art: vigorous, passionate creations that synthesize a fluent, international idiom with a decidedly folkloric, provincial one.

Johnson's early appreciation for the post-impressionist tendency to interject the self into one's work places him in the company of kindred artists (Georgia O'Keeffe, Arthur G. Dove, et al.) who also created visual/emotional bridges between themselves and their work. Johnson's career-long struggle to accommodate both himself and his subjects channeled his art away from total self-indulgence and, instead, toward a recognition of the spirtual dimensions of people, places, and things.

Johnson's concept of the "primitive," although initially just as narrow and skewed as that of the reigning moderns, became a powerful force in his work only when he linked it with an intimate knowledge of, and empathy for, the folk life and cultural expressions of selected marginalized peoples. The key to Johnson's success was his realization that, as an African-American artist who could bring to his art a vital, expressive point of view rooted in an elemental and traditional way of life, he could create work of major consequence for modern art.

Amid the ascendency of African-American artists during and just after World War II, Johnson was a special presence. As a committed professional who could conceptualize his paintings of Afro-America in a rhythmic, expressive, and *bluesy* manner, Johnson merits a special place in art history. In the 1940s, at the height of his powers, William H. Johnson—like Aaron Douglas in the 1920s, Jacob Lawrence in the 1940s, and Romare Bearden in the 1960s—discovered that one's work could be regarded as African-American only by embodying the same formal and thematic principles that governed other African-American folk expressions. Anticipating the antistyle orientations to painting of such contemporary black artists as Beverly Buchanan, Robert Colescott, and Faith Ringgold, Johnson introduced in his very last works a late-modernist perspective in African-

American art, in which form, theme, and artistic intent all promote a black, populist aesthetic.

In a career that mirrors the complexities of art and society between the two World Wars, William H. Johnson left an artistic legacy of *re-creation*: a moving away from an art of cultural fragmentation and displacement into one of cultural integrity and resolution. Johnson's individual search for a way out of "the valley" and toward "home" is only now being understood, for its personal significance and for its example to other modernists—e.g., Marsden Hartley and Archibald J. Motley, Jr., who also acknowledged the intrinsic value of the folk community to their art. William H. Johnson, in spite of the many years of invisibility and the uncertainty surrounding his place in the history of American art, is finally being recognized as a major figure whose importance to the development of American modernism can no longer be ignored.

Abbreviations

AAA   Archives of American Art, Smithsonian Institution, Washington, D.C.

ALLP, MSRC   Alain Leroy Locke Papers, Moorland-Spingarn Research Center, Howard University, Washington, D.C.

CABP, CHS   Claude A. Barnett Papers, Manuscript Division, Chicago Historical Society, Chicago, Illinois.

HFP, LC   Harmon Foundation Papers, Manuscript Division, Library of Congress, Washington, D.C.

NMAA   National Museum of American Art, Office of the Registrar, Smithsonian Institution, Washington, D.C.

WHJP   William H. Johnson Papers, Archives of American Art, Smithsonian Institution, Washington, D.C.

WHJP, SIA   William H. Johnson Papers, Smithsonian Institution Archives, Washington, D.C.

During the period that Johnson worked and exhibited in Scandinavia (ca. 1930–38), it was common practice for newspaper journalists to sign their articles using abbreviations (e.g., "Y.B." of Stockholm's *Dagens Nyheter*), given names (e.g., "Rita" of Trondheim's *Nidaros*), or distinctive pen names (e.g., "Dr. Rank" of Copenhagen's *Ekstrabladet*). In the following notes, the author of this book, rather than attempting to establish the various identities behind the pen names (which, in most cases, were known in the communities where each reviewer and journalist worked), instead presents these writers as they chose to appear in various Scandinavian publications in the 1930s.

In 1956, when the Harmon Foundation acquired William H. Johnson's estate and memorabilia, a few selected articles and reviews from foreign newspapers were translated into English by staff members of the American-Scandinavian Foundation. In most instances, the author of this book has revised those translations, taking into consideration our expanded knowledge of Scandinavian art criticism and the particulars of Johnson's art and career. Many of the articles that were not translated by the American-Scandinavian Foundation—both those already in the Harmon Foundation's possession and those that the author found through his own newspaper research in Denmark, Norway, and Sweden—were translated entirely by the author.

Notes

The Gate City: 1901–1918

1   For information on Florence and Johnson's early years there, the author is indebted to a number of sources. First, interviews (6–7 November 1985) with Florence historian Dr. G. Wayne King, as well as two books on Florence's history by Dr. King, were especially helpful. See *Rise Up So Early: A History of Florence County, South Carolina* (Spartanburg: The Reprint Company, 1981), and *Some Folks Do: A Pictorial History of Florence County* (Norfolk: The Donning Company, 1985). Second, interviews with longtime Florence citizens Laura Trusedell, Pearl McCleese, and Bertha Sumter (10 November 1985) recounted many important aspects of local black history. And finally, numerous city directories have supplied much information about Florence at the turn of the century. See *City Directory* (Florence: Board of Trade, 1905–06 and 1911, respectively). Unless otherwise noted, all accounts of local Florence history are from the above sources.

2   See J. P. McNeill, Jr., and John A. Chase, Jr., *Florence County: Economic and Social* (Columbia: Department of Rural Social Science, University of South Carolina, 1921), pp. 15–23.

3   See "Williamsburg Well May Weep," *The State* (Columbia, South Carolina), 23 February 1898, p. 1. Also see: "No Shred of Evidence," *The State*, 25 February 1898, p. 4; "A Damnable Record," *The Florence Daily Times* (Florence, South Carolina), as quoted in *The State*, 25 February 1898, p. 5; and "Richard Carroll Advises His Race," *The State*, 4 January 1898, p. 1.

4   Alice Johnson had informed the 1910 census gatherer that out of ten children born to her, only two of them, nine-year-old William and newborn Lacy, were living. See Bureau of the Census, *Thirteenth Census of the United States* (Washington, D.C.: Bureau of the Census, 1910), p. 36A.

5   When William H. Johnson applied for a passport to go overseas in 1926, he was initially prevented from doing so because he did not have a birth certificate. Curiously, the state of South Carolina kept no birth (or death) records of its residents until 1915. In lieu of a birth certificate, however, Johnson supplied the State Department with a sworn statement by Mrs. Mary Wilson, the midwife who attended to his mother at his birth in 1901.

6   Leona M. Webster, a former resident of Florence, wrote that Johnson's father was white. See letter to Adelyn D. Breeskin, 22 March 1971, WHJP, SIA. Another former Florence resident, James L. Robinson, told Evelyn Brown of the Harmon Foundation that Johnson was a "mulatto" (ca. October 1959), HFP, LC. When asked in Scandinavia about his ancestry, Johnson often told reporters that his mother was an American Indian and that his father was black. Johnson's acknowledgment of some mixed ancestry in his family suggests that he may have also believed these assertions. On the other hand, a sense of decorum and respect for his family would not have allowed Johnson to make any public mention of black-white miscegenation, despite its occurrence in American society.

7   Lillian Cooper's use of the racial term "mustee" in describing her mother, Alice Johnson, seems to reaffirm her belief that Alice was of American Indian and African-American ancestry. Interview with author, 7 November 1985.

8   Leona M. Webster, letter to Adelyn D. Breeskin, 22 March 1971, WHJP, SIA.

9   Narcissa Dargan, interview with author, Florence, 9 November 1985. Correspondence between Johnson and Louise Fordham Holmes, ca. 1930, appears in Johnson's scrapbook of clippings, letters, and other memorabilia. Scrapbook, WHJP.

Artistic Beginnings: 1918–1926

1   The prospects of greater job opportunities, higher wages, more individual rights, and a better education motivated over 100,000 southern blacks to move to various northern cities between 1915 and 1940. The creation of Harlem, in the context of these new, black urban populations, is discussed in Gilbert Osofsky, *Harlem: The Making of a Ghetto* (New York: Harper Torchbooks, 1971), pp. 17–34, and Jervis Anderson, *This Was Harlem: A Cultural Portrait, 1900–1950* (New York: Farrar, Strauss & Giroux, 1982), pp. 49–71, 121–27.

2   See William H. Johnson, quoted in a typed draft for *Human Interest Facts on the Artists Receiving Harmon Awards* (ca. 1929), HFP, LC.

3   See National Academy of Design vertical file, National Museum of American Art/National Portrait Gallery Library, Smithsonian Institution, Washington, D.C., and The School of the National Academy of Design Archives, New York City. William H. Johnson's academic records were generously made available to the author by National Academy of Design historian Abigail Booth Gerdts.

4   Francis Costa, interview with author, New York City, 8 October 1986.

5   See Ilya Bolotowsky, interview with Paul Cummings, 24 March 1968, Ilya Bolotowsky Papers, AAA; Helen Rennie, interview with author, Washington, D.C., 25 October 1985; and Francis Costa, interview with author, 8 October 1986.

6   William H. Johnson, in Kay P., "Med Kerteminde-Malerier til U.S.A. Negermaleren fortæller om Kunst og Race," *Demokraten* (Aarhus, Denmark), 7 December 1934, p. 3.

7   See Edwin H. Blashfield, "Academy Ideals," Edwin H. Blashfield vertical file, National Museum of American Art/National Portrait Gallery Library, Smithsonian Institution, Washington, D.C. Also see Lois Marie Fink, *Academy: The Academic Tradition in American Art* (Washington, D.C.: Smithsonian Institution Press, 1975), pp. 13–14, 17–19, 59.

8   Hong Ting Wong was a colleague of Johnson's both at the N.A.D. and at the Cape Cod School of Art. Born in Canton, China, in 1898, Wong eventually settled in Provincetown, Massachusetts, and operated the town's only Chinese restaurant for many years. I am grateful to Henry Hensche, former student of, and assistant to, Charles Hawthorne, for identifying Wong and supplying basic biographical information on him. Henry Hensche, interview with author, Provincetown, Massachusetts, 6 August 1986.

9   Biographical information on Hawthorne is from several sources: Elizabeth McCausland, *Charles W. Hawthorne: An American Figure Painter* (New York: American Artists Group, Inc., 1947); *Hawthorne Retrospective* (Provincetown, Mass.: The Chrysler Art Museum at Provincetown, 1961); and Janet A. Flint, *Charles W. Hawthorne: The Late Watercolors* (Washington, D.C.: National Museum of American Art, Smithsonian Institution, 1983). I am also indebted to Mr. Joseph Hawthorne, the artist's son, for

allowing me to interview him. Joseph Hawthorne, interview with author, Provincetown, Massachusetts, 6 August 1986.

10 Duncan Phillips, "Charles W. Hawthorne," *The International Studio* 61 (March 1917): xix–xxiv.

11 Ilya Bolotowsky, interview with Paul Cummings, 24 March 1968, AAA, and Prentiss Taylor, interview with author, Washington, D.C., 30 July 1986.

12 After Charles Hawthorne's death in 1930, his class notes and lectures on painting were compiled and published by his wife; see *Hawthorne on Painting* (1938; reprint, New York: Dover Publications, 1960), p. 21. Unless otherwise noted, all Hawthorne quotations are from this source.

13 Bolotowsky spoke at length in his 1968 interview about the conservative strain in N.A.D. teachers. Although most students were aware of Cézanne and Van Gogh, Bolotowsky recalled that students were "warned against them in various lectures." Ilya Bolotowsky, interview with Paul Cummings. Bolotowsky also described the subtle resentment that many of the conservative teachers had for the ever-popular Hawthorne. (These sentiments were corroborated by similar observations from Francis Costa, Henry Hensche, Helen J. Rennie, and former N.A.D. student Herbert Sanborn, in various interviews with author.)

14 Elizabeth McCausland, *Charles W. Hawthorne*, p. 38.

15 Prentiss Taylor, interview with author, 30 July 1986.

16 Helen Rennie, interview with author, 25 October 1985.

17 Ibid. Also Prentiss Taylor, interview with author.

18 American graphic arts expert Janet A. Flint describes Hawthorne's late watercolors as "markedly original" for their time. "In many respects," she continues, "Hawthorne's late watercolors reflect the continuation of an earlier American tradition of highly individualistic, even idiosyncratic, watercolors." Janet A. Flint, *Charles W. Hawthorne*, pp. 14–16.

19 In a 1967 interview, Umberto Romano said that Ivan G. Olinsky was "the most sympathetic instructor" he had at the N.A.D. Umberto Romano, interview with Karl Fortess, 25 August 1967, Umberto Romano Papers, AAA.

20 Both Herbert Sanborn and Francis Costa remembered that Johnson was, by far, one of the most talented students at the school during those years. Sanborn recalled that during the late 1920s, one of Johnson's nude studies (possibly fig. 11) hung in the painting studio at the school. Francis Costa, interview with author, 8 October 1986; Herbert Sanborn, interview with author, 25 October 1985; and Ilya Bolotowsky, interview with Paul Cummings.

21 Joseph Hawthorne's biographical essay on his father (written in 1959) mentions Hawthorne's support for Johnson: "Besides providing this large number of scholarships at his school, he was instrumental in helping talented students in other schools, and also did such things as get up a purse to start off a gifted young Negro painter in Europe, since he would have no opportunity on this side of the Atlantic." Joseph Hawthorne, in *Hawthorne on Painting*, pp. xii–xiii.

22 For a historical survey of African-American artists who lived and worked in Paris during the twenties, see Michel Fabre, *La Rive Noire: De Harlem à la Seine* (Paris: Lieu Commun, 1985), pp. 47–131. For a larger discussion about American artists in Paris during the 1920s, see Elizabeth H. Turner, *American Artists in Paris, 1919–1929* (Ann Arbor: UMI Research Press, 1988).

23 The antics of George B. Luks are legendary in American art history. Many of these stories appear in Bennard B. Perlman, *The Immortal Eight* (New York: Exposition Press, 1962), pp. 74–81,

87–92. Also see Mahonri Sharp Young, *The Eight: The Realist Revolt in American Painting* (New York: Watson-Guptil Publications, 1973), pp. 110–25.

First Successes: 1926–1930

1 "Around the Studios," *New York Herald* (Paris Edition), 14 November 1927, p. 5.

2 William H. Johnson, letter to Charles W. Hawthorne, 13 August 1928, Charles W. Hawthorne Papers, AAA.

3 George Avril, "Art et Lettres: La Peinture à la Galerie Alban" Nice, France, ca. spring 1929).

4 In a 1929 interview for a Danish newspaper, Holcha talks about her scholarly and artistic interests in weaving. Madame, "Vævekunstens Renæssance," *Fyns Stiftidende* (Odense, Denmark), 1 December 1929, pp. 6–7.

5 William H. Johnson, biographical sketch of Holcha Krake Johnson, ca. 1946, WHJP.

6 William H. Johnson, letter to Charles W. Hawthorne, 13 August 1928, Charles W. Hawthorne Papers, AAA.

7 Charles W. Hawthorne, letter to William H. Johnson, 9 April 1929, HFP, LC.

8 Johnson states that his first meeting with the legendary Tanner, at the artist's country home in "Porte de Calais," was a memorable event. William H. Johnson, undated handwritten resume (ca. 1938), WHJP. Artist Palmer C. Hayden, who was in France around the same time as Johnson, told Adelyn D. Breeskin that "Henry O. Tanner . . . thought very highly of Johnson's work." Palmer C. Hayden, letter to Adelyn D. Breeskin, 23 January 1971, WHJP, SIA.

9 See Evelyn S. Brown, letter to Dr. David W. Scott, 19 July 1967, NMAA. Also see William H. Johnson's nomination blank for the Harmon Awards, 6 December 1929, and the official checklist for the 1929 Harmon Awards Applicants, HFP, LC.

10 See Hazel Spencer Phillips, *William Elmer Harmon* (Lebanon, Ohio: Warren County Historical Society, 1962). For a more in-depth look at the Harmon Foundation and its various levels of support for black artists, see Gary A. Reynolds and Beryl J. Wright, *Against the Odds: African-American Artists and the Harmon Foundation* (Newark: The Newark Museum, 1989).

11 "Exhibition To Be Held of Work of Negro Artists," Press Release, 4 January 1930, HFP, LC.

12 *Human Interest Facts on the Artists Receiving Harmon Awards*, ca. December 1929, HFP, LC.

13 Of the many articles that recorded Johnson's ascent in the American art world, one is of special note: "Is William H. Johnson, Negro Prize Winner, Blazing a New Trail?" *Art Digest* 4, no. 8 (15 January 1930): 13. These and other words of praise, however, were countered in critiques that questioned Johnson's relationship to European and Euro-American models. The most notable of these is William Auerbach-Levy, "Negro Painters Imitate Whites," *New York World*, 5 January 1930.

14 "Negro Artists," *New York Amsterdam News*, 8 January 1930, editorial page.

15 Gary A. Reynolds, "American Critics and the Harmon Foundation Exhibitions," in Reynolds and Wright, *Against the Odds*, pp. 107–19.

16 William H. Johnson, letter to Dr. George E. Haynes, 31 March 1930, HFP, LC.

17 For various accounts of this myth, see Adelyn D. Breeskin, *William H. Johnson, 1901–1970*, p. 14, and *Harlem Renaissance: Art of Black America* (New York: Harry N. Abrams, 1987), p. 182.

18 Lillian Cooper, interview with author, 7 November 1985.

19 Numerous Danish and Norwegian informants recall that Johnson "danced" as he painted. Sverre Engeset, a seventy-six-year-old inhabitant of Volda, Norway, remembered that Johnson would attract as many as ten to fifteen spectators while he painted the surrounding landscape. When it became too much of a sideshow, Johnson would pack up his painting equipment and leave in search of a less conspicuous site. Frantzen Sennett, a Danish elder from Kerteminde, Denmark, said that when Johnson painted, "he moved in a special way: graceful, self-assured, like an animal." Sverre Engeset, interview with author, Volda, Norway, 19 February 1985, and Frantzen Sennett, interview with author, Kerteminde, Denmark, 5 November 1984.

20 In a discussion about Johnson's Florence subjects, Alain Locke also recognized their capacity for subtle, social commentary. Referring to *Jacobia Hotel* and *Sonny* (another portrait of a black youth), Locke writes: "His ironic picture of the town hotel paints the decadence of the old régime, and his quizzical portrait study of *Sonny*, a Negro lad with all the dilemma of the South written in his features, is a thing to ponder over, if one believes that art has anything important to say about life." Alain Locke, "The American Negro as Artist," *The American Magazine of Art* 23 (September 1931): 217–18.

21 "Y.M.C.A. Officers Announce Exhibit by Negro Artist," *Florence Morning News*, 13 April 1930, p. 8; and "Artist Johnson," *Florence Morning News*, 15 April 1930, p. 4.

22 Locke's reputation as a key player in the "Negro" art world (ca. 1925–35) is confirmed in Arnold Rampersad's thorough, extensive biography of Langston Hughes, one of Locke's most celebrated associates. See *The Life of Langston Hughes*, Vol. I (New York: Oxford University Press).

23 Apparently, Hughes eventually reciprocated by sending Johnson a copy of his latest book, *Fine Clothes to the Jew*, which Johnson mentioned in a letter to Locke. William H. Johnson, letter to Alain Locke, 28 August 1930, ALLP, MSRC.

A Painter in the World: 1930–1938

1 Johanne-Marie Esbjerg, interview with author, Odense, Denmark, 28 April 1985, and Helga Ejsing, interview with author, Copenhagen, Denmark, 6 June 1985.

2 Holcha Krake/William H. Johnson prenuptial agreement, 28 May 1930, WHJP.

3 William H. Johnson, biographical sketch of Holcha Krake Johnson, ca. 1946, WHJP. According to Gregers Krake (a nephew of Holcha Krake), the Sørensen family name was changed to Krake around 1925, following a nationwide movement that encouraged families with the fairly common "-sen" names (Jensen, Olsen, Sørensen, etc.) to switch to more distinctive-sounding names. The very unusual name of "Krake" came from one of several characters found in old Scandinavian folktales. Gregers Krake, interview with author, Odense, Denmark, 26 April 1985.

4 Johanne-Marie Esbjerg, interview with author.

5 Sophie Breum, Kr. Kragh and V. Woll, *Kerteminde og Omegn* (Copenhagen: H. Aschehoug and Company, 1922). Information was also supplied by Kerteminde town officials: Erland Porsmose, Chief Curator, Kerteminde Museum, and the late Hans Hviid, Town Archivist, interviews with author, Kerteminde, Denmark, 1 May 1985.

6 Kerteminde, like many small, northern European towns, had its share of people who disapproved of nonwhites (like Johnson) moving there. Yet Danish racism, rather than being a social vice that discriminated *negatively* against people of color, was then more often the type that viewed blacks as exotic curiosities to be catered to in a ceremonious, overly inflated fashion. The blacks who loomed largest in Danish public consciousness in the early 1930s—classical singer Marian Anderson, jazz musician Louis Armstrong, and cabaret performer Josephine Baker—in many ways oriented the Danish public toward seeing *all* African-Americans as artistic creatures of sorts, to be ogled and fawned over. This Danish form of indulgent racism toward blacks was perhaps best described in a semi-autobiographical novel (set partially in Copenhagen) by Nella Larsen, an African-American novelist of the Harlem Renaissance era: *Quicksand and Passing*, ed. Deborah E. McDowell (1928; reprint, New Brunswick, N.J.: Rutgers University Press, 1986).

7 William H. Johnson, letter to Alain Locke, 28 August 1930, ALLP, MSRC.

8 William H. Johnson, letter to Alain Locke, 1 November 1930, ALLP, MSRC.

9 Niels Hansen, interview with author, Kerteminde, Denmark, 1 May 1985.

10 Niels Due, as quoted in the television documentary, *Manden der troede Jesus var sort*, written and produced by Per Mossin, for Danmarks Radio, 1983.

11 An-dre, "Stor Kunstner fra lille By," *Aarhus Stiftstidende* (Aarhus, Denmark), 26 November 1934, p. 2.

12 R.G., "Maleriudstilling," *Aarhus Stiftstidende* (Aarhus, Denmark), 30 November 1934, p. 3.

13 E.W., "Kunstudstillingen i Mageløs," *Fyns-Social Demokraten* (Odense, Denmark), 28 November 1930, p. 4.

14 K.P., "Neger-Kunstner i København," *Politiken* (Copenhagen, Denmark), 27 April 1933, p. 6.

15 For passing comments by Johnson on contemporary Danish art and artists, see Thomasius, "Chinos-Maleren i Kerteminde," *Fyns Stiftstidende* (Odense, Denmark), 9 July 1930, p. 3, and Dr. Rank, "Kunstnerisk Krydsning Kulmineret i København." *Ekstrabladet* (Copenhagen, Denmark), 18 April 1933, p. 6.

16 Frema, "Herr Johnson—han smiler," *Odense Avis* (Odense, Denmark), 5 December 1932, p. 7, and Dr. Rank, "Kunsterisk Krydsning," p. 6.

17 Helga Ejsing, interview with author, 6 June 1985.

18 Niels Juhl Andersen, as quoted in the television documentary, *Manden der troede Jesus var sort*.

19 Gunvor Jeppsen and Lars Tvedskov, interview with author, Kerteminde, Denmark, 29 April 1985; Frantzen Sennett, interview with author, 5 November 1984; and Helga Ejsing, interview with author..

20 Holcha's grandniece, Johanna Voll, after years of hearing about "Willie and Holcha" from her grandmother, Erna, and mother, Karen, summed up the couple's relationship in three words: "They were one." Johanna Voll, interview with author, Skodsborg,

Denmark, 5 October 1984. Also Gunvor Jeppsen and Lars Tvedskov, interview with author, and Niels Hansen, interview with author.

21 Bodil Bech, "En 'Indian-Negro' Maler i Kerteminde," *Tidens Kvinder* 9 (10 November 1931):10.

22 The book in question was probably one of two books on Kokoschka, published several years prior to the completion of Johnson's *Still Life*: Paul Westheim, *Oskar Kokoschka* (Berlin: Paul Cassirer, 1925) or Hans Heilmaier, *Oskar Kokoschka* (Paris: Editions G. Cres & Cie, 1929). Kokoschka's emphasis on intuiting the truth from a subject's head, facial expressions, and gestures correlates to Johnson's feeling that the exterior characteristics of a sitter, even his or her clothing, ere mirrors to the soul, containing "throbbing, vital human life."

23 Bodil Bech, "En 'Indian-Negro' Maler," p. 10.

24 Thomasius, "Chinos-Maleren," p. 3.

25 For a brief discussion of Johnson's blending into Tunisian society, see Thomasius, "Dagens Interview: Med Indianer—og Negerblod i Aarene. Chinos-Maleren William H. Johnson fortæller lidt om sin Afrikarejse, primitiv Kunst, m.m.," *Fyns Stiftstidende* (Odense, Denmark), 27 November, 1932, p. 3.

26 Miss D. "Fra Kerteminde til Nordafrika," *Aarhus Stiftstidende* (Aarhus, Denmark), 4 December, 1934, p. 4.

27 William H. Johnson, biographical sketch of Holcha Krake Johnson.

28 See, for example, Helen Engelstad, *Dobbeltvev i Norge* (Oslo: Gyldendal Norsk Forlag, 1958), and Irmtraud Reswick, *Traditional Textiles of Tunisia* (Los Angeles: Crafts and Folk Art Museum, 1985).

29 William H. Johnson, quoted by Ilya Bolotowsky, interview with Paul Cummings, 24 March 1968, Ilya Bolotowsky Papers, AAA.

30 In vain, Alain Locke tried to interest various collectors (including Edith Halpert of the Downtown Gallery) in Johnson's work, but with little success. In the following excerpt from a letter to Johnson, Locke explained the problem: "You probably think me very careless, but I have [not] had any definite news for you until recently. I have [been] doing all I could however . . . to present your work to the public and to try and sell some of it. At the present . . . there have been no results, except the one picture which the Harmon people already sold."

Similarly, Mary Beattie Brady of the Harmon Foundation was also at her wit's end concerning Johnson's work. "We have tried in a good many directions," she wrote to Locke, "but so far have not been successful. This is due, I think, first to the poor condition of the art market and second, because of the rather high prices we have had to carry on Mr. Johnson's work." Alain Locke, letter to William H. Johnson, 14 March 1931, ALLP, MSRC, and Mary Beattie Brady, letter to Alain Locke, 24 October 1932, HFP, LC.

31 When asked by an interviewer about the art and culture of Tunisia, Johnson replied, "There is no true painting tradition, only decorative arts. They have a century old ceramic industry. Their walls are covered entirely with splendid, painted tiles, but it is actually an altogether different form of color expression, and not painting." William H. Johnson, as quoted in Thomasius, "Dagens Interview," 1932, p. 3.

32 Ibid.

33 Wassily Kandinsky, "Reminiscences," trans. Hilla Rebay, in *Modern Artists on Art*, ed. Robert L. Herbert (Englewood Cliffs, N.J.: Prentice-Hall, Inc., 1964), p. 42.

34 "Conscious and exact imitation of nature does not create a work of art," said Nolde in his autobiographical notes, published in 1934. "A work becomes a work of art when one re-evaluates the values of nature and adds one's own spirituality." Emil Nolde, *Jahre der Kämpfe*, trans. Ernest Mundt, in *Theories of Modern Art*, ed. Herschel B. Chipp (Berkeley: University of California Press, 1968), pp. 146–51. Also see Stephen Eric Bronner, "Emil Nolde and the Politics of Rage," in *Passion and Rebellion: The Expressionist Heritage*, ed. Stephen Eric Bronner and Douglas Kellner (New York: Universe Books, 1983), p. 297. For Johnson's reference to Nolde, see: "Kunst og Gøgl," *Aarhusposten* (Aarhus, Denmark), 8 December 1934, p. 5.

35 DuBois's famous quote from the 1903 classic, *The Souls of Black Folk*, that the Negro American "ever feels his twoness—an American, a Negro; two souls, two thoughts, two unreconciled strivings; two warring ideals in one dark body, whose dogged strength alone keeps it from being torn asunder," would have at least been familiar, if not totally known, to Johnson, given his acquaintance with several members of the New Negro Renaissance movement in New York. W. E. B. DuBois, *The Souls of Black Folk* (1903; reprint, New York: Avon Books, 1965), p. 215.

36 Thomasius "Dagens Interview," p. 3.

37 Though Johnson's ideological allegiance with his Nordic brethren was similar to an orphan's attachment to an adoptive family, his artistic validation of the northern European cultural experience nevertheless illustrates a philosophical stance that was confirmed time and again among various Scandinavian and German aestheticians and artists in the years roughly between 1890 and 1917. Prompted in part by concurrent efforts at legislating class reforms and rehabilitating the national identities, many Scandinavian artists (especially toward the end of the nineteenth century) *Nordicized* their art by highlighting typical Scandinavian subject matter and regional themes. Kirk Varnedoe's "Nationalism, Internationalism and the Progress of Scandinavian Art," in the exhibition catalogue *Northern Lights: Realism and Symbolism in Scandinavian Painting, 1890–1910* (Brooklyn: The Brooklyn Museum, 1982), pp. 13–32, addresses the at times contradictory, at other times complementary, position of regionalism and internationalism in Scandinavia.

38 Dr. Rank, "Kunstnerisk, Krydsning," p. 6.

39 "My father was black and my mother is Indian," Johnson was fond of telling reporters, "and both of these people have in them an artistic tendency which clearly has culminated in me." William H. Johnson, quoted in Thomasius, "Chinos-Maleren," p. 3. The etymology of the racial descriptive *Chinos* has its roots, according to the Oxford English Dictionary, in the American-Spanish terminology for a "toasted" (or beige-colored) cotton twill cloth. *Chinos* as a racial term, according to historian Jack Forbes in *Black Africans and Native Americans: Color, Race and Caste in the Evolution of Red-Black Peoples* (New York: B. Blackwell, 1988), goes back to the colonial period in the Americas.

40 C.W.S., "Notes on Interview with William H. Johnson and Mrs. Johnson," unpublished manuscript, 24 March 1939, HFP, LC.

41 William H. Johnson, quoted in a memo from Evelyn S. Brown to Mary Beattie Brady, 17 January 1933, HFP, LC.

42 For a discussion of Johnson's relationship with the Harmon Foundation, see Richard J. Powell, "William H. Johnson and the Harmon Foundation: A Study in Afro-American Art Patronage," in *Against the Odds: African-American Artists and the Harmon Foundation*, ed. Gary A. Reynolds and Beryl J. Wright (Newark: The Newark Museum, 1989), pp. 89–97.

43 R.G., "Maleriudstilling," *Aarhus Stiftstidende* (Aarhus, Denmark), 30 November 1934, p. 3.

44 Kay P., "Kunstudstilling," *Demokraten* (Aarhus, Denmark), 30 November 1934, p. 2.

45 Helge Nilausen, interview with author, Copenhagen, 29 May 1985.

46 Herr Nat-og-Dag, "Ferniserings-Parade," *Dagens Nyheder* (Copenhagen, Denmark), 20 January 1935, p. 9.

47 "Neger og hvit hos Blomqvist: Utstillinger av Olaf Holwech og W. H. Johnson," *Arbeiderbladet* (Oslo, Norway), 18 March 1935, p. 4, and Um, "Sterke kontraster hos Blomqvist: Norsk natur og afrikanske urskoger," *Morgenbladet* (Oslo, Norway), 19 March 1935, p. 2.

48 "En neger-indiansk maler hos Blomqvist. William H. Johnson utstiller hot kunst," *Tidens Tegn* (Oslo, Norway), 19 March 1935, p. 6.

49 Leif Østby, "Olaf Holwech og W. H. Johnson hos Blomqvist," *Aftenposten* (Oslo, Norway), 23 March 1935, p. 3.

50 Pola Gauguin, "Blomqvist kunstutstilling," *Dagbladet* (Oslo, Norway), 25 March 1935, p. 4.

51 I am indebted to Jostein Nerbøvik, professor of Norwegian history at the Møre og Romsdal Distrikthøjskole in Volda, Norway, for helping me to identify these two paintings by Johnson.

52 Referring to both Rolf Stenerson and Edvard Munch, Johnson wrote: "One [of] the greatest collectors of Edvard Munch works did buy two of my paintings: a portrait and a landscape. He is to have a great museum of his collection in Oslo. I have . . . made [the] acquaintance of this great painter, as well as so few can say." William H. Johnson, letter to Mary Beattie Brady, 24 September 1937, HFP, LC.

53 Holcha Krake, quoted in Rita, "Eksotisk maler utstiller i Trondheim," *Nidaros* (Trondheim, Norway), 15 September 1937, p. 2.

54 "Neger og hvit hos Blomqvist," p. 4.

55 Turid Riste, interview with author, Volda, Norway, 21 February 1985.

56 Jostein Nerbøvik, interview with author, Volda, Norway, 18–24 February 1985.

57 During my ten-month stay in Scandinavia, various members of the Tjensvoll family—Sigrid and Torbjørg Bondo in Odense, Denmark; Liv Drabløs in Volda, Norway; Bothild Hagstrøm in Farsta, Sweden; and Eivind Tjensvoll in Nesbru, Norway—shared countless stories about William and Holcha's two-year residency in Volda. I am indebted to all of them for helping me reconstruct a vivid picture of the Johnsons' life while living there.

58 W.K., "Langframand kunstnar held utstilling i Volda," *Sunnmørsposten* (Aalesund, Norway), 17 December 1935, p. 2.

59 Svanhild Øvrelid, interview with author, Volda, Norway, 19 February 1985.

60 For a fascinating study of northern European painters and their preoccupation with a mythic, symbol-ridden landscape, see Roald Nasgaard, *The Mystic North: Symbolist Landscape Painting in Northern Europe and North America, 1890–1940* (Toronto: University of Toronto Press, in association with the Art Gallery of Ontario, 1984).

61 Kay P., "Kunstudstilling," p. 2.

62 Ned, "Trio på Konsthallen," (newspaper, Gävle, Sweden), ca. December 1937.

63   Bothild Hagstrøm, interview with author, Farsta, Sweden, 25 February 1985.

64   Described by a reviewer from Volda as "the attractive little girl on Engeset [Lane], with the big, questioning eyes," Johnson's sitter was Liv Baarstad, a childhood friend of the Tjensvoll children. "I was not planning to paint any portraits," Johnson said, "but this little girl was so attractive that I knew I had no other choice." "Mälaren W. H. Johnson," *Møre* (Volda, Norway), 9 July 1936, p. 3. Sigrid and Torbjørg Bondo, interview with author, Odense, Denmark, 7 November 1984.

65   N.B., "Långväga Konstnärbesök," *Vastmanslands Folkblad* (Västerås, Sweden), 8 November 1937.

66   Sigrid and Torbjørg Bondo, interview with author, 7 November 1984.

67   Inngunn Steinnes, interview with author, Volda, Norway, 18 February 1985.

68   Nils Valnes, interview with author, Volda, Norway, 17 February 1985.

69   Eivind Tjensvoll, interview with author, Nesbru, Norway, 10 February 1985.

70   Holcha Krake Johnson, letter to the Tjensvoll family and friends, 22 August 1937, trans. by Bothild Hagstrøm, courtesy of Sigrid and Torbjørg Bondo, Odense, Denmark.

71   Y.B., "Konstkrönika," *Dagens Nyheter* (Stockholm, Sweden), 25 November 1937, p. 4.

72   Ernst Ludwig Kirchner, quoted in Donald E. Gordon, *Ernst Ludwig Kirchner* (Cambridge: Harvard University Press, 1968), p. 110.

73   V-e., "En Konstnärstrio på Konsthallen," *Arbetarbladet* (Gävle, Sweden), 14 December 1937, p. 5.

74   See Murre., "Hvor nordlandssommeren lyser en i møte," *Dagsposten* (Trondheim, Norway), 14 September 1937, p. 2.

75   William H. Johnson, letter to Mary Beattie Brady, 24 September 1937, HFP, LC.

76   In a letter written less than a year later, Johnson again prodded the Harmon Foundation on its seemingly ambivalent perceptions of his work. "Perhaps you are not interested in my exhibition," Johnson rhetorically suggested, "because it is not *negroid* enough—*colored*" (emphasis added). William H. Johnson, letter to Mary Beattie Brady, 25 February 1938, HFP, LC.

77   N.B., "Långväga Konstnärbesök."

78   "Färgrik vernissage," *Nya Dagligt Allehanda* (Stockholm, Sweden), 19 November 1937, p. 9.

79   For a recounting of Christoph Voll's professional demise in Nazi-era Germany, see Stephanie Barron, *German Expressionist Sculpture* (Los Angeles: Los Angeles County Museum of Art, 1983), pp. 200–05. Also see the exhibition catalogue *Entartete Kunst* (Berlin: Verlag für Kultur und Wirtschaftswerburg/Content: Fritz Kaiser, Munich, 1937), pp. 11, 19.

80   William H. Johnson, letter to Mary Beattie Brady, 22 August 1938, HFP, LC.

81   H-dy., "W. H. Johnson i Kunst Udstillingsbygningen," *Fyns Tidende* (Odense, Denmark), 23 October 1938, p. 14.

82   Egil., "Johnson vender hjem–men kun for en Visit," *Fyns Stiftstidende* (Odense, Denmark), 21 October 1938, p. 8.

Homecoming: 1938–1946

1   Helen Harriton, letter to Mary Beattie Brady, 30 September 1956, HFP, LC.

2   Evelyn S. Brown, interview with Adelyn D. Breeskin, ca. 1970, WHJP, SIA.

3   William H. Johnson, letter to Mary Beattie Brady, ca. 6 April 1939, HFP, LC.

4   See File of the Works Progress Administration/Federal Art Project Employment Records, Record Group 69, General Services Administration Files, National Archives, Washington, D.C.

5   See "Joins Staff: William H. Johnson Put On Art Center Staff," *New York Amsterdam News*, 10 June 1939, p. 20, and James H. Baker, Jr., "Art Comes to the People of Harlem," *The Crisis* 46 (March 1939): 78–80.

6   That Johnson was "reserved," "quiet," and "not the easiest person to get along with," was repeatedly confirmed in several interviews with artists of the Harlem arts community, circa 1939–45. Jacob Lawrence, telephone interview with author, Chicago, Illinois, 20 June 1984; Romare Bearden, telephone interview with author, Chicago, Illinois, 23 June 1984; and Elton Fax, telephone interview with author, Washington, D.C., 15 August 1986.

7   James Johnson Sweeney, ed., *African Negro Art* (1935; reprint, New York: Arno Press, 1969).

8   For a fascinating study of this time-honored black gesture, both in Africa and the New World, see Robert Farris Thompson and Joseph Cornet, *The Four Moments of the Sun: Kongo Art in Two Worlds* (Washington, D.C.: The National Gallery of Art, 1981), p. 171.

9   Picasso was undoubtedly the most visible artist in New York during Johnson's first year back in the United States. Marie Harriman, Perls, Bignou and Valentine galleries all showed Picasso's art in exhibitions between January and June of 1939. These smaller shows were immediately followed by Picasso's featured role in the "Art of Our Times" exhibition in the Museum of Modern Art's new building and, later that year, in a major retrospective also at MOMA.

10   On a U.S. passport application and U.S. consular affidavit (both dated 5 January 1935), Johnson states that his professional name is *Mahlinda*. Application and affidavit, courtesy of the U.S. State Department, Washington, D.C. Investigations into an Arabic and/or Berber source for this unusual sounding name (based on the possibility that Johnson could have taken the name during his three-month stay in Tunisia) have proved fruitless. *Ma'lemba*, which is documented as being a common male personal name among the Gullah-speaking blacks of coastal South Carolina and Georgia (not too far afield from Florence, South Carolina, Johnson's hometown), might be a more likely source. See Lorenzo Dow Turner, *Africanisms in the Gullah Dialect* (1949; reprint, Ann Arbor: University of Michigan Press, 1974), p. 128.

11   "Ragcutters Find Harlem 'Heaven,'" *New York Amsterdam News*, 8 April 1939, p. 20.

12   This quote, and another passage that depicts Harlemites on a subway platform as "so still and silent that they clash with the crowd in their very immobility; standing noisy in their very silence," perfectly describe Johnson's street fashion paintings. Ralph Ellison, *Invisible Man* (New York: Random House, 1952), pp. 332–35.

13   Locke's futile efforts to sell Johnson's works, coupled with Johnson's overall dissatisfaction with the arrangement, apparently led to the complete dissolution of their business *and* personal relationship. For Locke's complete reversal on Johnson and his art,

see: "Advance on the Art Front," *Opportunity* 17 (May 1939): 132–36.

14 Fritzi Weisenborn, "Pier Exhibit Poses Some Questions," *Chicago Sunday Times*, 21 July 1940, sec. M, 13.

15 Alain Locke, Foreword, *Contemporary Negro Art* (Baltimore: The Baltimore Museum of Art, 1939).

16 Alain Locke, "Advance on the Art Front," pp. 133–36.

17 "Long John," sung by "Lightning" and a group of black convicts at Darlington State Prison Farm, Sandy Point, Texas, 1934. Recorded by John A. and Alan Lomax, *Afro-American Spirituals, Work Songs and Ballads*, Library of Congress Recording, AFS L3.

18 William and Holcha were probably introduced to Graham sometime around 1940 by collector, gallery owner, publisher, and author Alma Reed. The Alma Reed Galleries (formerly known as the Delphic Studios) published Graham's *System and Dialectics of Art* in 1937 and gave Johnson his first solo exhibition in New York in May 1941. Undoubtedly, the Johnsons initially met Graham not later than June 1941, since Holcha mentioned to a friend around that same time that she and William had just visited Graham's place. Holcha Krake Johnson, postcard to Onya La Tour, 24 June 1941, Onya La Tour Papers, AAA.

19 John D. Graham, *System and Dialectics of Art* (New York: Delphic Studios, 1937) pp. 84–85, 132–37.

20 William H. Johnson, Rosenwald Fellowship Application, 6 January 1941, HFP, LC.

21 The diary of collector/arts administrator Onya La Tour contains many enlightening observations on William and Holcha Johnson and their colorful circle of Greenwich Village friends. Onya La Tour Papers, AAA. Also see Ellen W. Lee, "The Onya La Tour Collection," in *Recent Accessions, 1966–1972* (Indianapolis: Indianapolis Museum of Art, 1972), p. 38.

22 For a discussion about African sensibilities in black Atlantic textile arts, see Robert Farris Thompson, *Flash of the Spirit: African and Afro-American Art and Philosophy* (New York: Random House, 1983), p. 209.

23 Carlyle Burrows, "Notes and Comments on Events in Art: Negro Life," *New York Herald Tribune*, 11 May 1941, sec. 6, 5.

24 Howard Devree, "A Reviewer's Notebook: Brief Comments on Some of the Recently Opened Shows in the Galleries," *New York Times*, 11 May 1941, sec. 8, 1.

25 Arguing on behalf of a more visible black presence on the frontlines of the war, one journalist wrote in 1942 that while it is "perfectly true that U.S. Negroes have never had a square deal from the U.S. majority, . . . they know their lot would be far worse under the racial fanatics of the Axis. . . . Now, when their country needs them," he optimistically continues, "they are glad to work and fight and die alongside their white fellow citizens." "Negroes at War," *Life* 12 (15 June 1942): 89. Taking a more pessimistic view of black involvement in the war effort is Charles Williams, "Harlem at War," *The Nation* 156 (16 January 1943): 86–88. Also see "Black Division," *Time* 38 (29 December 1941): 49.

26 Robert Beverly Hale, "The Passing Shows," *Art News* 42 (1–14 May 1943): 22.

27 Robert Lockwood, Jr., "Little Boy Blue," quoted in *The Blues Line: A Collection of Blues Lyrics*, ed. Eric Sackheim (New York: Grossman Publishers, 1969), p. 425.

28 Howard Devree, "A Reviewer's Notebook: Brief Comments on Some of the Recently Opened Shows in the Galleries," *New York Times*, 2 May 1943, sec. 2, p. 8.

29 Emily Genauer, "Latest Johnson Works Placed on Exhibition," *New York World-Telegram*, 1 May 1943, p. 9.

30 On both sales, see Adelyn D. Breeskin, exhibition research notes, WHJP, SIA.

31 The author is grateful to John Hutton, Registrar at the Studio Museum in Harlem, for bringing this painting and its owner to light.

32 "Harlem Disorder Brings Quick Action by City and Army," *New York Times*, 2 August 1943, pp. 1,16. Also see the chapter entitled "Harlem Explodes," Jervis Anderson, *This Was Harlem* (New York: Farrar, Strauss and Giroux, 1982), pp. 295–298.

33 James A. Porter, *Modern Negro Art* (1943; reprint, New York: Arno Press, 1969), pp. 124–25.

34 Aaron Douglas, letter to Langston Hughes, 21 December 1925, Langston Hughes Papers, James Weldon Johnson Memorial Collection of Negro Arts and Letters, Beinecke Rare Book and Manuscript Library, Yale University, New Haven, Connecticut; Archibald J. Motley, Jr., quoted from a Guggenheim Fellowship application form, 1929, Archibald J. Motley, Jr. Papers, AAA; William H. Johnson, quoted in Thomasius, "Dagens Interview," p. 3; Ralph Ellison, "Modern Negro Art," *Tomorrow* 4 (November 1944): 92–93.

35 William H. Johnson, postcard to Thora and Nanna Krake, 18 June 1945, Courtesy of Gregers Krake, Odense, Denmark.

36 Quotations and recollections by Helen Harriton are from the following sources: letter to Nanna Krake, 31 October 1947, Courtesy of Gregers Krake, Odense, Denmark; letter to Mary Beattie Brady, 30 September 1956, HFP, LC; and interview with Adelyn D. Breeskin, ca. 1970, WHJP, SIA.

37 See James Weldon Johnson and J. Rosamond Johnson, eds., *The Books of American Negro Spirituals*, Book II (New York: Da Capo Press, Inc., 1985), pp. 144–46.

38 Ibid., Book I, pp. 62–63.

39 Historian Lawrence Levine discusses this process of familialization as seen in slave-era sermons, spirituals, and other documented sources:

> The heroes of the Scriptures—"Sister Mary," "Brudder Jonah," "Brudder Moses," "Brudder Daniel"—were greeted with . . . intimacy and immediacy. . . . The world described by the slave songs was a black world in which no reference was ever made to any white contemporaries. The slave's positive reference group was composed entirely of his own peers: his mother, father, sister, brother, uncles, aunts, preachers, fellow "sinners" and "mourners" of whom he sang endlessly, to whom he sent messages via the dying, and with whom he was reunited joyfully in the next world.

Lawrence Levine, *Black Culture and Black Consciousness* (Oxford: Oxford University Press, 1977), p. 37. The author also greatly benefited from discussions with Dr. Levine in Bellagio, Italy, 12–14 June 1990.

40 David C. Driskell, quoted in the television documentary, *Manden der troede Jesus var sort*, written and produced by Per Mossin, for Danmarks Radio, 1983.

41 Johnson and Johnson, *The Books of American Negro Spirituals*, Book I, p. 59.

42 Describing the ladder imagery in this song as "the *ultimate* stage of Afro-American spirituality," Joseph Brown connects the enigmatic, droning stanzas of "We Am Clim'in Jacob's Ladder" with a sense of heavenly entitlement:

> The singer-prophet of ["We Am Clim'in' Jacob's Ladder"] is comfortable with the voice of God and is allowed to do more

than see the angels; the singer is allowed—through the strength of the self-constructed image-assertion—to become one of God's angels. . . . Angels climb that particular ladder in the Bible. Afro-Americans climb that same ladder in their songs. . . . The song is the message: "no one who is called upon to deliver a message from God need feel alone. I know, I had a message and a confirmation and a trip to heaven to prove what I say. You go, and I'll go with you.

Joseph A. Brown, S.J., "Voices Stirring the Waters: Reflections on the Religious Impulse of Afro-American Art" (M.A. thesis, Yale University, 1983), p. 96. Conversations with Dr. Brown over the last ten years have greatly informed the author's interpretations of Johnson's religious paintings.

43 Recollections by James Johnson are from an interview with author, Florence, South Carolina, 9 November 1985.

44 Gospel music's growth during the Depression years and throughout the 1940s was no doubt a by-product of this period's economic uncertainty for blacks. In Pearl Williams-Jones's essay on Gospel music luminary Roberta Martin, she makes special note of "the concept of Jesus giving satisfaction" as a key message from the Gospel songwriters and singers. Pearl Williams-Jones, "Roberta Martin: Spirit of an Era," in *Roberta Martin and the Roberta Martin Singers: The Legacy and the Music* (Washington, D.C.: Smithsonian Institution, 1982), p. 16. The Golden Gate Quartet's "The Sun Didn't Shine" (recorded in 1941) can be heard on the anthology album, *The Gospel Sound*, vol. 1 (Columbia G31086).

45 Giving his Danish in-laws the latest on his life and work without Holcha, Johnson wrote; "I am still at my ship yard, painting, doing my own work—all good art I'm doing now, thanks to my Radio. In my free time I have it going [from] the time I get into bed—[to] . . . when I am getting up. " William H. Johnson, letter to Thora and Nanna Krake, 15 November 1945, Courtesy of Gregers Krake, Odense, Denmark.

46 Howard Devree, "Among the New Exhibitions," *New York Times*, 17 December 1944, sec. 2, p. 4.

47 A.Z. Kruse, "At the Art Galleries: Marquié Gallery," *Brooklyn Eagle Sun*, 17 December 1944, 26.

48 Else Hvistendahl, "Negerkunstneren Johnson som kjenner Norge som få nordmenn har reist og malt overalt i landet," *Nordisk Tidende* (Brooklyn, New York), 25 January 1945.

49 See Alain Locke, "Up Till Now," in *The Negro Artist Comes of Age: A National Survey of Contemporary American Artists* (Albany: Albany Institute of History and Art, 1945).

50 Recounting his progress during this period, Johnson wrote:
I [have] now completed it all from my people's phite [sic] early 1800 to date. Spirituals, poor workers, sharecroppers, city lives, jitter bugs, dancers, war scenes, Red Cross, religious themes, family's [sic] down south—portraits of all I could paint [of] history's Great men, women—fighter[s] for Freedom. I . . . depicted the character[s] who accomplished great deeds for the Freedom phite [sic]—up to the United Nations. Now all this completed—all!
William H. Johnson, letter to Thora and Nanna Krake, 28 September 1946, Courtesy of Gregers Krake, Odense, Denmark.

51 Johnson's painting is based on a photograph of Chiang Kai-shek, Roosevelt, and Churchill that appeared in newspapers and magazines soon after their widely reported conference in Cairo. John-

son's clipping file contained a copy of this photograph, which was cut out of the magazine article, "Fighting Friends in Teheran," *Life* 15 (20 December 1943): 25, 32.

52 Helen Harriton, letter to Mary Beattie Brady, 30 September 1956, HFP, LC.

53 Nora Holt, "Primitives on Exhibit," *New York Amsterdam News*, 9 March 1946, p. 16.

54 William H. Johnson, letter to Emily Genauer, ca. February 1946, Emily Genauer Papers, AAA.

55 William H. Johnson, letter to Thora and Nanna Krake, 26 March 1946, Courtesy of Gregers Krake, Odense, Denmark.

56 Johnson wrote: "I do want to get all my [things] in your office—I am taking all my pictures back with me to Denmark"; letter to Evelyn Brown, ca. April 1946, HFP, LC. Ten years later, Mary Beattie Brady recounted the circumstances of Johnson's 1946 request in a letter to an associate: "When Johnson went back to Europe the last time he was pretty mad at everybody and everything in the United States, and came and asked for work that he had formerly given us. . . . We bore him no ill-will, but were sorry that he was in such an antagonistic state of mind." Mary Beattie Brady, letter to Claude A. Barnett, 28 June 1956, CABP, CHS.

57 Langston Hughes, letter to William H. Johnson, 26 September 1946, Scrapbook, WHJP.

58 Passport application, 26 August 1946. Office of Program Support/Passport Services, Department of State, Washington, D.C.

59 Helen Harriton, letter to Nanna Krake, 31 October 1947, Courtesy of Gregers Krake, Odense, Denmark.

60 William H. Johnson, letter to Thora and Nanna Krake, 28 September 1946, Courtesy of Gregers Krake, Odense, Denmark.

61 Helen Harriton, letter to Mary Beattie Brady, 30 September 1956, HFP, LC.

Professional and Personal Decline: 1946–1947

1 Johnson described (in English and bits of broken Danish) the process of putting this painting together in a letter to Thora and Nanna Krake:
From all my studies in Kerteminde I thought [of] my *Remembrance* of Kerteminde. I lay the studies I had on the floor: little Mor in midt, Mayor Hansen, fisker Jon Due, fisker Nielsen, Jorgen, . . . and Fru Old Winters; there are 8 portraits against a cerulean blue background with Kerteminde's landmarks.
William H. Johnson, letter to Thora and Nanna Krake, 15 November 1945, Courtesy of Gregers Krake, Odense, Denmark. For a larger discussion about this painting, see Richard J. Powell, "William H. Johnson's *Minde Kerteminde*," *Siksi: The Nordic Art Review* 1 (1986): 17–23.

2 Johanna Voll, interview with author, 5 October 1984; and Onni Fahrenholtz, interview with author, Aarhus, Denmark, 16 June 1985.

3 Johanna Voll, ibid.

4 Johanne-Marie Esbjerg, interview with author, 28 April 1985.

5 Ibid.

6 Ibid.

7 Fast, "William Johnson—En amerikansk Maler," *Land og Folk* (Copenhagen, Denmark), 12 March 1947, p. 7. A second review did, in fact, appear, but in an Odense newspaper: J.M.E., "De

farvedes Problem i kunstnerisk Belysning," *Fyns Tidende* (Odense, Denmark), 17 April 1947.

8 Botolf Folkestad, interview with author, Volda, Norway, 20 February 1985.

9 Torbjørg Bondo, interview with author, 7 November 1984.

10 The author's conversations with Elka Spoerri, curator of the Adolf Wölfli Collection at the Bern Kunstmuseum (in Bern, Switzerland, on 15 January 1985) and James L. Foy, M.D., of Georgetown University (in Washington, D.C., on 18 August 1985) were instrumental in arriving at these conclusions. Also see "Dagens Interview," p. 3.

11 Nanna Krake, letter to Helen Harriton, 2 July 1950, HFP, LC.

12 Records from the American Embassy, Oslo, Norway, Record Group 84, Washington National Record Center, Suitland, Maryland.

13 See Verne Dyson, *The History of Central Islip* (Brentwood, N.Y.: The Brentwood Village Press, 1954), p. 20. Also see Fred B. Charatan, "A Century of Care," *Central Islip Psychiatric Center/Media* 4 (Winter 1989): 7. The author is also indebted to James E. Ramseur, Executive Director of the Central Islip Psychiatric Center, and Frank Nichols, Media Chairman, for providing much information about the history of the hospital.

14 Nanna Krake, letter to Helen Harriton, 15 December 1947, Courtesy of Gregers Krake, Odense, Denmark; Helen Harriton, letter to Nanna Krake, 19 June 1950, Courtesy of Gregers Krake.

Resurrection: 1955–The Present

1 Helen Harriton, letter to Nanna Krake, 16 February 1955, HFP, LC.

2 In a letter of 28 June 1956 to Claude A. Barnett, the director of the Associated Negro Press, Mary Beattie Brady discusses the circumstances surrounding the Harmon Foundation's acceptance of Johnson's estate. CABP, CHS.

3 Helen Harriton, letter to Nanna Krake, 16 February 1955, HFP, LC.

4 Mary Beattie Brady, letter to Claude A. Barnett, 28 June 1956, CABP, CHS.

5 Evelyn S. Brown, letter to David W. Scott, 16 June 1966, NMAA.

6 David W. Scott, letter to Mary Beattie Brady, 16 September 1966, NMAA.

7 Adelyn D. Breeskin, quoted in the television documentary, *Manden der troede Jesus var sort*, written and produced by Per Mossin, for Danmarks Radio, 1983.

8 See Lillian Cooper, interview with author, 7 November 1985. According to Cooper, a cousin of hers who resided in New York, would often visit William in his early years at Central Islip.

9 Romare Bearden, letter to Adelyn D. Breeskin, 11 March 1971, WHJP, SIA. See also Romare Bearden, telephone interview with author, 23 June 1984.

10 Lillian Cooper, quoted in Jeannette Smyth, "Tribute to an Artist," *The Washington Post*, 5 November 1971. See also Lillian Cooper, interview with author, 8 November 1985.

11 Ibid.

12 Joshua C. Taylor, Foreword, in Adelyn D. Breeskin, *William H. Johnson, 1901–1970* (Washington, D.C.: Smithsonian Institution, 1972), p. 7.

Chronology

1901 William Henry Johnson born in Florence, South Carolina, on 18 March.

1907–17 Attends the Wilson School for Negroes. Brothers Lacy and James and sisters Lucy and Lillian born. Holds odd jobs at the Florence Railroad Station and YMCA.

1918 Moves to New York City with the assistance of uncle, Willie Smoot. Lives with uncle and aunt at 146 West 128th Street.

1918–26 Works in New York as a hotel porter, short-order cook, and stevedore.

1921 Is admitted in October to the School of the National Academy of Design in the Preparatory Class under Charles L. Hinton; promoted to the Antiques-on-Probation class in December.

1922 Is promoted to the Antiques-in-Full class in January and the Life-in-Probation class in March. Awarded an Honorable Mention for work in the Antiques School (May).

Begins Life-in-Probation class with George Willoughby Maynard (September) and is promoted to Maynard's Life-in-Full class in December.

1923 Continues Life-in-Full studies with Charles Curran. Is Awarded second prize for work in the Advanced Still Life class (May).

1923–26 Beginning in September (and for the remainder of tenure at the School of the National Academy of Design), continues Life-in-Full studies with Charles Webster Hawthorne.

1924 Receives the Cannon Prize for work in Painting from the Nude, as well as an Honorable Mention for work in the Life School (April).

1924–26 Spends the next three summers at Charles Webster Hawthorne's Cape Cod School of Art in Provincetown, Massachusetts.

1925 Is awarded the Hallgarten Prize for work in the Painting School, as well as a School Prize for Advanced Still Life painting (April).

Has work in "Exhibition of Paintings" at the Provincetown Art Association (August–September).

Is awarded a full scholarship for the 1925–26 school year (September).

1926 Receives another Cannon Prize for work in Painting from the Nude, as well as a School Prize for work in the Still Life class (May).

After failing to win the coveted Pulitzer Traveling Scholarship, receives about one thousand dollars from Charles W. Hawthorne to help finance a year of independent study abroad.

Works briefly in the New York studio of painter George B. Luks (ca. August–October).

Leaves for Paris around November. Lives and works in Montparnasse, at 86, rue Notre-Dame-des-Champs.

1927 Visits painter Henry Ossawa Tanner in Trépied, Pas de Calais, France.

Rents a studio for the summer in Moret-sur-Loing, south of Paris, and starts painting landscapes.

Returns to Paris in the fall and holds first solo exhibition at the Students and Artists Club on the Boulevard Raspail (November).

1928 Travels to the south of France and settles in Cagnes-sur-Mer (January).

1928–29 Has solo exhibition at Galerie Alban, Nice, France.

1929 While living in Cagnes-sur-Mer, meets Danish weaver Holcha Krake. Joins Holcha, her sister Erna, and Erna's husband, the German sculptor Christoph Voll, on a month-long tour of Corsica (May). For the entire summer, continues to travel with Holcha Krake and the Volls throughout Europe.

Returns to New York in November and rents a loft at 311 West 120th Street. Meets with George Luks, who encourages him to apply for the 1929 Harmon Foundation Award for Distinguished Achievements Among Negroes in the Fine Arts.

1930 Is awarded the Harmon Foundation's Gold Medal.

Is included in "Exhibit of Fine Arts by American Negro Artists" at the International House, New York (January).

Has solo exhibition ("Exhibition of Paintings by William H. Johnson") at the Peter White Public Library, Marquette, Michigan (March).

Returns to Florence, South Carolina (March). While there, paints several landscapes, portraits, and has a one-day exhibition at the Florence YMCA (15 April).

En route to New York, stops briefly in Washington, D.C., and visits Alain Locke.

Leaves the United States in May. Travels to Denmark to marry Holcha Krake. Settles with wife in Kerteminde, Denmark (on the island of Funen).

Has a two-person exhibition (with Holcha) at the Tornøes Hotel, Kerteminde (July).

Is included in a four-person exhibition at Weimanns Udstillingslokaler, Odense, Denmark (November).

1930–37 Is included in numerous Harmon Foundation-sponsored exhibitions of works by Negro artists, which travel throughout the United States.

1931 Has work in "Traveling Art Exhibit of Paintings by Negro Artists," in Capetown, South Africa (April–May).

Has exhibition (with Holcha) at Mageløs, Odense (November).

1932 Travels with Holcha to Tunisia, North Africa, via Hamburg, Amsterdam, Cologne, Paris, and Marseille. During the couple's three-month stay in Tunisia (ca. April, May, and June), they visit several cities, including Nabeul (where they study ceramics) and Kairouan (where Johnson paints many watercolors).

Return to Kerteminde, Denmark, via Martigues and Paris (where they visit Henry Ossawa Tanner).

Participates (with Holcha) in a two-person exhibition at the local library, Kerteminde (ca. October).

Has two-person exhibition (with Holcha) at Albanitorv 9, Odense (November–December).

1933 Has exhibition (with weavings and ceramics by Holcha) at the Christian Larsen Gallery, Copenhagen, Denmark (April).

Father, Henry Johnson, dies (ca. October/November).

Has two-person exhibition (with Holcha) at Vestergade 82, Odense (November–December).

1934 Bicycles across western Denmark (Jutland), camping along the way. Has two-person exhibition in Aarhus, Denmark (November–December).

1935 Travels to Copenhagen (January) where he visits Paul Robeson and African art collector Carl Kjersmeier.

Leaves for Oslo, Norway, in late January. While in Oslo, paints and makes woodcuts of the city, and holds a two-person exhibition (with Norwegian painter Olaf Holwech) at Blomqvist (March). Through art critic Pola Gauguin and local collector Rolf E. Stenersen, meets Norwegian painter Edvard Munch.

Spends the summer painting and sightseeing in Norway's Gudbrandsdal region.

By September, settles with Holcha in the western fjord town of Volda, where they reside with friends for the next two years.

Has two-person exhibition (with Holcha) at Uppheim, Volda, Norway (December).

1936 Is included in "Exhibition of Fine Art Productions by American Negroes" for the Hall of Negro Life of the Texas Centennial, Dallas, Texas (June–November).

Has two-person exhibition (with Holcha) in Aalesund, Norway (December).

1937 Has two-person exhibition (with Holcha) in Volda (May).

In June, travels with Holcha by coastal steamer from Aalesund to Tromsø, where they have an exhibition at the Handicrafts Society. While on the steamer, they meet their future New York friends and patrons, Helen and David Harriton. Visits Lofoten Islands for the rest of the summer to paint the landscape under the midnight sun.

Has solo exhibition at the Trondheim Art Society (September). Travels to Sweden, where two-person exhibitions (with Holcha) are held in November in Västerås and in Stockholm. With Holcha and Swedish artist/friend Allan Ebeling, has three-person exhibition in Gävle, Sweden (December).

1937–38 Is included in a three-person traveling exhibition (with painters Palmer Hayden and Malvin Gray Johnson), organized by the American Federation of Arts.

1938 Returns to Norway in January and stays in Oslo for the next several months. In the spring, travels to the Hardangerfjord region to paint the blossoming apple and cherry orchards.

Returns to Kerteminde in the summer and has last two-person exhibition (with Holcha) before moving to the United States (October).

Arrives in New York on Thanksgiving Day, met by Helen and David Harriton. After staying with the Harritons for several weeks, finds an apartment at 27 West 15th Street.

1939   Is included in "Exhibition of Sculpture and Painting" at the Labor Club, New York (February–March).

"Exhibition: Watercolors, Woodcuts (Colored) from Travels in Europe and Africa by William H. Johnson and Tapestries and Ceramics by Holcha Krake" is held at the Artists' Gallery, New York (February).

Is assigned to the WPA/FAP, New York, to teach painting at the Harlem Community Arts Center (May).

Has work in the Harlem Artists Guild Annual Exhibition at the Harlem Community Arts Center (June).

Brother-in-law, German sculptor Christoph Voll, dies, 16 June. Sister-in-law and her daughter flee to Denmark.

Is included in "Water Water Everywhere!" at Contemporary Arts Gallery, New York (September).

1940   Is included in "United American Artists Annual" at A.C.A. Gallery, New York (May–June) and in "Exhibition of the Art of the American Negro (1851–1940)" at the American Negro Exposition, Chicago, Illinois (July–September).

Exhibits *Chain Gang* in "Art of the WPA Projects" at the New York World's Fair (October–November).

Is included in "Onya La Tour Presents A Rotating Exhibition of Modern Art" in the Steele Galleries at Indiana University, Bloomington, Indiana (October–November).

Is included in the "Buy American Art Week" exhibition at the American Fine Arts Society, New York (November–December).

Is included in "Seventy-Five Years of Freedom; Commemoration of the 75th Anniversary of the Proclamation of the 13th Amendment to the Constitution of the U.S.," Library of Congress, Washington, D.C. (December–January).

1941   Is included in "The Creative Art of the American Negro," Library of Congress, Washington, D.C. (February).

"Paintings: William H. Johnson" is held at Alma Reed Galleries, New York (May).

Is included in "Contemporary Negro Art" at McMillen Inc., New York (October–November).

1941–42 Is included in "American Negro Art: Nineteenth and Twentieth Centuries" at The Downtown Gallery, New York (December–January).

1942   Is included in "American Artists' Record of War and Defense" at the National Gallery of Art, Washington, D.C. (February–March). Exhibition circulated in the U.S. through the year.

Is included in "Exhibition of Paintings by Negro Artists of America" at Atlanta University, Atlanta, Georgia (April–May).

Is included in "American Red Cross National Competition" at the National Gallery of Art, Washington, D.C. (May).

Receives a Certificate of Honor in Recognition of his "Distinguished Service to America in Art," in conjunction with National Negro Achievement Day Festivities, 27 June, New York.

Leaves WPA/New York City Art Project Division. Is reclassified as a Lab Assistant, 25 November.

Moves from 27 West 15th Street to a larger loft in Greenwich Village. Within a week, fire destroys building (December). After salvaging their belongings, William and Holcha temporarily move in with friends.

1943   Resigns from the WPA, 13 January.

Moves to a loft at 79 East 10th Street (February).

"Tempera Paintings by William H. Johnson" is held at Wakefield Gallery, New York (April–May).

Holcha is diagnosed as having breast cancer (September).

Places Holcha in public hospital, New York (December).

1944   Transfers Holcha to a hospice in the Bronx (January).

Holcha Krake Johnson dies, 13 January.

Is included in "Third Annual Atlanta University Exhibition," Atlanta, Georgia (March–April).

Is included in "American Negro Art: Contemporary Painting and Sculpture" at the Newark Museum, Newark, New Jersey (April–May).

"Small Oil Paintings by William H. Johnson" is held at Wakefield Gallery, New York (May).

Is included in "New Names in American Art" at the G Place Gallery, Washington, D.C. (May).

Visits mother in Florence, South Carolina (June).

Is included in "30 Pictures/30 Artists" at Mortimer Brandt Gallery, New York (October–November).

"Oil Paintings by William H. Johnson/Art Textile and Ceramic by Holcha Krake" is held at Marquié Gallery, New York (December).

1944–46 Works as a laborer at the Naval Ship Yards, New York.

1945   Is included in "The Negro Artist Comes of Age: A National Survey of Contemporary American Artists" at the Albany Institute of History and Art, Albany, New York (January–February).

1946   Has solo exhibition at the 135th Street Branch of the New York Public Library, in conjunction with "National Negro History Week" (February–March).

Leaves for Denmark, taking all of his and Holcha's art (October).

1946–47 Stays with in-laws in Odense and Copenhagen (October–April).

1947　Has solo exhibition, Kunsthallen, Copenhagen (March).

　　　Travels to Oslo, Norway. Shortly thereafter, is picked up for vagrancy and placed in a hospital. Diagnosed as suffering from paresis (April).

　　　Under the jurisdiction of the U.S. Department of State, is shipped back to New York. Art and personal effects placed in storage in lower Manhattan warehouse (November).

　　　Is admitted to Central Islip State Hospital, Long Island, New York, 1 December.

1948–70　Is confined to Central Islip State Hospital, unable to paint or lead a normal life again.

1956　Decision is reached by courts to destroy the contents of the rented storage space in lower Manhattan. The Harmon Foundation intervenes and agrees to accept responsibility for the work, acquiring the Johnson estate (January–February).

1956–57　"William H. Johnson: A Retrospective Exhibit" is held at the Countee Cullen Branch of the New York Public Library (December–March).

1957–60　"William H. Johnson: An Artist of the Work Scene," a traveling exhibition of selected works and educational materials, tours nationally.

1959　Mother, Alice Smoot Johnson, dies (ca. October/November).

1964　Is included in "The Portrayal of the Negro in American Painting" at the Bowdoin College Museum of Art, Brunswick, Maine (May–July).

1967　With the Harmon Foundation's closing, a gift of 1,154 works by William H. Johnson is made to the National Collection of Fine Arts, Smithsonian Institution, Washington, D.C. (April).

　　　Is included in "The Evolution of Afro-American Artists: 1800–1950" at the Great Hall, City College, New York, (October–November).

1967–73　Gifts of paintings, drawings, and prints made to selected black college and university art collections, small regional art museums, and to the Johnson family in Florence, South Carolina.

1968　"William H. Johnson" is held at the College Museum, Hampton Institute, Hampton, Virginia (March–April).

1968–69　Is included in "Invisible Americans: Black Artists of the 30s" at the Studio Museum in Harlem, New York (November–February).

1970　Is included in "Dimensions of Black" at the La Jolla Museum of Art, La Jolla, California (February–March).

　　　Is included in "Afro-American Artists Abroad" at the University Art Museum, University of Texas, Austin, Texas (March–May).

　　　"William H. Johnson, Afro-American Painter," an exhibition from the Atlanta University Art Collection and other repositories, is held at the John D. Rockefeller, Jr., Fine Arts Building, Spelman College, Atlanta, Georgia (April).

　　　Dies of acute pancreatitis, on 13 April, in Central Islip, Long Island, New York.

Posthumous Exhibitions

1971　"Black Artists: Two Generations," The Newark Museum, Newark, New Jersey (May–September).

　　　"William H. Johnson," George Washington Carver Museum, Tuskegee Institute, Tuskegee, Alabama (June).

1971–73　"William H. Johnson, 1901–1970," National Collection of Fine Arts, Smithsonian Institution, Washington, D.C. (November 1971–January 1972). Tours Africa and Europe (1972–1973) under the auspices of the United States Information Agency.

1973　"Highlights from the Atlanta University Collection of Afro-American Art," High Museum of Art, Atlanta, Georgia (November–December). Tours nationally through 1976.

1974–75　"The Barnett-Aden Collection," Anacostia Neighborhood Museum, Smithsonian Institution, Washington, D.C. (January–May 1974). Travels to the Corcoran Gallery of Art, Washington, D.C. (January–February 1975).

1975–76　"Jubilee: Afro-American Artists on Afro-America," Museum of Fine Arts, Boston, Massachusetts (November–January).

1976　"William H. Johnson, Paintings and Graphics," Carl Van Vechten Gallery of Art, Fisk University, Nashville, Tennessee (February).

　　　"America as Art," National Collection of Fine Arts, Smithsonian Institution, Washington, D.C. (April–November).

　　　"The American Spirit," Pennsylvania Academy of the Fine Arts, Philadelphia, Pennsylvania (April–December).

　　　"Two Centuries of Black American Art," Los Angeles County Museum of Art, Los Angeles, California (September–November). Tours nationally in 1977.

1977　"Perceptions of the Spirit in Twentieth Century American Art," Indianapolis Museum of Art, Indianapolis, Indiana (September–November). Tours nationally in 1977 and 1978.

1978–79　"William Carlos Williams and the American Scene, 1920–1940," Whitney Museum of American Art, New York (December–February).

1979　"Black Artists/South," Huntsville Museum of Art, Huntsville, Alabama (April–June).

1979–80　"Impressions/Expressions: Black American Graphics," Studio Museum in Harlem, New York (October–January). Tours nationally for the next four years.

1980　"William H. Johnson (1901–1970)," Ramapo College Art Gallery, Mahwah, New Jersey (September–October). Travels to selected U.S. colleges and universities in 1980 and 1981.

1982　"Ritual and Myth: A Survey of African American Art," Studio Museum in Harlem, New York (June–November).

　　　"William H. Johnson: The Scandinavian Years," National Museum of American Art, Smithsonian Institution, Washington, D.C. (September–November).

1983　"Painting in the South, 1564–1980," Virginia Museum of Fine Arts, Richmond, Virginia (September–November). Tours nationally in 1984 and 1985.

1984   "A Blossoming of New Promises: Art in the Spirit of the Harlem Renaissance," Emily Lowe Gallery, Hofstra University, Hempstead, Long Island, New York (February–March).

"William Henry Johnson, 1901–1970," Jamaica Arts Center, Queens, New York (January–March).

"Since the Harlem Renaissance: Fifty Years of Afro-American Art," Center Gallery, Bucknell University, Lewisburg, Pennsylvania (April–June). Tours nationally in 1984 and 1985.

"Artists of the 'Thirties and 'Forties," Museum of African American Art, Los Angeles, California (June–September). Travels to Chicago, Illinois, in 1984 and 1985.

1985   "Art in Washington and Its Afro-American Presence: 1940–1970," Washington Project for the Arts, Washington, D.C. (March–May).

"Hidden Heritage: Afro-American Art, 1800–1950," Bellevue Art Museum, Bellevue, Washington (September–November). Tours nationally through 1988.

1986   "Choosing: An Exhibition of Changing Perspectives in Modern Art and Art Criticism by Black Americans, 1925–1985," Museum of Science and Industry, Chicago, Illinois (February).

"Treasures from the National Museum of American Art," Seattle Art Museum, Seattle, Washington (February–April). Tours nationally in 1986 and 1987.

"Naivety in Art," Setagaya Art Museum, Tokyo, Japan (March–June). Travels to the Tochigi Prefectural Museum of Art, Utsunomiya, Japan (June–August).

1987   "The Portrayal of the Black Musician in American Art," California Afro-American Museum, Los Angeles, California (February–June). Tours nationally in 1987.

"Harlem Renaissance: Art of Black America," Studio Museum in Harlem, New York (February–August). Tours nationally in 1987 and 1988.

1989   "The Blues Aesthetic: Black Culture and Modernism," Washington Project for the Arts, Washington, D.C. (September–December). Tours nationally in 1990.

"Afro-American Artists in Paris, 1919–1939," Bertha and Karl Leubsdorf Art Gallery, Hunter College, City University of New York, New York (November–December).

1990   "Against the Odds: African-American Artists and the Harmon Foundation," The Newark Museum, Newark, New Jersey (January–April). Tours nationally in 1990.

"Novae: William H. Johnson and Bob Thompson," California Afro-American Museum, Los Angeles, California (May–August). Tours nationally in 1990 and 1991.

1991   "Homecoming: William H. Johnson and Afro-America, 1938–1946," National Museum of American Art, Smithsonian Institution, Washington, D.C. (September–March). Tours nationally and internationally in 1992 and 1993.

Public Collections

Aaron Douglas Collection, Amistad Research Center, New Orleans, La.

The Atlanta University Collection of Afro-American Art, Clark Atlanta University, Atlanta, Ga.

The Barnett-Aden Collection, Tampa, Fla.

Carl Van Vechten Gallery of Art, Fisk University, Nashville, Tenn.

Carolina Art Association/Gibbes Museum of Art, Charleston, S.C.

Columbia Museum of Art, Columbia, S.C.

DuSable Museum of African American History, Chicago, Ill.

Florence Museum, Florence, S.C.

Gallery of Art, Howard University, Washington, D.C.

Greenville County Museum of Art, Greenville, S.C.

Hampton University Museum, Hampton, Va.

I. P. Stanback Museum, South Carolina State College, Orangeburg, S.C.

Kerteminde Museum/Johannes Larsen Museet, Kerteminde, Denmark

Länsmuseet, Gävle, Sweden

Library of Congress, Washington, D.C.

Moderna Museet, Stockholm, Sweden

Morgan State University Gallery of Art, Baltimore, Md.

The Museum of African American Art, Los Angeles, Calif.

Museum of Art, North Carolina Central University, Durham, N.C.

National Museum of American Art, Smithsonian Institution, Washington, D.C.

The Newark Museum, Newark, N.J.

Trøndelag Kunstgalleri, Trondhjems Kunstforening, Trondheim, Norway

Tuskegee University, Tuskegee, Ala.

Select Bibliography

Archives

Archives of American Art, Smithsonian Institution, Washington, D.C.

Bureau of Vital Records and Statistics, Department of Health, N.Y.

Central Islip Psychiatric Center, Central Islip, Long Island, N.Y.

Chicago Historical Society, Chicago, Ill.

Department of State, Washington, D.C.

Hatch-Billops Collection, Inc., N.Y.

James Weldon Johnson Collection, Beinecke Rare Book and Manuscript Library, Yale University, New Haven, Conn.

Kerteminde Museum/Johannes Larsen Museet, Kerteminde, Denmark

Library of Congress, Washington, D.C.

Moorland-Spingarn Research Center, Howard University, Washington, D.C.

National Academy of Design, N.Y.

National Archives, Washington, D.C.

National Museum of American Art, Smithsonian Institution, Washington, D.C.

National Museum of Denmark, Copenhagen, Denmark

Powell, Richard J. Interviews and Notes, 1983–90

Provincetown Art Association, Provincetown, Mass.

The Schomburg Center for Research in Black Culture, New York Public Library, N.Y.

Smithsonian Institution Archives, Washington, D.C.

Washington National Record Center, Suitland, Md.

Books

Anderson, Jervis. *This Was Harlem.* New York: Farrar, Strauss and Giroux, 1982.

Barron, Stephanie, ed. *German Expressionism, 1915–1925: The Second Generation.* Munich: Prestel-Verlag, 1988.

Bastin, Bruce. *Red River Blues: The Blues Tradition in the Southeast.* Urbana and Chicago: University of Illinois Press, 1986.

Bodelsen, Merete, and Povl Engelstoft, eds. *Weilbachs Kunstnerleksikon.* Vol. 2. Copenhagen: Aschehoug Dansk Forlag, 1949.

Breum, Sophie, Kr. Kragh, and V. Woll. *Kerteminde og Omegn.* Copenhagen: H. Aschehoug and Company, 1922.

Bronner, Stephen Eric. "Emil Nolde and the Politics of Rage." In *Passion and Rebellion: The Expressionist Heritage.* Edited by Stephen Eric Bronner and Douglas Kellner. New York: Universe Books, 1983.

Brown, Milton W. *American Painting from the Armory Show to the Depression.* Princeton, N.J.: Princeton University Press, 1972.

Campbell, Mary Schmidt. *Harlem Renaissance: Art of Black America.* New York: The Studio Museum in Harlem and Harry N. Abrams, Inc., 1987.

Clark, Eliot. *History of the National Academy of Design, 1825–1953.* New York: Columbia University Press, 1954.

Crew, Spencer. *Field to Factory: Afro-American Migration, 1915–1940.* Washington, D.C.: Smithsonian Institution Press for the National Museum of American History, 1987.

Dover, Cedric. *American Negro Art.* Greenwich, Conn.: New York Graphic Society, 1960.

DuBois, W. E. B. *Black Reconstruction in America.* 1935. Reprint. New York: Atheneum, 1983.

———. *The Souls of Black Folk.* 1903. Reprint. New York: Avon Books, 1965.

Ellison, Ralph. *Invisible Man.* New York: Random House, 1952.

Engelstad, Helen. *Dobbeltvev i Norge.* Oslo: Gyldendals Norsk Forlag, 1958.

Fabre, Michel. *La Rive Noire: De Harlem à la Seine.* Paris: Lieu Commun, 1985.

Fink, Lois Marie. *Academy: The Academic Tradition in American Art.* Washington, D.C.: Smithsonian Institution Press for the National Collection of Fine Arts, 1975.

Franklin, John Hope and Alfred A. Moss, Jr. *From Slavery to Freedom: A History of Negro Americans.* New York: Alfred A. Knopf, 1988.

Gee, Malcom. *Dealers, Critics, and Collectors of Modern Painting: Aspects of the Parisian Art Market, between 1910 and 1930.* New York: Garland Press, 1977.

Goldwater, Robert J. *Primitivism in Modern Art.* Cambridge: The Belknap Press for Harvard University Press, 1986.

Gordon, Donald E. *Ernst Ludwig Kirchner.* Cambridge: Harvard University Press, 1968.

Graham, John D. *System and Dialectics of Art.* New York: Delphic Studios, 1937.

Green, Christopher. *Cubism and Its Enemies: Modern Movements and Reactions in French Art, 1916–1928.* New Haven: Yale University Press, 1987.

Grohmann, Will. *E.L. Kirchner.* New York: Arts, Inc., 1961.

Hawthorne, Charles W. *Hawthorne on Painting.* 1938. Reprint. New York: Dover Publications, Inc., 1960.

Heilmaier, Hans. *Oskar Kokoschka.* Paris: Editions G. Cres and Cie, 1929.

Hermand, Jost. "Artificial Atavism: German Expressionism and Blacks." In *Blacks and German Culture.* Edited by Reinhold Grimm and Jost Hermand. Madison: University of Wisconsin Press, 1986.

Igoe, Lynn Moody. *Two Hundred Fifty Years of Afro-American Art: An Annotated Bibiliography.* New York: R. R. Bowker Company, 1981.

Jensen, Johannes V. *Nye Himmerlandshistorier.* Copenhagen: Gyldendals, 1940.

Joachimides, Christos M., Norman Rosenthal, and Wieland Schmied, eds. *German Art in the Twentieth Century: Painting and Sculpture, 1905–1985*. Munich: Prestel-Verlag, 1985.

Johnson, Clifton H., ed. *God Struck Me Dead: Religious Conversion Experiences and Autobiographies of Ex-Slaves*. Philadelphia : Pilgrim Press, 1969.

Johnson, James Weldon, and J. Rosamond Johnson, eds. *The Books of American Negro Spirituals*. Vols. 1 and 2. New York: Da Capo Press, 1985.

Kandinsky, Wassily. "Reminiscences." In *Modern Artists on Art*. Edited by Robert L. Herbert. Translated by Hilla Rebay. Englewood Cliffs, N.J.: Prentice-Hall, Inc., 1964.

King, G. Wayne. *Rise Up So Early: A History of Florence County, South Carolina*. Spartanburg, S.C.: The Reprint Company for the Florence County Historical Commission, 1981.

———. *Some Folks Do: A Pictorial History of Florence County*. Norfolk: The Donning Company Publishers, 1985.

Kjersmeier, Carl. *Centres de Style de la Sculpture Nègre Africaine*. 4 Vols. Paris: A. Morance, 1935–38.

———. *Paa Fetischjagt i Afrika: 6000 km. i automobil gennem Fransk Sudan, Øvre Volta og Guinea*. Copenhagen: Povl Branner, 1932.

Landgren, Michael E. *Years of Art: The Story of the Art Students League*. New York: Robert M. McBride and Company, 1940.

Larsen, Nella. *Quicksand and Passing*. Edited by Deborah E. McDowell. New Brunswick, N.J.: Rutgers University Press, 1986.

Levine, Lawrence. *Black Culture and Black Consciousness*. New York: Oxford University Press, 1977.

Lewis, David Levering. *When Harlem Was in Vogue*. New York: Alfred A. Knopf, 1981.

Lhote, André. *La Peinture, le coeur et l'esprit*. Paris: Denoel et Steele, 1933.

Littlefield, Daniel C. *Rice and Slaves: Ethnicity and the Slave Trade in Colonial South Carolina*. Baton Rouge: Louisiana State University, 1981.

Locke, Alain. *The Negro in Art*. 1940. Reprint. New York: Hacker Art Books, 1979.

———. *The New Negro*. 1925. Reprint. New York: Atheneum Press, 1970.

Long, Richard A. *Africa and America: Essays in Afro-American Culture*. Atlanta: Atlanta University, 1981.

McCausland, Elizabeth. *Charles W. Hawthorne: An American Figure Painter*. New York: American Artists Group, Inc., 1947.

McNeill, J. P., Jr., and John A. Chase, Jr., *Florence County: Economic and Social*. Columbia: University of South Carolina, 1921.

Mead, Chris. *Champion—Joe Louis: Black Hero in White America*. New York: Charles Scribner's Sons, 1985.

Nolde, Emil. "Jahre der Kämpfe." In *Theories of Modern Art*. Edited by Herschel B. Chipp. Berkeley: University of California Press, 1968.

Nørregaard-Nielsen, Hans Edvard, ed. *Dansk Kunst*. Vols. 1 and 2. Copenhagen: Gyldendals Bogklub, 1983.

Osofsky, Gilbert. *Harlem: The Making of a Ghetto*. New York: Harper Torchbooks, 1971.

Ottley, Roi. '*New World A-Coming': Inside Black America*. New York: Houghton Mifflin Company, 1943.

Paalen, Wolfgang. *Form and Sense: Problems of Contemporary Art*. New York: Wittenborn and Company, 1945.

Perlman, Bennard B. *The Immortal Eight*. New York: Exposition Press, 1962.

Phillips, Hazel Spencer. *William Elmer Harmon*. Lebanon, Ohio: Warren County Historical Society, 1962.

Porter, James A. *Modern Negro Art*. 1943. Reprint. New York: Arno Press, 1969.

Rampersad, Arnold. *The Life of Langston Hughes*. Vol. 1, *1902–1941: I, Too, Sing America*. New York: Oxford University Press, 1986.

Rand, Harry. *Arshile Gorky: The Implication of Symbols*. Montclair, N.J.: Abner Schram, 1981.

Reswick, Irmtraud. *Traditional Textiles of Tunisia*. Seattle: University of Washington Press, 1985.

Rosenblum, Robert. *Modern Painting and the Northern Romantic Tradition: Friedrich to Rothko*. London: Thames and Hudson, 1975.

Rosengarten, Theodore. *All God's Dangers: The Life of Nate Shaw*. New York: Alfred A. Knopf, 1975.

Rossel, Sven H. *Johannes V. Jensen*. Boston: Twayne Publishers, 1984.

Sackheim, Eric, ed. *The Blues Line: A Collection of Blues Lyrics*. New York: Grossman Publishers, 1969.

Santini, Pier Carlo. *Modern Landscape Painting*. London: Phaidon, 1972.

Schiefler, Gustav. *Edvard Munchs Graphische Kunst*. Dresden: Arnolds Graphische Bücher, 1923.

Scott, Gail R. *Marsden Hartley*. New York: Abbeville Press, 1988.

Seldes, Gilbert. *The Seven Lively Arts*. New York: Harper and Brothers, 1924.

Still, William. *The Underground Railroad*. 1872. Reprint. Chicago: Johnson Publishing Company, Inc., 1970.

Taylor, Joshua C. *America as Art*. Washington, D.C.: Smithsonian Institution Press for the National Collection of Fine Arts, 1976.

Thompson, Robert Farris. *Flash of the Spirit: African and Afro-American Art and Philosophy*. New York: Random House, 1983.

Toomer, Jean. *Cane*. 1923. Reprint. New York: Harper and Row, 1969.

Turner, Elizabeth H. *American Artists in Paris, 1919–1929*. Ann Arbor: UMI Research Press, 1988.

Turner, Lorenzo Dow. *Africanisms in the Gullah Dialect*. 1949. Reprint. Ann Arbor: University of Michigan Press, 1974.

Walls, Dwayne E. *The Chickenbone Special*. New York: Harvest Books, 1971.

Werenskiold, Marit. *The Concept of Expressionism: Origin and Meta-morphoses.* Oslo: Universitetsforlaget, 1984.

Westheim, Paul. *Oskar Kokoschka.* Berlin: Paul Cassirer, 1925.

Williams-Jones, Pearl. "Roberta Martin: Spirit of an Era." In *Roberta Martin and the Roberta Martin Singers: The Legacy and the Music.* Washington, D.C.: Smithsonian Institution Press, 1982.

Wingler, Hans Maria. *Oskar Kokoschka: The World of the Painter.* Salzburg: Galerie Welz, 1958.

Young, Mahonri Sharp. *The Eight: The Realist Revolt in American Painting.* New York: Watson-Guptil Publications, 1973.

Exhibition Catalogues

American Artists' Record of War and Defense. Washington, D.C.: National Gallery of Art, Smithsonian Institution, 1942.

American Negro Art: Nineteenth and Twentieth Centuries. New York: The Downtown Gallery, 1941.

Barron, Stephanie. *German Expressionist Sculpture.* Chicago: University of Chicago Press for the Los Angeles County Museum of Art, 1983.

Breeskin, Adelyn D. *William H. Johnson: 1901–1970.* Washington, D.C.: Smithsonian Institution Press for the National Collection of Fine Arts, 1971.

Christoph Voll, 1897–1939. Mannheim: Stadtischen Kunsthalle, 1960.

Contemporary Negro Art. New York: McMillen, Inc., 1941.

Dillenberger, Jane and John Dillenberger. *Perceptions of the Spirit in Twentieth-Century American Art.* Indianapolis: Indianapolis Museum of Art, 1977.

Driskell, David C. *Two Centuries of Black American Art.* New York: Alfred A. Knopf for the Los Angeles County Museum of Art, 1976.

Entartete Kunst. Berlin: Verlag für Kultur und Wirtschaftswerburg, 1937.

The Evolution of Afro-American Artists: 1800–1950. New York: City University of New York, 1967.

Exhibit of Fine Arts by American Negro Artists. New York: Harmon Foundation, 1930.

Exhibition of Sculpture and Painting Presented by The Labor Club. New York: The Labor Club, 1939.

Finsen, Hanne. *Katalog over Den Hirschsprungske Samling af dansk Kunstneres arbejder.* Copenhagen: Den Hirschsprungske Samling, 1982.

Flint, Janet A. *Charles W. Hawthorne: The Late Watercolors.* Washington, D.C.: Smithsonian Institution Press for the National Museum of American Art, 1983.

Fransk genombrottskonst fran nittonhundratelet. Utställningar i Stockholm, Oslo, Göteborg och Köpenhamn. Stockholm: Konsthall, 1931.

Frommhold, Erhard. *Christoph Voll: Radierungen und Holzschitte.* Munich: Galleria del Levante, 1981.

Gordon, Allan M. *Echoes of Our Past: The Narrative Artistry of Palmer C. Hayden.* Los Angeles: Museum of African American Art, 1988.

Hammond, Leslie King. *Ritual and Myth: A Survey of African American Art.* New York: Studio Museum in Harlem, 1982.

Haskell, Barbara. *Marsden Hartley.* New York: New York University Press for the Whitney Museum of American Art, 1980.

Hawthorne Retrospective. Provincetown, Mass.: The Chrysler Art Museum at Provincetown, 1961.

Kloss, William. *Treasures from the National Museum of American Art.* Washington, D.C.: Smithsonian Institution Press for the National Museum of American Art, 1985.

Lee, Ellen W. *The Onya La Tour Collection.* In *Recent Accessions, 1966–1972.* Indianapolis: Indianapolis Museum of Art, 1972.

LeFalle-Collins, Lizetta, ed. *Novae: William H. Johnson and Bob Thompson.* Los Angeles: California Afro-American Museum, 1990.

Locke, Alain. *Contemporary Negro Art.* Baltimore: The Baltimore Museum of Art, 1939.

Long, Richard A. *Highlights from the Atlanta University Collection of Afro-American Art.* Atlanta: High Museum of Art, 1973.

———. *William H. Johnson, Afro-American Painter.* Atlanta: Spelman College, 1970.

Maleriudstilling af den amerikanske maler William H. Johnson, New York. Copenhagen: Christian Larsen, 1933.

Måleriutställning av den amerikanske Målaren William H. Johnson från New York. Västerås: Nya Posthuset, 1937.

Mules and Mississippi. Jackson, Miss.: Department of Archives and History, 1980.

Naivety in Art. Tokyo: Setagaya Art Museum, 1986.

Nasgaard, Roald. *The Mystic North: Symbolist Landscape Painting in Northern Europe and North America, 1890–1940.* Toronto: University of Toronto Press in association with the Art Gallery of Ontario, 1984.

The Negro Comes of Age: A National Survey of Contemporary American Artists. Albany: Albany Institute of History and Art, 1945.

Onya La Tour Presents a Rotating Exhibition of Modern Art. Bloomington, Ind.: Steele Galleries, Indiana University, 1940.

Oskar Kokoschka (1886–1980): Memorial Exhibition. New York: Marlborough Gallery, Inc., 1981.

Paintings: William H. Johnson. New York: Alma Reed Galleries, 1941.

Park, Marlene and Gerald E. Markowitz. *New Deal for Art.* Hamilton, N.Y.: Gallery Association of New York State, Inc., 1977.

Reynolds, Gary A. and Beryl Wright, eds. *Against the Odds: African-American Artists and the Harmon Foundation.* Newark: The Newark Museum, 1989.

Rubin, William, ed. *"Primitivism" in Twentieth Century Art: Affinity of the Tribal and Modern.* New York: Museum of Modern Art, 1984.

Scandinavian Modernism: Painting in Denmark, Finland, Iceland, Norway and Sweden, 1910–1920. New York: Rizzoli International Publications, 1989.

Since the Harlem Renaissance: Fifty Years of Afro-American Art. Lewisburg, Pa.: The Center Gallery, Bucknell University, 1985.

Sweeney, James Johnson, ed. *African Negro Art.* 1935. Reprint. New York: Arno Press, 1969.

Thompson, Robert Farris and Joseph Cornet. *The Four Moments of the Sun: Kongo Art in Two Worlds.* Washington, D.C.: The National Gallery of Art, 1981.

Tuchman, Maurice. "Chaim Soutine (1893–1943)." In *Chaim Soutine (1893–1943).* Edited by Ernst-Gerhard Güse. London: Arts Council of Great Britain, 1982.

Tunesien: Tradition und Tourismus. Lübeck: Museum am Dom/Museum für Kunst und Kulturgeschichte der Hansestadt, 1976.

Varnedoe, Kirk. "Nationalism, Internationalism and the Progress of Scandinavian Art." In *Northern Lights: Realism and Symbolism in Scandinavian Painting, 1890–1910.* Brooklyn: The Brooklyn Museum, 1982.

Wheat, Ellen. *Jacob Lawrence: American Painter.* Seattle: University of Washington Press for the Seattle Art Museum, 1986.

Journal Articles

"American Negro Art Given Full Length Review in New York Show." *Art Digest* 16 (15 December 1941).

"Art by Negroes." *Art Digest* 16 (15 October 1941).

Baker, James H. "Art Comes to the People of Harlem." *The Crisis* 46 (March 1939): 78–80.

Bech, Bodil. "En 'Indian-Negro' Maler i Kerteminde." *Tidens Kvinder* 9 (10 November 1931): 10.

"Black Division." *Time,* 29 December 1941, 49.

Boswell, Helen. "57th Street in Review: William H. Johnson Exhibits." *Art Digest* 15 (1 May 1941): 31.

Boswell, Peyton. "Fable of the Jitterbugs." *Art Digest* 14 (15 January 1940): 3.

Charatan, Fred B. "A Century of Care." *Central Islip Psychiatric Center/Media* 4 (Winter 1989): 7.

E. I. "Utstillinger i Oslo." *Kunst og Kultur* 21 (1935): 191–92.

Ellison, Ralph. "Modern Negro Art." *Tomorrow* 4 (November 1944): 92–93.

"Fighting Friends in Teheran." *Life,* 20 December 1943, 25–32.

Frost, Rosamund. "Art." *Town and Country,* May 1941, 74.

Halasz, Piri. "Figuration in the '40s: The Other Expressionism." *Art in America* 70 (December 1982).

Hale, Robert Beverly. "The Passing Shows." *Art News* 42 (1–14 May 1943): 22.

———. "The Passing Shows." *Art News* 43 (15–31 December 1944): 21.

"Is William H. Johnson, Negro Prize Winner, Blazing a New Trail?" *Art Digest* 4 (15 January 1930): 13.

Landy, Jacob. "William H. Johnson: Expressionist Turned 'Primitive.' " *Journal of the American Association of University Women* 52 (March 1958): 167–70.

Locke, Alain. "Advance on the Art Front." *Opportunity* 17 (May 1939): 132–36.

———. "The American Negro as Artist." *American Magazine of Art* 23 (September 1931): 210–20.

Lowe, Jeannette. "Paintings by William Johnson: Arts and Crafts by Holcha Krake." *Art News* 37 (25 February 1939): 14.

———. "The Passing Shows: Four Artists." *Art News* 40 (15–31 May 1941): 25.

"Negro Artists: Their Works Win Top U.S. Honors." *Life,* 22 July 1946, 62–65.

"Negro Prize Winners." *Art Digest* 4 (1 January 1930): 11.

"Negroes at War." *Life,* 15 June 1942, 89.

Phillips, Duncan. "Charles W. Hawthorne." *The International Studio* 61 (March 1917): xix–xxiv.

Powell, Richard J. "William H. Johnson's *Minde Kerteminde.*" *Siksi: The Nordic Art Review* 1 (1986) : 17–23 .

Riley, Maude. "Art Notes: William H. Johnson." *Cue* 10 (10 May 1 1944): 24.

Rydbeck, Ingrid. "Stockholms-Krönika." *Konstrevy* 14 (1938): 39.

"Survey of the Month: Negro Artist Gives One-Man Show in New York City Gallery." *Opportunity* 19 (May 1941): 153.

Tandstad, Kjetil. "Verdskunst med Volda-motiv." *Voldaminne* (1983) : 6–13 .

"Tempera Paintings by Johnson Shown in New York." *Opportunity* 21 (July 1943).

Vaughan, Malcom. "The Passing Shows." *Art News* 43 (15–31 May 1944): 21.

Watson, Jane. "News and Comment: The Red Cross Challenges the Artist." *Magazine of Art* 35 (February 1942): 74–76.

Williams, Charles. "Harlem at War." *The Nation,* 16 January 1943, 86–88.

Newspapers

Many of the articles from French, Danish, Norwegian, and Swedish newspapers were originally found in William H. Johnson's scrapbook. Because these articles were collected and clipped over a fifteen-year period by Johnson in an unsystematic fashion, many lack newspaper titles, dates, and/or other identifying references. While every effort has been made to identify as many of these articles as possible, some are still not fully identified. At the very least, however, each European article has been given an approximate date, city, and country of publication.

An-dre. "Stor Kunstner fra lille By." *Aarhus Stiftstidende* (Aarhus, Denmark), 26 November 1934, 2.

"Around the Studios." *New York Herald (Paris Edition)*, 14 November 1927, 5.

"Artist Johnson." *Florence Morning News*, 15 April 1930, 4.

Auerbach-Levy, William. "Negro Painters Imitate Whites." *New York World*, 5 January 1930, 1M.

Avril, Georges. "Art et Lettres: La Peinture à la Galerie Alban." (Nice, France), ca. spring 1929.

Burrows, Carlyle. "Notes and Comments on Events in Art: Negro Life." *New York Herald Tribune*, 11 May 1941, sec. 6, 5.

C.U. "En god maler: William H. Johnson." (Aalesund, Norway), ca. December 1936.

Dalerik. "Fyrverkeri ur målarskrin." *Gefle-Posten* (Gävle, Sweden), 15 December 1937, 5.

"A Damnable Record." *The Florence Daily Times*, as quoted in *The State*, 25 February 1898, 5.

Devree, Howard. "Among the New Exhibitions." *New York Times*, 17 December 1944, sec. 2, 4.

———. "A Reviewer's Notebook: Brief Comments on Some of the Recently Opened Shows in the Galleries." *New York Times*, 11 May 1941, sec. 8, 1.

———. "A Reviewer's Notebook: Brief Comments on Some of the Recently Opened Shows in the Galleries." *New York Times*, 2 May 1943, sec. 2, 8.

E.W. "Kunstudstillingen i Mageløs." *Fyns-Social Demokraten* (Odense, Denmark), November 28, 1930, 4.

E-son. "Konst: Utställningara i konstgalleriet och i nya 'posthuset.'" *Vestmandlands Läns Tidning* (Västerås, Sweden), 12 November 1937, 7.

Egil. "Johnson vender hjem—men kun for en Visit." *Fyns Stiftstidende* (Odense, Denmark), 21 October 1938, 8.

"Färgrik Vernissage." *Nya Dagligt Allenhanda* (Stockholm, Sweden), 19 November 1937, 9.

Fast. "William Johnson—En amerikansk Maler." *Land og Folk* (Copenhagen, Denmark), 12 March 1947, 7.

Frema. "Hr. Johnson—han smiler. Thi han og Konen har rivende Afsœtning paa deres Udstilling." *Odense Avis* (Odense, Denmark), 5 December 1932, 7.

G.S-d. "Färgexplosion på Konsthallen." *Gefle-Dagblad* (Gävle, Sweden), 13 December 1937, 6.

Gauguin, Pola. "Blomqvist Kunstutstilling." *Dagbladet* (Oslo, Norway), 25 March 1935, 4.

Genauer, Emily. "Johnson at Marquié." *New York World-Telegram*, 23 December 1944, 6.

———. "Latest Johnson Works Placed on Exhibition." *New York World-Telegram*, 1 May 1943, 9.

Gnist. "Eiendommelig Kunstnerbesøk: Sioux-etling med blond frue i Kunstforeningen. Kunstnere som føler Norge som en eneste inspirasjonskilde. 'Sammenlignet med Norge blir Sveits some et postkort!'" *Adresseavisen* (Trondheim, Norway), 15 September 1937, 5.

Gold, Barbara. "William Johnson: Learning to Be Primitive." *The Baltimore Sun*, 2 April 1972, D6.

H-dy. "W. H. Johnson i Kunst Udstillingsbygningen." *Fyns Tidende* (Odense, Denmark), 23 October 1938, 14.

H:son. "William H. Johnsons utställning." *Westmanlands Allehanda* (Västerås, Sweden), 10 November 1937, 5.

"Harlem Disorders Bring Quick Action by City and Army." *New York Times*, 2 August 1943, 1, 16.

"Harmon Award Winner Depicts Latest World in Modern Art, Critic Asserts." *New York Amsterdam News*, 8 January 1930, 2.

Herr Nat-og-Dag. "Ferniserings-Parade." *Dagens Nyheder* (Copenhagen, Denmark), 20 January 1935, 9.

Holt, Nora. "Primitives on Exhibit." *New York Amsterdam News*, 9 March 1946, 16.

Hvistendahl, Else. "Negerkunstneren Johnson som kjenner Norge som få nordmenn har reist og malt overalt i landet." *Nordisk Tidende* (Brooklyn, N.Y.), 25 January 1945.

"Internasjonalt kunstnerpar i Aalesund." *Sunnmørsposten* (Aalesund, Norway), 3 December 1936, 8.

J.M.E. "De farvedes Problem i kunstnerisk Belysning." *Fyns Tidende* (Odense, Denmark), 17 April 1947, 5.

"Johnson og Krake: En Duet i Kunstbygi001ningen." *Aarhus Amtstidende* (Aarhus, Denmark), 30 November 1934, 4.

"Joins Staff: William H. Johnson Put on Art Center Staff." *New York Amsterdam News*, 10 June 1939, 20.

Jones, Kellie. "No Second Fiddle." *The Village Voice*, 14 April 1987, 92.

K.P. "Neger-Kunstner i København," *Politiken* (Copenhagen, Denmark), 27 April 1933, 6.

Kay P. "Kunstudstilling." *Demokraten* (Aarhus, Denmark), 30 November 1934, 2.

———. "Med Kerteminde-Malerier til U.S.A. Negermaleren fortæller on Kunst og Race." *Demokraten* (Aarhus, Denmark), 7 December 1934, 3.

Kruse, A. Z. "At the Art Galleries: Marquié Gallery." *Brooklyn Eagle Sun*, 17 December 1944, 26.

"Kunst og Gøgl." *Aarhusposten* (Aarhus, Denmark), 8 December, 1934, 5.

L.T. "Kunstutstilling." *Møre* (Volda, Norway), 29 April 1937, 3.

Madame. "Vævekunstens Renæssance." *Fyns Stiftstidende* (Odense, Denmark), 1 December 1929, 6–7.

"Målären W. H. Johnson." *Møre* (Volda, Norway), 9 July 1936, 3.

Miss D. "Fra Kerteminde til Nordafrika." *Aarhus Stiftstidende* (Aarhus, Denmark), 4 December 1934, 4.

Murre. "Hvor nordlandssommeren lyser en i møte." *Dagsposten* (Trondheim, Norway), 14 September 1937, 2.

N.B. "Långväga Konstnärbesök." *Vastmanlands Folkblad* (Västerås, Sweden), 8 November 1937.

Ned. "Trio på Konsthallen." (Gävle, Sweden), ca. December 1937.

"Neger og hvit hos Blomqvist: Utstillinger av Olaf Holwech og W. H. Johnson." *Arbeiderbladet* (Oslo, Norway), 18 March 1935, 4.

"En neger-indiansk maler hos Blomqvist. William H. Johnson utstiller 'hot' kunst. " *Tidens Tegn* (Oslo, Norway), 19 March 1935, 6.

"Negro Artists." *New York Amsterdam News*, 8 January 1930, Editorial page.

"No Shred of Evidence." *The State*, 25 February 1898, 4.

"Norsk og neger-indiansk maleri hos Blomqvist." *Aftenposten* (Oslo, Norway), 18 March 1935, 2.

Østby, Leif. "Olaf Holwech og W. H. Johnson hos Blomqvist." *Aftenposten* (Oslo, Norway), 23 March 1935, 3.

Ostrow, Joanne. "Mr. Johnson's Varied and Vivid Vision." *The Washington Post*, 17 September 1982, W29.

Perinax. "William Johnson og Holcha Krake Johnson." *Fyns Venstreblad* (Odense, Denmark), 26 November 1933.

pr. "Udstilling: Neger-Indianeren William H. Johnson." (Copenhagen, Denmark), ca. April 1933.

R.G. "Maleriudstilling." *Aarhus Stiftstidende* (Aarhus, Denmark), 30 November 1934, 3.

"Ragcutters Find Harlem 'Heaven.'" *New York Amsterdam News*, 8 April 1939, 20.

Rank, Dr. "Naar man er Solen naer: Kunstnerisk Krydsning Kulmineret i København. Hvad Fiskerne i Kerteminde og Nordafrikas Arabere betyder. Neger-Indianeren og hans danske Hustru udstiller paa Højbroplads. William H. Johnson fortæller." *Ekstrabladet* (Copenhagen, Denmark), 18 April 1933, 6.

Richard, Paul. "Finding a Place in the Midnight Sun." *The Washington Post*, 18 September 1982, C1, 8.

———. "Spirit of William H. Johnson." *The Washington Post*, 8 November 1971, B1, 6.

"Richard Carroll Advises His Race." *The State*, 4 January 1898, 1.

Rita. "Eksotisk maler utstiller i Trondheim. Og lærer oss å se vart eget lands farveprakt." *Nidaros* (Trondheim, Norway), 15 September 1937, 2.

Smyth, Jeannette. "Tribute to an Artist." *The Washington Post*, 5 November 1971, B8.

"Some Prize Winning Exhibits." *New York Age*, 11 January 1930, 3.

Thomasius. "Chinos-Maleren i Kerteminde: Interview med den berømteamerikanske Chinos-Maler William H. Johnson, der sammen med sin Hustru Kunstvæverksen Holcha Krake, udstiller paa Tornøes Hotel." *Fyns Stiftstidende* (Odense, Denmark), 9 July 1930, 3.

———. "Dagens Interview—Med Indianer og Negerblod i Aarene. Chinos-Maleren William H. Johnson fortæller lidt om sin Afrikarejse, primitiv kunst, m.m." *Fyns Stiftstidende* (Odense, Denmark), 27 November 1932, 3.

"U.S.A.-ministern ser på U.S.A.-konst." *Stockholms-Tidningen* (Stockholm, Sweden), 26 November 1937, 14.

"Udstilling af Malerier og Kunstvævning. Kunstner parret William og Holcha Johnson aabnede i Dag en interessant Udstilling paa Tornøes Hotel." *Kjerteminde Avis* (Kerteminde, Denmark), 8 July 1930, 2.

Um. "Sterke kontraster hos Blomqvist. Norsk natur og afrikanske urskoger." *Morgenbladet* (Oslo, Norway), 19 March 1935, 2.

Upton, Melville. "New Talent Has Its Day." *The New York Sun*, 30 December 1944, 9.

V-e. "En Konstnärstrio på Konsthallen." *Arbetarbladet* (Gävle, Sweden), 14 December 1937, 5.

"Verdens udstiller i Aarhus." *Aarhus Amtstidende* (Aarhus, Denmark), 27 November 1934, 4.

W.K. "Langframand Kunstnar held utstilling i Volda." *Sunnmørsposten* (Aalesund, Norway), 17 December 1935, 2.

Weisenborn, Fritzi. "Pier Exhibit Poses Some Questions." *Chicago Sunday Times*, 21 July 1940, M13.

"Williamsburg Well May Weep." *The State*, 23 February 1898, 1.

Y.B. "Konstkrönika." *Dagens Nyheter* (Stockholm, Sweden), 25 November 1937, 4.

"Y.M.C.A. Officers Announce Exhibit by Negro Artist." *Florence Morning News*, 13 April 1930, 8.

"Young Florence Negro Wins $400 Fine Arts Prize." *Florence Morning News*, 4 January 1930, 8.

Theses and Dissertations

Brown, Joseph A., S.J. "Voices Stirring the Waters: Reflections on the Religious Impulse of Afro-American Art." Master's thesis, Yale University, 1983.

Halasz, Piri. "Directions, Concerns and Critical Perceptions of Paintings Exhibited in New York, 1940–1949: Abraham Rattner and His Contemporaries." Ph.D. diss., Columbia University, 1982.

Hammond, Leslie King. "The Life and Work of William Henry Johnson, 1901–1970." Ph.D. diss., Johns Hopkins University, 1975.

Powell, Richard J. "William H. Johnson: Expressionist and Artist of the Blues Aesthetic." Ph.D. diss., Yale University, 1988.

Stoelting, Winifred L. "Hale Woodruff, Artist and Leader: Through the Atlanta Years. " Ph.D. diss., Emory University, 1978.

Video and Sound Recordings

Afro-American Spirituals, Work Songs and Ballads. Library of Congress Recording. LP AFS L3.

The Gospel Sound, Vol. 1. Columbia. LP G31086.

Mossin, Per. *Manden der troede Jesus var sort*. 55 minutes. Danmarks Radio, 1983. Videocassette.

Credits

Unless otherwise noted, all photographs are from the William H. Johnson Papers, Archives of American Art, Smithsonian Institution, Washington, D.C.

Half-title pg.   NMAA 1967.59.1118

p. xiii   photo courtesy of the National Archives, Washington, D.C.

Fig. 1   photo courtesy of Dr. G. Wayne King

Fig. 2   photo courtesy of the author

Fig. 3   photo courtesy of the Archives of American Art, Smithsonian Institution

Fig. 4   photo courtesy of the National Academy of Design Archives, New York

Fig. 5   NMAA 1967.59.469

Fig. 6   photo courtesy of the Juley Collection, National Museum of American Art/National Portrait Gallery Library, Smithsonian Institution, Washington, D.C.

Fig. 7   photo courtesy of the National Academy of Design, New York City

Fig. 8   NMAA 1967.59.679

Fig. 9   The Chrysler Museum at Norfolk, Norfolk, Virginia

Fig. 10   Dallas Museum of Fine Arts, Dallas, Texas

Fig. 11   photo courtesy of the National Academy of Design, New York City

Fig. 12   NMAA 1967.59.684

Fig. 13   photo courtesy Helen J. Rennie Papers, Archives of American Art, Smithsonian Institution, Washington, D.C.

Fig. 15   NMAA 1967.59.84

Fig. 16   NMAA 1985.88

Fig. 17   photo courtesy of the Department of State, Washington, D.C.

Fig. 18   National Gallery of Art, Washington, D.C. Gift of Chester Dale

Fig. 19   NMAA 1967.59.694

Fig. 20   Collection of Steve Harvey, San Francisco, California

Fig. 21   NMAA 1967.59.686

Fig. 22   photo courtesy of the National Archives, Washington, D.C.

Fig. 23   Philadelphia Museum of Art, Philadelphia, Pennsylvania

Fig. 24   Hampton University Museum, Hampton, Virginia

Fig. 25   NMAA 1967.59.691

Fig. 26   photo courtesy of the Archives of American Art, Smithsonian Institution, Washington, D.C.

Fig. 27   NMAA 1967.59.702

Fig. 28   photo courtesy of Johanna Voll, Skodsborg, Denmark

Fig. 29   photo courtesy of Johanna Voll, Skodsborg, Denmark

Fig. 30   Robert Gore Rifkind Collection, Beverly Hills, California.

Fig. 31   photo courtesy of the Archives of American Art, Smithsonian Institution, Washington, D.C.

Fig. 32   photo courtesy of the Archives of American Art, Smithsonian Institution, Washington, D.C.

Fig. 33   photo courtesy of the Archives of American Art, Smithsonian Institution, Washington, D.C.

Fig. 34   NMAA 1967.59.693

Fig. 35   NMAA 1975.87

Fig. 36   Statens Museum for Kunst, Copenhagen, Denmark

Fig. 37   photo courtesy of the National Archives, Washington, D.C.

Fig. 38   NMAA 1967.59.762

Fig. 39   NMAA 1967.59.748

Fig. 40   NMAA 1967.59.747

Fig. 41   NMAA 1967.59.744

Fig. 42   NMAA 1967.59.741.

Fig. 43   Gallery of Art, Howard University, Washington, D.C.

Fig. 44   photo courtesy of the National Archives, Washington, D.C.

Fig. 45   photo courtesy of the National Archives, Washington, D.C.

Fig. 46   NMAA 1967.59.725

Fig. 47   NMAA 1967.59.720

Fig. 48   Ny Carlsberg Glyptotek, Copenhagen, Denmark

Fig. 49   NMAA 1967.59.528

Fig. 50   photo by H. and H. Jacobsen, Kerteminde, Denmark

Fig. 51   Fyns Kunstmuseum, Odense, Denmark

Fig. 52   Florence Museum, Florence, South Carolina

Fig. 53   photo courtesy of Helga and Niels Ejsing, Copenhagen, Denmark

Fig. 54   NMAA 1967.59.773

Fig. 55   The Atlanta University Collection of Afro-American Art, Clark Atlanta University, Atlanta, Georgia

Fig. 56   Neue Galerie der Stadt Linz/Wolfgang Gurlitt Museum, Linz, Austria

Fig. 57   photo courtesy of the Archives of American Art, Smithsonian Institution, Washington, D.C.

Fig. 58   Gallery of Art, Morgan State University, Baltimore, Maryland

Fig. 59   NMAA 1967.59.750

Fig. 60   NMAA 1967.59.34

Fig. 61   Kerteminde Museum, Kerteminde, Denmark

Fig. 62   photo courtesy of the Archives of American Art, Smithsonian Institution, Washington, D.C.

Fig. 63   NMAA 1967.59.860

Index

Note: Page numbers in italics refer to captions.

VENABLE ELEMENTARY SCHOOL
406 14th STREET N.W.
CHARLOTTESVILLE, VA 22903